The Gale of Life

There, like the wind through woods in riot,
Through him the gale of life blew high;
The tree of man was never quiet:
Then 'twas the Roman, now 'tis I.

A.E. Housman, *A Shropshire Lad*, XXXI

The Gale of Life
Two Thousand Years in South-West Shropshire

There, like the wind through woods in riot,
Through him the gale of life blew high;
The tree of man was never quiet:
Then 'twas the Roman, now'tis I.

A.E. Housman, *A Shropshire Lad*, XXXI

Edited by
John Leonard, David Preshous, Marion Roberts, John Smyth and Christopher Train

South-West Shropshire
Historical and Archaeological Society
in association with
Logaston Press

LOGASTON PRESS
Little Logaston, Logaston, Woonton,
Almeley, Herefordshire HR3 6QH

First published by Logaston Press 2000
Reprinted 2000
Copyright © SWSHAS 2000

ISBN 1 873827 36 9

Set in Times and Baskerville by Logaston Press
and printed in Great Britain by
The Cromwell Press, Trowbridge

Cover illustrations
Front: Offa's Dyke by Noel Sheperdson
Rear (clockwise from top left): Bury Ditches; Clun Castle;
Red House and Cockpit, Lydbury North; Eaton Station, Bishop's
Castle Railway with the Long Mynd in the background

Contents

Dedicated to the late Keith Ritherden, founder of the
Bishop's Castle Historical Research Group,
and to the many other devoted scholars and enthusiasts
in the county (past and present) who have
pioneered research into the history and archaeology
of south-west Shropshire and the Welsh Border.

Acknowledgements

This publication is the fruit of many hours of research and investigation. We are most grateful to all our contributors for their hard work, energy and enthusiasm in the composition of the essays, and in the production of many of the maps and illustrations that accompany them.

The Editorial Committee members, John Leonard, David Preshous, John Smyth and Christopher Train, wish to acknowledge and express particular thanks for the patient and painstaking support, wisdom, and generous encouragement of our Historical Adviser, Marion Roberts.

We gratefully acknowledge the generous financial support given to this publication by The Marc Fitch Fund, Oxford, and The Walker Trust, Shrewsbury. We also thank the South-West Shropshire Historical and Archaeological Society committee for backing the project, Enterprise House, Bishop's Castle, for technical help and advice, and Andy Johnson of Logaston Press for his excellent work in the publication of this book.

We thank the following institutions, which have granted permission for the reproduction of copyright material: the Society of Authors as the literary representative of A.E. Housman for the verse of his poem 'On Wenlock Edge' (*A Shropshire Lad, XXXI*) which is incorporated in our title; the Clwyd-Powys Archaeological Trust for their fine aerial photographs (Plates 1 CPAT 84-C-436; 2 CPAT 90-C-366; 3 CPAT 84-C-436; 7 CPAT 90-C-241; and rear cover CPAT 89-C-224); the Oxford University Press for the map reproduced as Fig. 9 (from Davies, R.R. *The Age of Conquest (Wales 1063-1415)*, OUP 1991); and The National Monuments Record (English Heritage) for the photograph reproduced as Plate 13. Other photographs used in the text and on the rear cover were supplied by Robert Anthony, John Leonard, and David and Janet Preshous.

The author of chapter 9 is indebted for archaeological detail and much else besides to Philip Barker and Robert Higham who have probably done more than anyone else to advance the study of timber castles and to restore them to their rightful place in the history of fortification.

The author of chapter 16 is indebted in the compilation of this essay to the kind help and advice of Dr J.F.A. Mason and Mrs Marion Roberts.

Finally, we were delighted to be given permission to reproduce Noel Shepherdson's lovely painting of Offa's Dyke under snow as our cover picture.

Preface

South-west Shropshire has never been particularly populous or, by national standards, prosperous. It is overwhelmingly rural. Its rugged hills do not lend themselves readily to the kind of large-scale arable farming which in the lowlands has destroyed hedgerows and excluded birds, insects and mammals from the landscape. The district has its centre in Bishop's Castle, indisputably an urban community throughout its history. Clun also has a claim to be urban, both in the past and in the present. The scale of the castle and the grid plan of the streets suggest that its medieval lords had urban ambitions for the community, and in 2000 it retains more shops and pubs than a village with the same population. It is curious that talented civil servants came in the mid-1830s to create a poor law union for the area based on its acknowledged market town, they called it the Clun Union, but its centre of administration, the workhouse, was built in Bishop's Castle.

It is tempting when describing south-west Shropshire in the twenty-first century to use terms like 'unchanging', 'timeless', 'unspoiled' or 'time warp'. It is easy and sometimes pleasurable to be impressed by some of the historic features of the area, by the ironmonger's shop in Bishop's Castle, of a kind that has disappeared from many other market towns, by Plowden Hall, described in Madge Moran's contribution to this volume, a house with phases of each century since the fourteenth, by pubs which make their own splendid beers. Nevertheless it is the task of the historian to seek to increase our understanding of the past, not just to wallow in the quaint and nostalgic. As in any other part of Britain, there have been periods of startling change in south-west Shropshire, some of which are explored in this volume.

One such period was the first century AD, when the arrival in the area of the Roman army was quickly followed by the appearance of Roman miners, who practised large-scale techniques like hushing. Roger White's analysis of the Roman lead workings at Linley displays not only the suddenness of the change which came over the area when the miners arrived, but how much has been added to our knowledge of that period in recent decades. The Roman pig of lead kept at Linley Hall, bearing the inscription of the Emperor Hadrian is one of the most astonishing historic artifacts in the district. It represents a cataclysm in the area's past. A native who knew the area before the arrival of the Romans who returned after the commencement of lead mining would not have described it with words like 'unchanging'.

The equally sharp changes of the Dark Ages are more difficult to discern. Margaret Gelling remarks that most parish names probably refer to settlements that were long-established when English-speaking rulers came to control the area, and that they were renamed in the language of the new governors. Words—in this case place names—can raise questions which illuminate our understanding of the past as effectively as artifacts like pigs of lead. Structures can be equally powerful stimulants to the posing of fruitful historical questions, and there is no more stimulating structure than Offa's Dyke. I first learned about the Dyke when a student, through reading Sir Cyril Fox's book in the Bodleian Library in preparation for an essay on the Mercian kings. It seemed very remote, and Fox's scholarship seemed authoritative. To explore the Dyke has proved one of the great pleasures of more than three decades' residence in Shropshire. There are few more satisfying moments for the lover of the Shropshire landscape than to attain the summit of the strength-sapping, stitch-inducing climb from the crossing of the Ceiriog upstream from Chirk, and to see almost all the county spread out like a map, framed by its great hills. To follow the exposed line of the great earthwork across Llanfair Hill is a different but equally powerful experience. David Hill shows in his chapter how our understanding of the Dyke has changed, how some of Fox's suppositions have been shown by the evidence of excavation to be false, how the Dyke may not even have extended from sea to sea. What remains evident is that the building of the Dyke, like the establishment of the Roman lead mines, was a period of sudden, far-reaching change, perhaps brought about by the same governors who re-named the area's communities.

Other new governors, the Norman kings, also brought changes to the area. John Smyth's contribution considers the origins and siting of motte and bailey castles, while Maurice Young details the remnants of Norman work in the castle and church at Clun. But the rulers of England in the eleventh and twelfth centuries, lay barons and monastic foundations as well as the crown, built towns as well as castles. Our understanding of many aspects of the history of towns in the Borderland was transformed by the publication of Maurice Beresford's *New Towns of the Middle Ages* in 1967, and the useful exposition by Sally Chappell and Anne Lawrence of the evidence for the plantation of Bishop's Castle is one of the many fruits of Beresford's scholarship. It is also evidence of dramatic change. There was doubtless a morning when surveyors began to peg out the burgage plots on the High Street, and the local inhabitant who left the night before and returned 20 years later would not have uttered words like 'timeless'.

It is difficult to assess the impact of the Civil Wars of the 1640s, but Peter Bigglestone's contribution to this volume brings out the brutality of such incidents as the storming of Hopton Castle, and the prevailing uneasiness caused by the presence of loosely-disciplined troops that continued throughout war.

Some of the great changes of more recent times have occurred gradually. The range of shops in Bishop's Castle, much greater at the limits of living memory than it is now, developed slowly. There were few shops in the modern sense in the seventeenth century. Shoemakers, tailors and cabinet makers, butchers and bakers provided for most local needs, while fabrics, haberdashery, sugar, tea, spices, books and paper could be obtained from the town's one or two mercers. Over two centuries the range of shops developed with national changes in the transport system, and probably reached a peak in the first half of the twentieth century, when consignments of goods for shops might arrive on the Bishop's Castle Railway, and before road transport drew away shoppers to larger towns. Senior citizens may remember with pleasure the shops of the 1930s or 1950s, and regret the demise of many of them, but they were the culmination of a long period of retailing growth, not part of an unchanging past.

Similarly in the countryside, we know relatively little of the process of enclosure on the hills of Clun Forest, or of the landscape which preceded the patterns of large, straight-sided fields which we can now see. Most parts of the area were enclosed during the nineteenth century, and we can readily read the Acts of Parliament which authorised the re-shaping of the landscape, and there are some records of the work of the commissioners who did the work. We can look at the results of their work, often accomplished within a year or so of the passing of the relevant Act, and reflect that this was another period of rapid change in the area's history, and ask questions about the ways in which the re-casting of the landscape affected the lives of those who lived in the area.

On 8 April 1941 it might have been possible to stand on Cranberry Rock and to reflect that the Second World War had only marginally affected south-west Shropshire, farming practices might be changing, there were evacuees from Merseyside in most schools, although many had returned home, and there were fewer cars on the roads. Twenty-four hours later the Stiperstones Ridge was under large-scale attack from Goering's Luftwaffe. Successive waves of bombers showered the hill with flares, incendiary bombs and high explosives, in the belief, perhaps fostered by British intelligence, that it was a strategically significant target. The war had certainly arrived in south-west Shropshire. Both world wars represent times of marked change. The First World War is perhaps best reflected on the area's many memorials to those killed, chiefly in Flanders and on the Somme. Local communities, like those elsewhere in Britain and in many other European countries, felt bitterly the loss of almost a whole generation of young men. The effects of the Second World War were more immediate. A large proportion of the nation's armed forces were in Britain between the time of Dunkirk and D-Day, and they were joined during 1942 by a huge army and air force from the United States. Government was deeply involved in every aspect of daily life, setting standard rations, requisitioning mansions for the use of troops, building hostels for the Women's Land Army, stockpiling shells on roadside verges. Many aspects of wartime, when changes were set in train which have shaped many aspects of the society in which we live, can only be recorded through the recollections of those who lived through the period. It is be hoped that the mid-twentieth century will be recorded through oral recollections as effectively as Janet Preshous has recorded the century's earlier years.

Those of us alive in 2000 may feel ourselves lucky that large parts of our lives have been spent in what the Chinese proverb would define as uninteresting times. We can reflect on the changes brought about in south-west Shropshire by the motor car—commuting, shopping at a distance, tourism. These have not been as dramatic as some of the changes of past centuries. We can admire in the area a landscape that is unspoiled, although not unchanged over centuries. We can enjoy a way of life that is less frenetic than that of big cities. We should be aware that when we look at the past we must expect to find, even in an area of this kind, periods of dramatic change as well as evidence of continuity.

Barrie Trinder

South-west Shropshire and the adjacent parts of Montgomeryshire may not unreasonably boast a certain uniqueness. This section of the Welsh Marches, with the Severn Valley to the west, the Long Mynd to the east, the Teme valley to the south, and the Shropshire/Cheshire plain to the north, remains one of the most unspoilt and quietly inspiring places in Britain. It has played a full part in the progress of two thousand years of History, and yet retains its natural beauty and keeps its secrets. The purpose of this work is not to present a comprehensive historical picture, but to focus upon some distinctive contributions that the area has made to the story of the past two millennia.

At the beginning of the Christian era, the steep hills and narrow valleys of south-west Shropshire were quite intensively occupied by Iron-Age farmers. A great number of the hilltops were crowned with impressive earthworks which survive today as a spectacular testimony to the culture which flourished here at the time of Christ. The hillforts raise intriguing questions about the nature of the society which built and used them.

CHAPTER 1

Celtic Hillforts and Settlements in the Iron Age
by Neil Hird

Originally from the upper Danube, the Celts migrated in the first millennium B.C. east and west across northern Europe. By 500 B.C. the Celtic people dominated Europe north of the Alps. Greek and Roman classical writers of that period described them as barbarian headhunters who loved warfare. However, the Celts were an enigmatic people: they were warlike but they were also competent seamen and farmers, traders and craftsmen skilled in working gold, copper, bronze and iron. It was the skilled Celtic smiths whose iron-using technology inaugurated the Iron Age in the western World. By the seventh century B.C. the Celts had settled in the Severn Valley, and in south-west Shropshire and the surrounding central Marches they left some of the area's most impressive monuments—their magnificent Iron Age hillforts.

There are about 1,500 Iron Age hillforts in England and Wales. The description 'Iron Age' can be misleading because hillfort construction and development in Britain overlapped the Late Bronze Age, the Iron Age itself and the Roman occupation period. The hillfort-dominated zone is a broad crescent stretching from Anglesey south through the Welsh Marches to the Salisbury Plain and then east along the Downs to the Kent coast. There are over 50 striking hillforts in south-west Shropshire, eastern Montgomeryshire and northern Herefordshire. This small area, barely 25

Pl.1: Caer Caradoc, Chapel Lawn

miles across, has one of the highest concentrations of hillforts in England and Wales. Each hillfort appears to be individually planned and built, and Celtic origins are supported by their names. Clee Burf, which was eradicated by quarrying, was one of the Brown Clee's three hillforts. 'Burf' is thought to be derived from the Celtic word '*bruarth*' meaning an enclosure.

Hillforts with one ditch and rampart are described as 'univallate' and those with multiple ditches and ramparts as 'multivallate'. The Roveries Hill Camp, Caer Din and Titterstone Clee Hill Camp are examples of univallate hillforts. Norton and the two Caer Caradocs are multivallate hillforts; one Caer Caradoc is located east of Church Stretton, the other, also called Gaer Ditches, is near Chapel Lawn. The area's hillforts are 'contour' type forts—the Celts took advantage of topography and built the ramparts to follow the contours. If the hill's natural slope was steep, then few or no ramparts were built. At Stretton's Caer Caradoc, an eastern rampart links up with the summit's natural rock outcrops. The 'elliptical' Bury Ditches, the 'pear-shaped' Burrow Hill Camp and the 'D-shaped' Norton are examples of contour type hillforts. Not all the area's hillforts were built on high hills; at 533 metres Titterstone Clee Hill Camp overlooks its neighbour Caynham Camp built at 174 metres above sea level.

Though some were constructed in the late Bronze Age, most were built after 600 B.C and in stages. Excavations at the Breidden, Ffridd Faldwyn, Caynham Camp and the Roveries indicate that these were each built in four stages. The Breidden might have been built over a 1,000 year period. Excavations indicated that in about 900 B.C. an enclosed settlement with an irregular double-timber palisade was formed, while the outer enclosure appears to have been constructed between the second and fourth centuries A.D. To build a hillfort manually would have required a large, well organised and skilful work force. Everybody in the community would have been involved, including the women, children and slaves. The Celts' tools were simple: flint, stone or bronze axes cleared the hilltop trees and prepared them as timber, deer-antler picks cleared stones, whilst cattle shoulder blade shovels were used to dig the earth and soil from the quarry ditches and to build the ramparts. Earth, turf and stone were carried manually in woven baskets. Likewise heavy timbers were moved by manpower, possibly with the assistance of ox-drawn carts. Stone hammers were used to drive in the palisade's timbers and shape the stones used as revetments.

The rampart's design and the materials used can indicate when a hillfort's first defences were built. The earliest enclosure had a simple timber palisade embedded in single or double rows with no frontal ditch or bank. Excavations at Titterstone Clee indicate that first a timber wall was built and then a stone rampart which was revetted every ten feet with three foot diameter timbers. Hauling the timber to the top of Titterstone Clee would have been a considerable operation. The stone rampart had no ditch but was fronted by large, loose basalt blocks. Chapel Lawn's Caer Caradoc, Bury Ditches and the Roveries, hillforts probably built between the seventh and the fifth centuries B.C., had vertically faced ramparts. These were revetted by timber or stone and separated from each other by ditches or 'berms' — flat platforms. After the fourth century B.C. hillforts such as Pontesford Hill Lower Camp and Wapley Camp, near Presteigne, had dump or 'glacis' ramparts of loose material on a sloping angle which ran into a deep ditch and were topped with wooden palisades. This type of rampart was easier to build and maintain and was a better defence.

Later ramparts were more widely spaced from each other. Wapley's south-east ramparts are 90 metres apart and separated by wide flat-bottomed ditches. This style, described as a 'Frécamp' rampart after its French origin, was more common in northern France and southern England in the first century A.D. and is unusual in the Marches. Wapley's Frécamp rampart might have been built to create a cattle holding area. Alternatively, aware of the advancing Romans after 43 A.D. the Celts, to improve Wapley's defences and keep any Roman onager (or catapult) as far away as possible from the hillfort's interior, built the Frécamp rampart. Hillforts were not continuously occupied and some were re-occupied and developed after a period of absence. A dump rampart could indicate that older defences had been rebuilt or strengthened. In some the ramparts occupied a large proportion of the structure's area. Pontesford Hill's ramparts cover almost three quarters of the total area.

Few hillforts had more than two entrances. possibly because the entrance was the weakest part of the defences. The earlier entrance struc-tures were simple with a short in-turned entrance and a single wooden gate which was vulnerable to both an attacker's battering-ram and fire. Considerable thought and planning went into the construction of later inge-nious entrances. The Roveries' in-turned north-west entrance was built in three stages. It is approached by a causeway 100 metres long and 5 metres wide which curves to the right. The actual entrance has 20 metres of care-fully worked thin dry stone walling. This leads to two stone-walled guard houses built behind a dual portal gateway, the guard-house sentries control-ling the traffic entering the hillfort. This type of guard house is called a 'Cornovian' guard house after the Roman name given to the Celtic people living in the area. The entrance was levelled and paved to assist access. To the east of the entrance is a berm 60 metres long and 6 metres wide. This berm steepens the hill's natural slope and possibly was built to strengthen the entrance's defences. Bury Ditches has two strong, elaborate entrances which are both unusual in the Marches. At the north-east the entrance is in-turned and at the south-west out-turned. The 30 metre north-east entrance is a straight corridor with indications of two guard houses at the end of the corridor on the southern rampart. At the curving south-west out-turned entrance, which is particularly impressive, north-west ramparts sweep round and overlap by 91 metres the south-east bank, ditch and counterscarp bank. The overlap might have been longer but the overlapping rampart has been truncated by a forest road. Another unusual feature is the entrance's 21 metre wide barbican. A possible explanation is that Bury Ditches' defenders could hold their half-wild cattle in the barbican and then release them down the sloping entrance into the compacted attackers. Bury Ditches' entrances could have had a timber tower and 'fighting' bridge spanning the entrance passageway.

'Hornwork', often in the form of claw-like out-works and with gates, gave entrances additional protection. The western entrance of Chapel Lawn's Caer Caradoc has hornwork which stands higher than the entrance, allowing a sentry to view the complete western entrance and its approaches. It would have been an excellent missile platform for spear, arrow, stone or sling-stone throwing. The sling, a simple, effective leather weapon was used in hunting or warfare and projected stones up to 70 metres. The ramparts here have visible sections of stone walling.

Wapley is a semi-contour hillfort with a magnificent main southern entrance. This 90 metre in-turned corridor entrance turns left at the top of a rise to a hidden gate position. An attacker coming up the corridor could not have seen the gate at its end. Also it would have been difficult to use a battering-ram up the angled slope. In the long corridor an attacker would have been harassed from both sides by defenders positioned high above him on the ramparts and armed with stones, rocks, spears and arrows. The question must be asked if such elaborate hillfort entrances, built after the fourth century B.C., were not only to improve defences but also to reflect their Celtic builders' social status.

Hillforts' interior areas vary considerably. Roundton, near Church Stoke, has an interior of about 1,000 square metres while Titterstone Clee, south Shropshire's largest hillfort, has an interior of almost 29 hectares. Only a few hillfort interiors have been excavated. Unfortunately, because of the acidic nature of the area's soil, when excavations are made few bone, leather, grain, wooden or pottery artifacts are found. Pottery, mainly Neolithic and Bronze Age, was found at the Roveries, Ffridd Faldwyn, the

Pl.2: Burrow Hill, Hopesay

Breidden and Caynham, near Ludlow. Close to Mitchell's Fold Bronze Age stones there is evidence of ploughing from that period. Bronze Age farmers would have found the south Shropshire hills' lighter soils easier to till and the climate then was warmer. The Neolithic and Bronze Age finds, and part of an even earlier Mesolithic macehead found at the Roveries, all indicate that some of the area's hillfort sites could have been occupied 2,500 years before the Celts started to build their hillforts on them.

The larger hillfort interiors could have contained farms or small settlements. With family units of up to ten people it is estimated that 180 to 250 people lived on one hectare in a central Marches Iron Age settlement. At Burrow Hill there is evidence of over 20 round houses. One circular rock-cut house platform had gullies to aid both construction and drainage, and post-holes for the timber frame. Celtic round houses were skilfully built— the roof timbers had ring-beams to prevent them forcing the house walls outwards, the roofs were thatched with reeds, straw or turf whilst the walls were made of timber or wattle-and-daub. They were often built close to the hillfort's inner rampart to protect them from the weather, and had central hearths but no chimneys, possibly because of the danger of up-draughts causing roof fires. The floors could have been bare stone or rammed earth covered with straw or reeds. The entrances usually faced south towards the households' livestock enclosures.

Excavations at Croft Ambrey revealed a hilltop settlement consisting of rectangular house platforms, the post-holes of four and six 'poster' storage huts, the huts of blacksmiths, butchers and potters and there was evidence of a street formation. The storage huts could have held grain, fleeces and skins and usually had floors built one metre off the ground to keep their contents dry and away from vermin. These storage huts were located away from the settlement's houses and working huts probably because of the danger of fire. The animal-bone finds at Croft Ambrey showed that sheep, of the Soay type, cattle and swine were kept in equal proportions. The animal bones also helped to explain Celtic pastoral, skinning and butchery practices. For example, from the age and sex of the animal-bone finds it is possible to ascertain if cattle were kept as a food source only; if sufficient cereals were grown to retain cattle throughout the winter months; if the ewes were kept for their wool only and if the swine were kept as a food source or to root the ground in the hillfort's vicinity. Croft Ambrey would have had workshops for smiths and tanners and tool storage huts in an industrial area, working and refuse pits and winter quarters for the community's livestock.

The absence today of a natural water supply in many hillforts raises the question - how could the Celts and their livestock have settled permanently in them? Burrow Hill, Stretton's Caer Caradoc, and Wapley have evidence of an internal water supply, but the age of Wapley's well is unknown. At the Breidden there is a square pond which could have been a rainwater reservoir. Clay-lined dew ponds may have been used in hillforts to collect water, but the close presence of streams and rivers to hillforts was important. For example the Roveries is situated close to the West Onny and the Camlad, and Bury Ditches is near to the Kemp and the Clun. The hillfort's women and children, as in sub-Saharan countries today, probably collected and carried water for their hillfort communities from these streams and were also responsible for driving the livestock to them for water.

What was the purpose of what appear to be annexes at the Breidden, the Roveries and Caynham hillforts? Were they additional defences? Such an explanation may be warranted at the Breidden where, to its south-east the ground rises to 1,000 feet blocking the view in that direction. A subsidiary enclosure was constructed on this rise in the second to the fourth centuries A.D. The Roveries has a small enclosure 200 yards to the north-west and access to it is very difficult. This enclosure's only man-made defensive work is a double ditch and bank on the western side, and its purpose is uncertain, indeed whether it was even contemporary with the hillfort. To the north, east and south the hillside falls away steeply. Access to

7

Caynham's adjoining annex is easy and it may have been a cattle enclosure. Radnor Wood's enclosure has no eastern rampart and forms an unusual horseshoe shape. Was it an unfinished satellite hillfort for nearby Bury Ditches, assuming they were contemporary Iron Age structures? It would appear that the hillforts were not necessarily individual communities, for example a ten mile routeway connected the Breidden, by way of Westbury, Farley and Pontesbury Hill to Earl's Hill hillfort.

It was a Celtic people, the Romans called them the Cornovii, who inhabited an area which today corresponds with Shropshire and Cheshire and parts of Wales east of the Clwyd hills. The Cornovii were one of the 25 Celtic speaking peoples or tribes of Britain at the time of the Romans' third invasion in 43 A.D. That these tribes were not united as one kingdom was very much to the Romans' advantage when they occupied Britain. The Cornovian capital might have been the Wrekin hillfort but Old Oswestry, Shropshire's largest hillfort, could also claim this title. There are signs that the Romans attacked the Wrekin, but no evidence of attacks on other Cornovian hillforts, though there is considerable speculation on the whereabouts of the hillfort where Caradoc (the Romans called him Caratacus) fought his last battle against the Romans (for a fuller discussion of this, see Chapter 2).

Around the hillforts, which must have been important focal points for tribal life, would have been farmsteads and small settlements. Aerial photography has revealed a number of rectangular enclosures in the Severn Valley, in the adjoining Rea, Roden and Tern river valleys and in southwest Shropshire. These enclosures could have been Iron Age farmsteads and excavations at Sharpstone Hill, south-east of Shrewsbury, have revealed isolated farmsteads. At Bromfield, before recent gravel-extracting operations, a ditch-enclosed farmstead has been identified close to the River Teme. Here were found the post holes of two small rectangular buildings called 'four posters', clay-lined retting or boiling tanks, evidence of hay trees, racks and Iron Age pottery. In 1976 Colstey Bank, north of Clun, was identified as a single bank and ditch Iron Age enclosure of about one acre with an earlier, inner enclosure. Pre-historic ranch boundaries can be traced on the Long Mynd, and Robury Ring, near Wentnor, might have been an Iron Age farmstead. Further evidence of hitherto undiscovered Iron Age farmsteads could well exist in south-west Shropshire.

Unlike other ancient civilizations the Celts did not leave behind a great material civilization but today their descendants speak western Europe's oldest languages. They also left, particularly in this area, their hillforts which remain prominent features of the landscape.

Bibliography

Cunliffe, B. *Iron Age Communities in Britain* Routledge & Kegan Paul, 1974

Darvill, T. *Prehistoric Britain* B.T. Batsford, 1992

Forde-Johnston, J. *Hillforts of the Iron Age in England and Wales* Liverpool University Press, 1976

Hogg, A.H.A. *Hillforts of Britain* Hart-Davis MacGibbon, 1975

Laing, L. *Celtic Britain* Routledge & Keegan Paul, 1979

Reid, M.L. *Prehistoric Houses in Britain* Shire Publications, 1993

Ross, A. *The Pagan Celts* B.T. Batsford, 1986

Salway, Peter *Roman Britain* Oxford University Press, 1990

Stanford, S.C. *The Archaeology of the Welsh Marches* S.C. Stanford, 1991

In the middle of the first century A.D., the Romans, moving north and west in their conquest of Britain, and establishing their base at *Viroconium* (Wroxeter), overcame the resistance focussed under the British chieftain, Caratacus. They then tightened their grip on the territory between the lands of the Welsh Ordovices and the more peaceable Cornovii of the Severn Valley. The evidence of their military movements in this sensitive border zone reveals their shrewd, peacekeeping strategy which remained effective here through their 350 year stay.

CHAPTER 2

The Roman Military Presence
by David Preshous

The Roman Conquest of Britain began in 43 A.D. in the reign of the Emperor Claudius with four legions (Legio II Augusta; Legio IX Hispana; Legio XIV Gemina; and Legio XX Valeria) under the command of Aulus Plautius. Swift and successful campaigns in southern and south-western Britain, and the capture of King Cunobelinus' city at Camulodunum (Colchester), capital of the Catuvellauni, laid open the way for legions to advance around 47 A.D. to bases in the South-West at *Glevum* (Gloucester - Legio XX) and in the Midlands at *Manduessedum* (Mancetter in Warwickshire - Legio XIV). Continuing resistance to the invaders in Wales or along the Border was concentrated at first under the leadership of Cunobelinus' son, Caratacus, among the tribes of South Wales (the Silures).

Between 47 and 51, the new governor of the province, Publius Ostorius Scapula, drove Caratacus northwards into the territory of the Decangi. S.C. Stanford argues that this may have been a tribe which occupied Herefordshire and which has been wrongly identified with the Deceangli of Clwyd. If this is so, evidence of destruction or dismantling of hillfort defences at Credenhill, Croft Ambrey and Midsummer Hill in Herefordshire may mark the passage of Scapula with all or part of Legio XX, on the trail of Caratacus. This theory has not, however, been widely accepted by other scholars. To the north, another Roman line of advance (Legio XIV) is indicated by a chain of forts from Mancetter to Wall

(*Letocetum*), Penkridge (*Pennocrucium*), Red Hill (*Uxacona*) and Wroxeter (*Viroconium*) or perhaps at first to the nearby camp at Leighton.

The site of Scapula's final confrontation with Caratacus has always been a popular archaeological mystery. The British chieftain's skilful choice of location and preparations to confront the Roman attack are described in detail in Book XII of the *Annales* of the Roman historian, Tacitus:

> He (Caratacus) chose a place for the battle where the approaches and escape-routes were to our disadvantage but favourable to his own forces. On one side there was a precipitously steep hill, and, where the gradient was gentler, he piled up rocks to form a rough rampart. There was also a river of uncertain depth (*vado incerto*) flowing by in front of his position, and here he stationed warriors to provide defence ... These eager preparations surprised the Roman commander. At the same time he was alarmed by the barrier created by the river, by the rampart which had been set up, by the threateningly steep mountain above, by the whole hostile aspect of the place, and by the crowds of defenders at all points.

Scapula's officers and men, however, did not share their commander's misgivings and enthusiastically demanded immediate battle. The outcome was never really in doubt:

> After a survey to discover which points in the defences were or were not penetrable, Scapula led out his eager troops, and crossed the river without difficulty. When they reached the rampart and while the fighting was still being carried on with missiles, our soldiers suffered more wounds and casualties, but afterwards, when they had formed a cover with their shields [the *testudo* or 'tortoise'], they tore down the roughly and irregularly constructed rampart of the Britons and joined battle on fairer terms at close quarters. The barbarians were compelled to retreat to the hilltops, but here also our soldiers closely followed up their attack.

Caution is necessary in the interpretation of this episode of Tacitus. Its vivid and heroic detail suggests the kind of literary embellishment which was acceptable to ancient historians, and accordingly it may be unwise to place too much reliance upon the geographical detail. Scholars who have ventured to use the proffered 'geographical indicators' have produced much speculation about the location of the battlefield. Several popular sites have been ruled out as failing to match Tacitus' descriptions. Neither of the imposing Caer Caradoc forts have an adjacent river *vado incerto*, unless one is prepared to accept a very substantial change since the First Century in the water-volume of the Cound or Redlake brooks!

A colourful contradictory hypothesis, put forward by Lt. Col. A.H. Burne in 1949, is that Caer Caradoc (Church Stretton) was Caratacus' advance camp, fronting Wroxeter (a base which he described as 'a pistol pointed at the heart of Wales'), Caer Caradoc (Chapel Lawn) was the main British base, and the actual battle took place above the River Clun on Purslow Hill. Colonel Burne's case is argued with great military panache and a good measure of imagination!

For geographical reasons, Coxall Knoll near Bucknell, and the Herefordshire Beacon on the Malverns have been rejected. Iron Age sites above the upper reaches of the Severn seem more promising, and John Peddie, another military author, supports an earlier suggestion by Dr. J.K. St. Joseph that the large hillfort on Cefn Carnedd above Llandinam, with a Roman fort nearby at Caersws, might be the battlefield site. Dolforwyn, and the Breiddens have also been proposed, but the current favourite appears to be the fort on Llanymynech Hill above the river Tanat.

The defeated Caratacus fled to northern Britain after the battle, only to be betrayed by the Brigantian Queen Cartimandua, and ended his days as a romantically defiant and honoured 'guest' of the Emperor Claudius in Rome.

From this victory the Romans were able to settle and defend the territory of the Cornovii with relative ease. The tribe itself appears to have submitted to Roman rule with little real resistance—the hillfort on the Wrekin is the only place located to date where archaeological evidence of serious fighting has been found (javelin heads and burnt huts).

Scapula's successors, Didius Gallus and Quintus Veranius, conducted further campaigns in southern and central Wales between 52 and 58 A.D. Their aims were to create and consolidate a frontier and to put a stop to the highly successful guerilla tactics of the Silures. Following their efforts, the next Governor, Suetonius Paulinus, moved the campaign into North Wales in 60 A.D. and attacked the Druidic stronghold of *Mona* (Anglesey). However, he was thwarted in the completion of this by having to retreat to deal with the violent and disastrous rebellion of the Iceni of East Anglia under Queen Boudicca.

Julius Frontinus, governor of Britain between 74 and 78, brought the Silures at last under control, establishing a new legionary fort at Caerleon

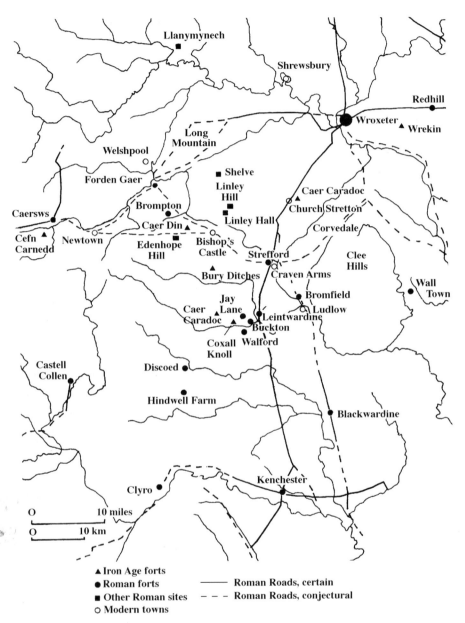

Fig.1 South-west Shropshire during the Roman Occupation

(*Isca*) for Legio II, and a network of associated forts guarding strategic river valleys in south and west Wales. Finally, in 78, Agricola, the father-in-law of the historian Tacitus and a veteran of two earlier campaigns in Britain (61 and 70-74 A.D.), completed the conquest of Wales with the capture of Anglesey.

Wroxeter, having been established as a major legionary base around 57 A.D. (Legio XIV and later Legio XX), was redeveloped in the Nineties as a civilian settlement and tribal capital, parts of the fort being absorbed into the town plan, and the legion moving up to Chester.

The permanent defence of the border area was concentrated on the legionary bases at Chester (*Deva* - Legio XX) and Caerleon (*Isca* - Legio II) , with satellite forts spaced out between, usually about 25-30 kms apart. Examples of these forts can be identified at Forden Gaer (*Lavobrinta*), Caersws (*Mediolanum*), Leintwardine (*Bravonium* or *Branogenium*) and Castell Collen near Llandrindod Wells.

The countryside of south-west Shropshire and adjacent areas of Powys and Herefordshire holds beneath its fields and hills considerable evidence of the passage of many Roman armies, but for most of the sites precise dating is difficult. Continuous farming over 1,900 years has rendered many earthworks invisible from ground level, although spectacular evidence is still revealed in crop-marks photographed from the air.

The Roman army on campaign had clearly laid-down strategies and techniques in the establishment of its bases, whether temporary or permanent, and these were adhered to quite strictly by commanders in the field. Overnight rectangular marching camps, with ditches and earth ramparts, were quickly set up during passage through uncertain or hostile territory, but these could be equally quickly abandoned, leaving as archaeological evidence only imposing but strictly standardised 'regulation' earthworks. In a number of strategically vital places forts were re-occupied, rebuilt, or extended for subsequent use, but it is often hard to establish an accurate chronological sequence for these manoeuvres.

The most important Roman military sites in south-west Shropshire, north Herefordshire and west Powys are where the rivers Onny and Teme meet, at Bromfield, near Ludlow; where the Clun and Teme meet, at Leintwardine, and nearby Jay Lane, Walford, Buckton, and Brampton Bryan; and in the Camlad/Caebitra/Mule/Severn valleys at Brompton, Glanmihell, and Forden. There are other Roman camps at Strefford (Craven Arms) and Wall Town (Cleobury Mortimer), and further south at Hindwell Farm (between Presteigne and Kington), covering the valleys of the Lugg and the Arrow. Small enclosures, arguably signal stations, are located on Linley Hill; Edenhope Hill (near Mainstone); Rowton and Woolston (near Craven Arms); and, according to Stanford, at The Sheet (Ludlow). A slightly larger rectangular earthwork at Caer Din near Bishop's Moat may be of Roman or earlier Iron Age origin. The Roman building complex at Linley Hall, near Bishop's Castle, is discussed more fully in Chapter 4.

Other sites conjectured as Roman camps at Discoed (Presteigne), Lydham (Bishop's Castle) and Bicton (Clun) have been generally discounted, and the existence of a fort at Westbury on the Roman road between Wroxeter and Forden is still based on very scanty archaeological evidence.

The 20 acre marching camp at Bromfield lies in an extraordinary concentration of archaeological sites, including Neolithic remains, Bronze Age burial mounds and a cemetery, an Iron Age farmstead, and an Anglo-Saxon cemetery. The area has been extensively explored, recorded and explained by S.C. Stanford. The Roman camp was first recorded in an aerial survey by Dr. J.K. St. Joseph in 1948, and excavated by Dr. Graham Webster in 1956. Evidence of its date and occupation remains inconclusive.

The other very large marching camps at Walford and Brampton Bryan suggest a movement of large forces up the Teme valley, and are possible evidence of Scapula's advance around 49/50 A.D., as he probed northwards from Gloucester to attack the Decangi and ultimately to pursue Caratacus. Strefford, a substantial marching-camp close to the line of Watling Street West at Craven Arms, probably also dates from these earliest Roman operations in the territory. Of the other forts in the Teme valley that at Jay Lane, west of Leintwardine may have been established subsequently by Scapula to consolidate his new frontier. This five acre fort was excavated by Stanford in 1968, and was revealed as having a single earth rampart and timber gate towers, a conventional format for first century satellite forts. Samian pottery found in this excavation appears to date from the period 50-70 A.D.

Dr. St. Joseph, in a small-scale exploratory excavation on the nearby Iron Age fort at Brandon Hill (Walford) in 1980, discovered evidence of a Roman granary and courtyard building, possibly dating to the campaign of Quintus Veranius in central Wales between 57 and 58 A.D.

Stanford suggests that Jay Lane may have been replaced c.80 A.D. on a site closer to the river Teme at Buckton. This fort, originally of earth and timber construction, was redesigned in the Trajanic period (98-117 A.D.) with stone gate-towers and double carriageways in all four walls. Such gateways are normally associated with legionary fortresses and are not found elsewhere in a small fort like this, which probably housed a single cavalry squadron. Aerial photography and excavation (1968) have also revealed gravel-surfaced internal roadways and stone-built central buildings.

Buckton fort (about 5.7 acres in area) appears to have been dismantled in the mid-second century, and a new fort built, apparently using some of its stone, at Leintwardine, and completed by about 170 A.D. This was a much larger (11 acre) fort, and was one of the group comprising also Caersws, Forden, and Castell Collen established as strategic links between the large, legionary garrisons at Chester and Caerleon. In a now settled province they would have provided adequate 'policing' of the area, and have served as depots for the support of local-based Roman economic activities. Leintwardine probably housed a cohort of about 500 soldiers, and a small bath-house (a feature of more 'comfortable' permanent forts) has been discovered outside the walls, close to the river Teme. Although a survey of the site (now very largely under the present village of Leintwardine) suggested specifically military use, it is probable that some civilian settlement existed here, associated with the Watling Street river crossing.

Leintwardine became a permanent civil settlement and probable supply depot for the area, remaining occupied until the third or fourth century. The maintenance of a military outpost here in the Teme / Clun valley would have been at least in part to defend the Roman road (Watling Street West) from Chester (*Deva*) and Wroxeter to Kenchester (*Magnis*) and Caerleon, as it crossed the open river valleys running down from the Welsh hills. A fuller account of the Roman road system appears in Chapter 3.

The group of forts in the Church Stoke / Montgomery area presents a similar pattern of temporary and permanent occupation, and suggests periodic reviews of the actual strategic needs of the locality. The large fort at Brompton is closely associated with three overlapping marching camps, which indicate occupation during more than one of the early campaigns. Dr. St. Joseph has identified a small marching camp about six miles west of Brompton at Glanmihell in the Mule valley. As at Leintwardine, a review of the requirements of the frontier led in the mid-second century (*c*.160 A.D.) to the rebuilding of the first century fort at Forden Gaer (*Lavobrinta*) as a more permanent base (7.75 acres) for the local garrison. As well as being one of the four substantial forts defending the central border, Forden would have controlled the ancient river Severn crossing at Rhydwhyman, on the Roman road from Wroxeter to Caersws.

Further afield, in north Herefordshire, there was probably a similar rationalisation of garrisons in the Presteigne / Kington area, with a succession of temporary camps around a larger one at Hindwell Farm, near Walton. This fort yielded some Samian pottery and a *ballista* (catapult) bolt which suggest occupation during the early campaigns.

In south-east Shropshire at Wall Town near Cleobury Mortimer a five acre site was excavated by the Kidderminster and District Archaeological and Historical Society in 1960-61, revealing, according to a subsequent examination of the evidence by Dr. Graham Webster, 'a sequence of Roman forts of a permanent character on the site'. Pottery evidence suggested that the site had been occupied from the first until at least the middle of the second century. This is one of the very few forts with remains (rampart and ditch) clearly visible at ground level. It was presumably built to watch over the upland area of the Clee Hills.

The smaller enclosures at Linley Hill, Edenhope, Woolston, and Rowton could only have held a handful of men, and are most convincingly described as signal-stations. They command good views and are probably the survivors of a more comprehensive chain. Such single earthworks can be easily 'ploughed out', and, although new sites continue to be found, many may well have already completely disappeared. The Linley Hill enclosure (96 feet square and without entrance apertures), surrounded by a ditch (4'6" deep) and a rampart (3' high, 18" wide) was investigated by the Shrewsbury Research Group in 1954. Their work was recorded by Dr. Graham Webster, but no finds were made to support any specific conclusions. Dr. Webster did, however, note that the site afforded views across to the high ground above the three local satellite forts at Forden, Caersws, and Leintwardine. It would be attractive to assume that this particular signal-station was placed here to keep an eye on the lead-mining operations in the Shelve and Gravels area which were one of the reasons for continuing Roman interest in the area. The Edenhope enclosure was found recently in an aerial survey, and it appears alongside the Linley signal-station in *Shropshire from the Air* by Mike Watson & Chris Musson.

In conclusion, it is possible to build up a general picture of Roman military operations in south-west Shropshire, from its violent beginnings in the campaign against Caratacus through further incursions into Wales, and culminating in the establishment of relatively small garrisons, a considerable distance apart, guarding the confluences of rivers, to provide early warning of raids from the Welsh mountains into the settled and increasingly prosperous territory of the Cornovii. Even this modest military presence was probably greatly reduced by the second century, with the legions based at Chester and Caerleon being considered adequate to secure the border territories.

Regrettably, the archaeological evidence does not yet permit a much clearer focus than this, since many sites have disappeared under the plough and others reveal occupation of a most temporary nature. Doubtless, continuing aerial survey, backed up by the new technological approaches to geophysics and archaeology will reveal new data about the existing sites and also lead to the discovery of some of those as yet unknown.

Bibliography

Burne, A.H. 'Caratacus' Last Battle', *Transactions of the Shropshire Archaeological Society (TSAS), Vol. LIII*, 1949

Clayton, P. *Companion to Roman Britain* Phaidon, 1980

Frere, S. *Britannia* Routledge & Kegan Paul, 1967

Peddie, J. *Conquest - The Roman Invasion of Britain* Bramley Books, 1987

Rivet, A.L.F. & Smith, C. *Place Names of Roman Britain* BCA, 1979

Stanford, S.C. *The Archaeology of the Welsh Marches* Collins, 1980

'Roman Marching Camp at Bromfield', *TSAS, Vol. LVIII*, 1965-68

'Bromfield Excavations', *TSAS, Vol. LXIV*, 1983-84

Cornelius Tacitus *Annals of Imperial Rome* Bks XII, XIV
                 Agricola

Watson, M. & Musson, C. *Shropshire from the Air* Shropshire Books, 1993

Webster, G. *The Cornovii* Alan Sutton, Revised Edition 1991
            Rome Against Caratacus BCA, 1981

'Investigation of Earthwork on Linley Hill', *TSAS, LV*, 1955-56

White, R. & Barker, P, *Wroxeter - Life and Death of a Roman City* Tempus, 1991

One of the great legacies of Roman civilisation to conquered countries was the establishment of an effective communications network through a system of military roads. Some remain apparent and are indeed still used today, others have to be traced through more elusive evidence.

CHAPTER 3

Roads and Communications in the Roman Period

by Christopher Train

It is a commonplace of history that one of the Romans' principal surviving contributions to the landscape of Western Europe is their road system. Every schoolboy, to deploy the ancient cliché, knew of those arrow-straight roads down which the legionaries marched to bring civilisation and subjection to the scattered and primitive British tribes, skulking in the few clearings of this forested land—'to create' in Tacitus' sardonic words, 'a wilderness and call it peace'. But how true is that image of the Roman past for this part of Shropshire and how useful for understanding its pattern of communications over those four centuries?

The starting point for this discussion must be the Ordnance Survey Map of Roman Britain. The Second Edition, of 1931, showed three roads in the area (for the purpose of this chapter the area viewed goes beyond south-west Shropshire, since the road system can be understood properly only if its points of origin and departure are taken into account). They were: the main Watling Street, coming north-west across England to Wroxeter before it turned north towards Chester; its extension westwards, passing to the south of Shrewsbury and climbing over the Long Mountain to a Roman fort which controlled the Severn crossing near Montgomery, called, in the 1931 Map, Caer Flos and now known as Forden Gaer; and the Watling Street

West running south-west from Wroxeter, by Church Stretton to Leintwardine, to Kenchester, west of Hereford, and ultimately to Caerleon-on-Usk in South Wales.

The fourth and latest edition of the Map, published in 1991, shows the same roads. The only difference is that the route west from Wroxeter is marked as uncertain throughout and has a branch running south of the Long Mountain through the Worthen gap. The policy of the Survey is to show only well authenticated roads and they include new information only when it has been verified by their Field Investigators. So, in the 60 years between these two editions, no further roads have been identified in this area to the satisfaction of the scholars who advise the Survey. Yet this period has seen massive advances in knowledge of the Roman occupation of Britain, advances to which the Maps bear vivid witness. A tract of country which, in 1931, was notable for its absence of signs of habitation was, by 1991, marked, not in profusion but nonetheless significantly, with a variety of the symbols testifying to the presence of the Romans, especially the evidence for military activity in forts and marching camps, most of these the product of aerial photography.

Aerial photography and modern archaeological techniques have, over the same period, added even more dramatically to our understanding of what this land, the territory of the Cornovii, was like when the Romans arrived. The lower lying country had long been cleared of forest, small farmsteads proliferating in the plain of the Severn and the valleys of its tributaries. Hillforts characterised the uplands, sometimes associated with or complementary to—the present state of knowledge makes this uncertain— the valley steadings. This was, as it is now, an agricultural, probably pastoral, society, measuring its wealth in livestock and land, but relatively undeveloped in material terms compared with the tribes of central and southern England, who were closer to the Continent and the trading opportunities which that gave. There was, undoubtedly, a developed pattern of trackways linking the various communities and serving the trade, of which there was some, with the world beyond the Severn and the Teme. None of these trackways can be confidently identified, unless the Clun-Clee Ridgeway remained in use, running from The Anchor to the south of the River Clun, to Clungunford, Onibury, Bromfield, Titterstone Clee Hill and Bewdley. This was suggested in the 1960s by Miss Lily Chitty as a trade route from mid-Wales to southern England from the late Stone Age onwards. It was not, then, to a pathless waste that the Romans came. And we may be sure that, though the Romans introduced their own lines of communication for their own military and economic purposes, these were superimposed on and did not remove the need for or the use of existing trackways. But were the three Roman roads which the Ordnance Survey accepts as authenticated the only ones which the Romans built here? The forts and occupation sites which appear, often unlinked, upon the face of the modern map tempt the curious eye to begin linking them both upon the map and upon the ground. And over the last forty years scholars have done that.

Before we turn to the product of that work, a cautionary word is necessary. Christopher Taylor, an investigator for the Royal Commission on Historical Monuments, wrote in the Introduction to his *Roads and Tracks of Britain* 'The fascination of roads and tracks, and the excitement that the process of tracing them onwards across country gives, have all too often in the past resulted in complete mental blocks and visual blindness ... The desire to trace a line of communication, any line, to a significant point, and to clothe it with romantic visions of prehistoric farmers, Roman soldiers or medieval travellers leads to greater and greater flights of fancy and in the end to total nonsense.'

Let us first look more closely at the roads whose authenticity even the cautious Survey acknowledges. The principal and earliest roads the Romans built were for military purposes, to link and supply legionary and auxiliary forts and to facilitate troop movement and military communications. Later many of these took on an economic and social purpose, enabling the resources of the country to be exploited and facilitating inward and outward trade. All the authenticated roads in this area were undoubtedly originally military roads; roads which had a specifically military purpose and were surveyed, laid out and built by the army. They display the typical features of such roads, being surveyed by simple means to produce broadly straight alignments, where the country allowed it, and built upon a low mound (called the *agger*) which was constructed from the spoil of roadside ditches to produce a firm and well-drained surface. They surely date from the early years of the Conquest, as the Romans came to a stand in order to face and then subdue the highland tribes of Wales. This was in the 30 years from the late 40s A.D. to 78 A.D.

The subjugation of Wales was the work of two legionary forces; in the south a legion based at Gloucester and from the mid-70s at Caerleon-on-Usk; and in the midlands and north-west, a legion based from about 57 A.D. at Wroxeter. The latter's communications to the rear were secured by the great arterial road, running up from London across central England—the Watling Street. Its line of advance beyond Wroxeter directly to the west, to

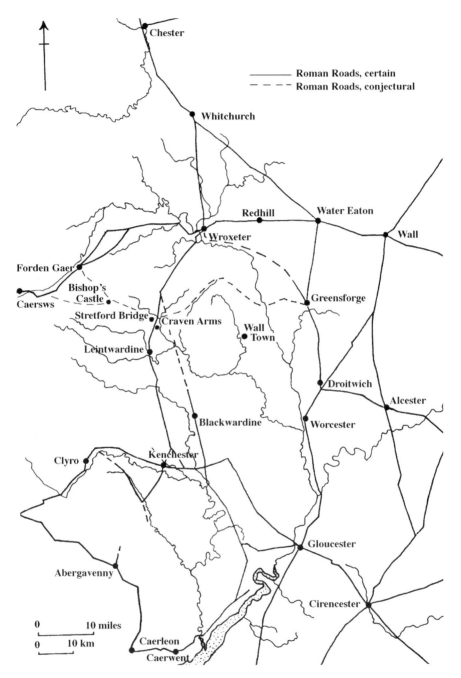

Fig.2 The Midlands and Welsh Border during the Roman Occupation

control the valley of the Severn as it emerges from central Wales, took it by way of Meole Brace, Yockleton, Westbury and, perhaps originally over the Long Mountain but later along the valley past Worthen and Marton, to the fort at Forden Gaer, at the Severn crossing by Rhydwhyman—a site chosen a thousand years later by the Normans for their castle at Hen Domen—and on to Caersws between Newtown and Llanidloes. Flanking this road between Yockleton and Westbury is Stoney Stretton (place names with some form of the word 'street' indicating the presence of a Roman road).

The road system to the north from Wroxeter does not concern us here. But, looking south-westward, the Romans needed to link their two forces and to secure communication along the border with Wales. The link was provided by the Watling Street West.

Leaving Wroxeter by a ford across the Severn, this heads south-west, crossing the Cound Brook north of Cound village, and aiming in a true alignment, from which it varies only marginally, for the Stretton Gap, on past Pitchford and Frodesley to the foot of Caer Caradoc. It turns south here and keeping to the eastern side of the valley passes the Strettons (again the names indicate the presence of the road). In places it coincides with the A49, before it turns away from the modern road at the Marshbrook level crossing and climbing onto the higher ground makes for Bushmoor, Leamoor Common, Wistanstow (the high bank on the eastern side of the lane as it comes into the village may be the remains of the *agger*) and the crossing of the River Onny near The Grove. Here it is realigned towards the western flank of View Edge and runs above the River Clun past Rowton, Shelderton and on to Leintwardine, just before which traces of the *agger* can be seen on the hillside south of Stormer Hall. The Romans chose this more westerly route in preference to that of the modern main north/south road, the A49, because it gave closer access to the pathways into the eastern hills of Wales, up the valleys of the Clun, the Teme, the Lugg and the Arrow, and, running as it did on the western flank of the limestone ridge which trends south for ten miles or so from View Edge, it commanded good lines of vision into the hills and valleys further west.

Beyond Leintwardine it leaves the modern road, running a little to its east by Paytoe, before coming close to it again to pass through the gap in the hills above Aymestrey, and then on past Kingsland, through Canon Pyon (so skirting to the west the steep escarpment of Dinmore Hill which the modern road has to surmount), before one branch veers westward by Credenhill to Kenchester. Having crossed the Wye, its course is clear down to the Golden Valley, but after that less certain, as it headed for Abergavenny, Usk and the legionary base at Caerleon-on-Usk.

So the Watling Street West in south-west Shropshire is a characteristic example of a Roman military road and of the Romans' abilities as road makers. It is well planned, surveyed and engineered to make the very best use of the lie of the country, both tactically and locally, as in its use of the flanks of the hills in the lower Clun Valley, and strategically and over the broader sweep of the land on its route to distant Caerleon, as in its use of the gaps through the hills past Stretton and down to Aymestrey.

So much for the authenticated roads. What of the others proposed for the area? Forty years ago Dr. A.W.J. Houghton identified two in particular. One is an extension north from an authenticated road which the Ordnance Survey shows in northern Herefordshire to the east of Leominster. This route came north-north-west from Gloucester to the east of Hereford and Leominster, ending on the map at Ashton about seven miles south of Ludlow. The second—a road accepted, unlike the first, as certain by Ivan Margary in his magisterial study *Roman Roads in Britain*—ran east/west across this area from a fort at Greensforge, to the west of Dudley, making for the forts on the Severn upstream from Welshpool and Newtown.

The first of these roads as it appears on the map of Roman Britain ends virtually in the middle of nowhere. It was coming from Gloucester, but where was it going? Dr. Houghton believed that it was heading for Wroxeter. On that basis, he suggested a route northwards, of uncertain line south of Ludlow, crossing the River Teme at a ford downstream from Ludford Bridge and passing over the Ludlow ridge on the line of Old Street and Corve Street. Beyond Ludlow its line has been lost in the construction of the railway and of more modern roads and does not re-emerge until the level crossing at Bromfield by Ludlow Race Course (a Roman marching camp was discovered and partially excavated here in the late 1950s), whence it continues as a lane to the east of the railway through to Onibury village. From Onibury it climbs away from the marshy valley of the River Onny and takes an almost straight line due north, below the hill to the west, on which stands Norton Camp, a fine Iron Age fort. It goes over the Craven Arms/Bridgnorth road at Greenway Cross and, traversing the western end of the Wenlock Edge escarpment, passes the Dinchopes before cutting down a narrow defile to ford the Byne Brook at Strefford (a name to which Dr. Houghton attached significance; as he also did to the fact that in an early map the Byne Brook was called the Strad Brook—'Strad' as in Strat- or Street- ford). At this point it is only a mile from the Watling Street West at Wistanstow, and there is a footpath which takes a direct line north-west to join that road at Leamoor Common. But Dr. Houghton suggested the

Roman road was on a northerly alignment set by the lane down which it had come from Lower Dinchope to the Strefford ford. He therefore traced it on to Upper Affcot, where another marching camp was detected in 1959, Felhampton, where excavation showed a solid stone surface extending under the hedge on the west of the A49, to Marsh Farm and on along the line of the Old Ludlow Road west of the railway to join the Watling Street West at Marshbrook. Again, excavation in Marsh Wood revealed a well made and level surface cut out of the bedrock.

The second of Dr. Houghton's proposed roads, that from the fort at Greensforge through the central Welsh Marches to the Upper Severn forts, crosses the Severn at Bridgnorth and comes into the Corvedale by Aston Eyre, where parts of the *agger* were reported in 1960 as very well preserved, and Monkhopton. A mile before Shipton the Roman road keeps to the south of the River Corve, running down a metalled lane for much of the way on a low ridge between the Corve and the Trow Brook before rejoining the modern road at Beambridge. Excavation here revealed that the road was some fifteen feet wide and set upon large stones. This alignment continues true, following the modern road past Munslow, Aston Munslow and Diddlebury, before swinging over the watershed between the Corve and the Onny and dropping towards Craven Arms. A footpath by Halford Vicarage indicates the line the road took north-west to ford the Onny by Newington and then to re-align up Long Lane, passing the site of a marching camp, crossing the Watling Street West, and climbing into the hills beyond.

From now on the lie of the land makes straight alignments less frequent on the route. Passing Wart Hill, an Iron Age hill settlement above the Hopesay Valley, and on through Round Oak, it drops steeply into the valley at Basford, climbs past Edgton and makes down hill to the Red House. Its path is now over Oakley Mynd above Lydbury North (a stretch along which flint implements have been found in profusion, so this may have been the line of a more ancient track following through from the Kerry Ridgeway and matching the Clun-Clee Ridgeway on the hills to the south), down Stank Lane into Bishop's Castle past the church and straight on, with only a minor kink, for Moat Hill and the ridge above the valley of the River Camlad.

By the motte and bailey at Bishop's Moat, the road forks. A branch down the side of the escarpment to the northwest may have been a Roman route heading for a fort close to the River Caebitra crossing at Brompton and on to Forden Gaer on the Severn. But the main line, with traces of the *agger* visible in places, keeps to the ridge above Mainstone, where Offa's

Dyke crossed it and where excavations turned up substantial remains of the *agger*, which was, to quote Dr. Houghton, 'constructed of rammed shale strengthened by pitched stone and ... immensely hard.' After this it proceeds to a further branch at Pantglas, where the Kerry Ridgeway turns off south-westward, the road straight on aiming for the defile below Pant Hill, coming by City to Sarn (the Welsh word for 'causeway') and thence to Kerry, Newtown and Caersws, a nodal point for the Roman routes in Central Wales.

The strands of evidence which suggest Roman development (or consolidation) and use seem much stronger for this road than for the proposed road from Ashton (the Ashton/Marshbrook link). It had an evident strategic value, linking the forts of middle Wales rather more directly to routes in central England than the roads which follow the line of the Severn round through Wroxeter. On several stretches the alignments remain clear and true; there are a number of traces of *agger* along the route. And the excavation evidence, where it is available, is not inconsistent with Roman construction. For the Ashton/Marshbrook link the evidence is less clear cut. The place name evidence at Strefford is significant, but there are fewer straight alignments, and Dr. Houghton cites no findings of the *agger*. The excavated sections are not certainly dateable as Roman. And the strategic need for a Gloucester/Wroxeter link by this route is not immediately obvious. One is tempted to suggest, although there is scant evidence on the ground, that the route after Ashton made for the forts and settlement at Leintwardine, especially if Dr. Webster's proposal is correct that there was a Roman route up the Teme valley towards the mid-Wales forts.

But this is to dally with the sort of speculation which Christopher Taylor warns against, as are, at present, any attempts to find road links to the apparently isolated first century fort at Walltown Farm two miles north-east of Cleobury Mortimer.

We can, indeed, be sure that south-west Shropshire was crossed by trackways—some age-old—which linked its scattered farms and minor and major settlements. We can be certain that the mines around Snailbeach and the Stiperstones would have roads for the transport of their products to southern England. We know the line of the main and authenticated military roads through south Shropshire. We may be reasonably confident of the east/west military route down the Corvedale and onwards to the Upper Severn. But beyond that, in the present state of knowledge, we cannot venture.

Bibliography

Houghton, Dr. A.W.J. *Transactions of the Shropshire Archaeological Society Vol. LVI (1960)*, p. 233 and *Vol. LVII (1961)*, p. 185

Margary, Ivan D. *Roman Roads in Britain* Revised Edition, 1967

Putnam, W.G. *The Roman Road from Westbury to Forden Gaer*

Montgomeryshire Collections, LXI, p. 89

Ordnance Survey *Ludlow, Wenlock and the surrounding area* (Landranger 137 - 1:50000).

Ordnance Survey *Roman Britain* Fourth Edition, 1991

Stanford, S.C. *The Archaeology of the Welsh Marches* Revised Edition, 1991

Taylor, C. *Roads and Tracks of Britain* 1979

Webster, G. *The Cornovii*, Revised Edition 1991

White, R. and Barker, P. *Wroxeter - Life and Death of a Roman City* Tempus, 1998

The reasons for the Roman invasion and long occupation of Britain have always been a cause for debate. One undisputed objective of the invaders was the search for valuable mineral resources. In south-west Shropshire, they found lead, and their short-lived but intensive investigation of the Stiperstones / Hope Valley / Linley area has left some intriguing archaeological evidence of their methods of locating, extracting and processing the metal deposits.

CHAPTER 4

The Roman Lead Workings at Linley

by Roger White

'Britain bears gold, silver, and other metals which are the prize of victory'. Tacitus, *Agricola, 12*

For Tacitus, writing at the end of the first century A.D., the aims, and fruits, of conquest were clear: to add further riches to the Imperial treasury and lustre to the glory of Rome. This, however, cannot be the simple explanation for the conquest of the area we now know as Shropshire. Once the Emperor Claudius decided to invade Britain, for his own political ambitions and to out-general Caesar himself, the natural geography of the island demanded the extension of Roman control beyond the generally low-lying south and east of Britain and into the more difficult terrain of the western and northern lands. Rome was already fully aware by the time of Augustus, at the beginning of the first millennium, that Britain's resources were unevenly distributed. While the south and east was the most productive part of the island for cereals and other arable crops, the south-west peninsula was rich in 'white lead' (the Roman term for tin) and lead, from the Mendip hills, while in the Welsh massif and its borders there were rich supplies of lead, copper, and gold. As Pliny the Elder himself noted, in Spain and Gaul, lead was mined with considerable effort, but in Britain 'it is found on the surface in such large quantities that there is a law limiting production'.[1] The Welsh Marches also harboured a more gentle pastoral aspect which raised much-needed reserves of livestock for the army and civilian populations.

The century following the Boudiccan revolt of 60 A.D. saw Britain making steady progress towards a fully Romanised state. In the Nineties, the army finally left Wroxeter for its new fortress in northern Cornovian territory, at Chester on the River Dee. Their fortress at Wroxeter was mostly levelled, although some of its buildings remained and its street grid was reused and extended to form the layout of the new town.[2] By the mid-second century, the town had constructed its principal public buildings: a forum (in modern terms a combined market and county hall) and a splendid public baths with combined shopping mall (*macellum*). The dedication to the forum, by the people of the tribe, was to the then Emperor, Hadrian (117-138), during his thirteenth regnal year, 129-130.[3] The same emperor appears, coincidentally, on one of the few tangible remains of the Roman lead industry in Shropshire: the lead pigs which bear his name, one of which still resides at Linley Hall.[4]

The history of Roman lead working in Shropshire is still unfortunately obscure, largely because so little work has been done on the subject. Some of the aspects may be fleshed out from other areas of Britain, but even so the detail remains elusive. Nonetheless, it is clear that the lead industry was one of great importance both locally and to the Roman Empire as a whole. There is little sign that the mineral had been worked in the Iron Age, although some must have been acquired since Iron Age metalsmiths knew that a small addition of lead to the basic constituents of bronze—copper and tin—would allow the alloy to flow more easily into the moulds demanded by the complex shapes so beloved in the later Iron Age. Presumably the small amounts used came from surface collection. Although the Romans were interested in British lead for its own sake, primarily for use in buildings as water pipes, pool-lining, and to cover roofs, but also to make coffins and as one of the constituent parts of the alloy pewter, a popular product of the later Roman period in Britain,[5] their initial and overriding interest came from the wish to acquire bullion. The lead found in the Shropshire hills, as in many of the other lead ores in Britain, was argentiferous so that if the ore was roasted in a furnace with bone ash at its base, the result was a bloom of lead, and silver fused with bone ash. This latter mixture was then further refined by burning away the bone leaving the silver behind. The process, called cupellation, was possibly known to the Iron Age peoples since it is an extremely simple technique, but was certainly used widely in Roman Britain as cupellation hearths are known at a number of sites, including Wroxeter.[6]

Naturally, since silver was, along with gold, the mainstay of the currency, mines producing bullion were under the exclusive control of the Emperor through his army. Thus, at major lead-working sites, such as that at Charterhouse-on-Mendip, there is a Roman fort whose garrison would have had responsibility for mining the lead ore and producing silver. The by-product, lead pigs, were invariably marked with the Emperor's name since they came from mines owned by the Imperial estate. Such dated lead pigs have been found from all the major lead-bearing areas of Britain: the Mendips, the Derbyshire Peaks, Shropshire, Yorkshire, and North Wales (Flintshire).[7] Indeed, lead pigs found in the Mendips carry the remarkably early date of 49 A.D., a mere six years after the conquest, arguing for an extremely rapid assessment of ore quality and subsequent exploitation.[8] The mining itself was carried out not by soldiers but by criminals or slaves, as witnessed by slave-gang chains found in the gold mine at Dolaucothi, the soldiers merely acting as their overseers. The lead, too, could be used by the army for their own purposes. One of the few contemporary inscriptions mentioning Britain's most famous governor, Iulius Agricola, was found on lead pipes from Chester's fortress.[9] However, the lead in this instance almost certainly came from the mines in Flintshire, the territory of the Deceangli, rather than from Shropshire since that source was not only closer to Chester but was also accessible by water, an important consideration when the weight of Shropshire lead pigs is 86 kg (190 lb.). Shropshire's lead ores are, however, rather low in silver content and it was known by the Romans that the closer the ore is to the surface, the higher the proportion of silver. Thus, the more lead ore was mined, the less profitable it became. Indeed, even at its best, the return from Shropshire's workings may have been so poor that silver extraction may not have been worthwhile at all.[10] When this point was reached, the mine might be let out to a concessionary who would pay a fee to the Imperial treasury in return for working the mine for his own profit. He would work the mine with slaves too, but probably not exclusively since some freemen are also attested, these presumably working in the mine for their own profit. This accounts for some of the pigs which bear not the name of the Emperor but of the lessee, usually an unknown individual, such as the citizen C. Nipius Ascanius who is attested on a lead pig from North Wales dated to 74 A.D.[11]

The soldiers working the mines at Linley and Shelve, the two sites known to be have been worked in the Roman period by the army, do not seem to have been based in a substantial fort like that known at Charterhouse. Instead, the nearest known military site is the tiny fort on the top of Linley Hill, north of the workings at Norbury.[12] This is large enough only to have held 16 men, the *turmae* of a cavalry regiment, who would presumably have patrolled the area. Given their isolated position, it is difficult to believe that these men can have been controlling the mine. Instead it may be suggested that the men in charge of the mining were based instead at Wroxeter since the fortress is less than one day's march from the lead mines. After about 90 A.D., there would have had to have been a reorganisation since the Wroxeter fortress was relinquished and it is perhaps at this date that the workings in the Linley area were leased out to civilians. Alternatively, the men supplying the garrison for the mine and for the fort on Linley Hill could have been drawn from the auxiliary fort at Brompton, only 10 km away, or Forden Gaer, the nearest permanently occupied auxiliary fort, 13 km west of Linley.

Whichever authority or lessee was working the lead ores, the techniques of working are still clear in the landscape even today, although much more has been lost to post-medieval reworking of the area, especially in the last century. The ores outcrop as bands or reefs which can easily be followed as veins across the landscape. The ore was thus simply quarried away by following the vein until it became too deep. Where veins lay more horizontally, they would be followed into the earth from their exposed face as drift-mines, as in the copper mine at Llanymynech. Reworking of these veins, as for example at the Roman Gravels Mine and at Shelve, have uncovered evidence of the Roman working in the form of lead pigs and, more astoundingly, some of their tools. Principal among these are two wooden shovels, carved from riven oak planks and fashioned to the shape of angular table-tennis bats, which survive still at Linley Hall.[13] Square holes cut into the centre of the blade show that these were mounted on short handles to be used as entrenching tools—the blade shovelling debris away and the 'handle' of the bat acting as a tool to rake out cracks. Their survival may be attributed to the dry atmosphere of the workings since wooden artifacts such as these are otherwise rarely preserved. To these may be added other items which one may guess were used but which have not survived. Wicker baskets, for instance, would have transported the ore and other debris away from the workings, while the rock face itself would have been broken up by fire-setting, an ancient mining technique involving the heating of rock through fire followed by its sudden drenching to cause the rock to shatter. The weakened rock would then be broken up with iron picks and wedges.

In those areas where veins were suspected, but could not be easily followed due to an overburden of thin soil and turf, another technique was used: hushing, or its related technique, ground-sluicing. First, narrow parallel trenches would be cut down a slope to break up the surface. The Roman term for these was *corrugi*, a term which amply conveys the impression of these trenches. Meanwhile, temporary reservoirs would be created up-slope of the area being worked upon, these being filled by natural streams diverted for the purpose. Where these were not available nearby, aqueducts consisting of V-shaped leats that could be either rock-cut or of timber, would bring water to the site. When sufficient water had been accumulated, the dams would be broken and the water would rush down the slope, washing away the loosened soil, exposing the rock (and its ore-

Pl.3 Marks of Roman hushing near Norbury Hill. Parallel lines are visible running across fields from left to right

veins) below. If successful, the ore veins thus exposed could then be followed easily.[14] Evidence for the system's use in the area survives dramatically on the slopes of Linley Hill, west of Norbury. Here, there are the thin grooves caused by the trenching and, more difficult to observe, the remains of the reservoirs surviving as platforms on the slope. The remains are very difficult to appreciate on the ground and are best seen from aerial photographs,[15] but the fact that they do survive shows that the prospecting, here at least, was unsuccessful since had substantial amounts of ore been discovered, the site would have been developed as an open-cast mine. (It is important to distinguish hushing or ground-sluicing from the related technique of hydraulicing. This is a mining operation used more commonly today, especially in the mining of kaolin in Devon and Cornwall, that consists of blasting away at a rock face with a high-pressure hose. This requires a means of building up and delivering water under high pressure, a technology the ancient world did not have.)

Once the ore had been mined, it would be carried away for processing. This would be done as near as possible to the site to avoid having to transport huge quantities of rock over long distances. The ore would be washed and sorted, the residue then being processed in separate buildings away from the mining area. These are almost certainly what the 'villa' buildings are at Linley Hall that were partially excavated in the mid-nineteenth century. The excavated buildings consisted of several small rooms with hypocausts—the Roman system of heating rooms by suspending the floor over a cellar, the floor being supported by numerous pillars that allowed hot air to circulate beneath. The size of the rooms, and the presence of an aqueduct, make it virtually certain that this was a bath house rather than some elaborate process for washing or otherwise treating the ore.[16] This bath house was located at the corner of a compound whose full extent was not found but which seems to have extended for several hundred metres to the west and north, towards the present hall. Within this compound, a few other buildings were located but these were not as thoroughly investigated as the bath house and their purpose and number remain unclear. Despite this, we can make a good guess that these other buildings were for accommodation, ore-processing and smelting. The details of the complex are necessarily unclear, but a very similar site has been excavated in modern times in north Wales. This is the site at Pentre Farm, just outside Flint and on the Dee estuary shoreline.

The Pentre Farm range of buildings, built in around 120 A.D. and occupied until about 240, was a complex site that produced some evidence for official construction and use.[17] Primarily, this came from the construction method used in the first phase buildings. These were made from prefabricated panels, a method identical to that seen in fort buildings throughout Britain and the other provinces. In a later phase, some tiles stamped with the name of the Twentieth Legion were found. These could only have been used on a military site since they were made by the legion in its tile factory at Holt, also on the River Dee. The buildings were not uncovered in their entirety and hence some uncertainty must surround their interpretation but the general character of the site is not in doubt. In the first phase, a simple accommodation block, not dissimilar to the barracks of a fort, were constructed. Surrounding this on three sides were a possible stable block and a house, the whole arranged around a court-yard. Later on, in the second half of the second century or beginning of the third, the complex was rearranged to provide a more substantial stone built accommodation block with the barrack block retained at one end and, parallel with it, a bath house with the rooms arranged in a row (*Reihentyp*, 'row-type').

The official, or quasi-official, nature of the site has been interpreted in two ways: the excavators see the site as the official residence of a mining official, or military officer serving the same function, who was adminis-tering the mining and shipping of lead out from the district with ore processing being carried out either on the same site or nearby. Ernest Black, however, sees the complex as a posting station along the coast road, a *mansio*, where officials might get a room for the night, a change of horses or oxen for their wagon, and a bath.[18] These were provided at government expense at regular intervals along the roads of the entire empire to allow the Imperial posting system to function. Whatever the true interpretation of the Pentre site (and it is not inconceivable that it changed from one function to another), the site provides a suggestive parallel for what might be expected in a mining area. One would expect a mining official, a *procurator*, to control the operations and to make sure that the mine operated to its full efficiency, and such a man would expect to be provided with accommoda-tion and comforts commensurate with his status. The buildings at Linley Hall, imperfectly understood though they are, probably represent just such a complex.[19]

For the moment, this is all we may hazard as to the operation of the mines in the Linley area. There is a considerable amount of work still to be done on the sites, and much that could be achieved through effective modern geophysical prospecting methods using machines that can detect buildings by differentiating minute variations in the earth's magnetic field caused by human activity (magnetometry survey) or by measuring the resistance to an electrical current passed through the ground (resistivity survey). Ideally, both should be used, in conjunction with a full measured survey of the fields both at Linley Hall and at Linley Hill. Such surveys are relatively quick, cheap, and easy to carry out, certainly in comparison with excavation which can be very costly, and of course ultimately destructive. If such a survey could be arranged, we would have a much clearer picture of the exploitation of this important resource in the Roman period.

*   *   *

One final word should be reserved for two categories of monument of undoubted Roman date in the area. The first are the carved fragments built into the garden wall at Linley Hall itself. These are variously of first to third century A.D. date and are all derived from funerary monuments of two types: ash chests (for cremations) and sarcophagi fragments. The ash chests are the earlier since inhumation was largely a rite of the later Roman period. The chests are decorated with garlands of flowers and with other symbols designed to invoke the otherworld and the triumph of the spirit over death. The same themes figure on the sarcophagi in the form of Dionysiac scenes that reminded the viewer of Dionysus' triumph over death itself. An isolated funerary inscription in green-veined *cippolino* marble in the Hall itself commemorates the death and burial of a veteran of the Imperial fleet at Misenum, on the Bay of Naples. These monuments are all clearly products of the Grand Tour of the eighteenth century and, although interesting in their own right, tell us nothing of the Roman site at Linley. In the other monument category, again almost certainly a Grand Tour import, are the geometric mosaic fragments to be found on either side of the font in More church. These are of such good quality and preservation that they are extremely unlikely to be of local derivation. Certainly, had they been found in the excavations at Linley Hall in 1856, they would have been mentioned in Wright's account.

References

1. Nat. Hist. Bk. XXXIV, 164. For the early knowledge of Britain's produce, the geographer Strabo (first century BC - first century A.D.) famously referred to exports of grain, cattle, hunting dogs, gold, silver and iron (Bk. IV, 5, 2).
2. R.H. White and P.A. Barker (1998) *Wroxeter, Life and Death of a Roman City*, Tempus (Stroud), 49-50 and 72-7.
3. D. Atkinson (1942) *Report on Excavations at Wroxeter (the Roman City of Viroconium) in the county of Salop, 1923-7* (Oxford), 177-84; The inscription is R.I.B. 288; *Roman Inscriptions of Britain, vol 1, Inscriptions on Stone* (1965), (eds.) R.G. Collingwood and R.P. Wright (Oxford U.P.), 97.
4. Three lead pigs are definitely known from Shropshire: R.I.B. 2404.28-30 (*Roman Inscriptions of Britain, vol. 11, fasc.* I Instrumentum Domesticum: *The Military* Diplomata; *Metal Ingots; Tesserae; Dies; Labels; and Lead Sealings* (1990), (eds.) S.S. Frere, M. Roxan and R.S.O. Tomlin, (Sutton, Stroud), 50-3. They were found at Aston (3 miles north-west of Bishop's Castle), Snailbeach (found at Snailbeach Farm) and Snead (found near The Roveries, an Iron Age and/or Romano-British enclosure). A fourth, reputed to be from the Gravels Mine, Shelve, is in fact that from Aston, this example being the pig now at Linley Hall (cf. G.C. Whittick (1932), 'The Shropshire pigs of Roman lead' *Trans. Shropshire Archaeol and Nat. Hist. Soc, Vol. XLVI*, 129-35, esp. 131).
5. N. Beagrie (1989), 'The Romano-British Pewter Industry' *Britannia* 20, 169-191.
6. R.F. Tylecote (1962), *Metallurgy in Archaeology. A Prehistory of Metallurgy in the British Isles.* (Arnold, London), 75-82. The Wroxeter hearth is mentioned in J.P. Bushe-Fox (1914), *Second Report on the Excavations on the Site of the Roman Town at Wroxeter, Shropshire 1913* Rep. Research Comm. Soc. Antiquaries London 2 (Oxford U.P.), I 1.
7. All those from Shropshire have identical inscriptions: IMP[ERATORIS] HADRIANI AVG[VSTI], i.e. [Property] of The Emperor Hadrian Augustus.
8. E.g. R.I.B. 240 1.1 from Wookey Hole, Somerset (*op. cit.* n.4, 38-9).

9. Conveniently illustrated in W.S. Hanson (1987), *Agricola and the Conquest of the North*, pl.4. The inscription reads: IMP. VESP. VIIII T. IMP VII COS. CN IVLIO AGRICOLA LEG. AVG. PR. PR., (which translates as 'Emperor Vespasian and Titus Imperator, consuls for the ninth and seventh times respectively [i.e. 79 A.D]. Gn. Iulius Agricola, Provincial legate of Augustus with Pro-praetorian powers').

10. On the poor quality of Shropshire's ores, and on the relative levels of silver in British lead ore, cf. Tylecote (*op. cit.* n. 6), 89-92.

11. R.I.B. 2404.38, *op. cit.* n.4, 56. This official is discussed by G. Webster in 'The lead mining industry in North Wales in Roman times', *Journal Flintshire Hist. Soc. (1953)*, 13, 5-33. The lead pigs from Shropshire carry the Emperor Hadrian's title and name, as already noted (n.7) but the pig from Aston at Linley Hall has an incuse mark bearing the initials MINB whilst that from Snailbeach carries the initials NSI. These cannot be further translated but presumably represent the *tria nomina* of a Roman citizen acting as a mining official, or even as a lessee (G. Webster (1991), *The Cornovii* (Sutton, Stroud), 114. All three pigs also bear another mark, a palm branch, cast at the time of manufacture. The significance of this is not known.

12. An excellent aerial photograph of this fort may be found in C.R. Musson and M.D. Watson (1993), *Shropshire from the Air, Man and the Landscape*, 43, photo 44 (Shrewsbury). The site was excavated in 1954, without conclusive dating evidence; G. Webster (1956), 'An investigation of an earthwork at Linley Hill, More' *Trans. Shropshire Archaeol. and Nat. Hist. Soc., Vol. LV*, 119-121.

13. All trace of the Roman workings have been removed by (mostly) Victorian reworking of these areas but accounts from the period refer to the discovery of Roman pottery and tools as deep as 50 ft at the Roman Gravels mine (Shelve) and pottery and a lead pig were found also at Snailbeach (F. Brook and M. Allbutt (1973), *The Shropshire Lead Mines* (Moorland publ., 32 and 65). For a contemporary description, *cf.* T. Wright (1856), 'An Excursion to the Roman Lead Mines in the parish of Shelve, and the Roman Villa at Linley Hall, Shropshire', *Illustrated London News*, 4th October 1856. The shovels are delightfully illustrated as woodcuts in the same account.

14. For an account of both fire-setting and hushing, see A. Woods (1987),'Mining' in (ed.) J. Wacher *The Roman World* vol. 2, 611-34, esp. 615-6 and 625 ff. For the term *corrugi*, see Pliny, *Nat. Hist. XXXIII*, 74).

15. As for example in M.D. Watson and C.R. Musson (1996), *Shropshire from the Air. An English County at Work*, 26 and White and Barker *op cit.* n.2, fig. 29. For a plan of the remains, see G.D.B. Jones and D. Mattingley *(1991), An Atlas of Roman Britain*, Map 6.9.

16. The plan and a description of the remains are conveniently to be found in T. Wright (1872), *Uriconium*, 24-9, itself largely a re-working of the 1856 article referred to in note 13. That account, however, also includes the only known illustration of the hypocausted building.

17. T.J. O'Leary (1989), *Pentre Farm, Flint, 1976-81*. British Archaeol. Rep., Brit. Ser. 207 (Oxford). For a visual summary of the phasing, see fig. 5. The military or official character of the site and its possible function is discussed in *ibid, 50-2*.

18. E.W. Black (1995), Cursus Publicus. *The Infrastructure of government in Roman Britain*, British Archaeol. Rep., Brit. Ser. 241 (Oxford), 32-4.

19. On the role of the procurator in the lead industry, see G. Webster, *op. cit.* n.11.

The coming of the Anglo-Saxon peoples to Britain brought another radical change to the language of the people – the imposition of Old English upon the existing indigenous languages. South-west Shropshire is an area not rich in physical evidence for the Saxon era, but a study of local place-names shows the extent and nature of their penetration.

CHAPTER 5

Place-Names
by Margaret Gelling

Since only a selection of the settlement-names of south-west Shropshire can be discussed in one chapter, those which acquired the special status of parish-names may conveniently be used as a basis for this study. They are marked on the accompanying map.

A very special interest attaches to those names which were adopted by English-speaking people from indigenous Welsh speakers. Here, as elsewhere, a great mystery surrounds the paucity of these pre-English names. It is not possible that in this part of England there were enough Germanic settlers in the post-Roman period to swamp the existing population, so there must have been a change in the language of place-names without a major change in the ethnic composition of the population. Settlement history is one of more or less continuous expansion and some of the places whose names appear on the map will indeed be new foundations of the Anglo-Saxon period. This is most likely in the region round Leebotwood where Haughmond Abbey was developing settlements in woodland even after the Norman Conquest. But the great majority of the parish-names are likely to refer to settlements which were long-established when English-speaking rulers gained control of this area, and what is reflected on the map must be largely a renaming in the language of the new governors.

The most notable of the pre-English items which did survive the language change is Clun, the name of the enormous manor which dominated the south-west corner of the county. This and the adjoining Clunbury and Clungunford are named from the river Clun, which bears a name of prehistoric antiquity identical in origin with rivers in other counties now called Clowne and Colne. In Clungunford the addition is a corruption of Gunward, the name of the last owner before the Norman Conquest, and in Clunbury it is an English word discussed below. Another pre-English river-name is Cound, from which are named the parishes of Cound and Condover ('flat-topped ridge by the River Cound').

Major rivers and large hills are the features most likely to retain ancient names when a change of language occurs, so there is nothing surprising about the survival of Clun and Cound. What is surprising is that they stand alone in this area. The River Corve is of similar size to the Cound, and this and the Rea Brook might also have been expected to retain pre-English names, but in fact Corve is from Old English *corf* 'a cutting', and Rea is from an Old English phrase meaning 'at the river' (Old English *æt thære ie* becoming Middle English *atter e*, with mistaken transference of the *-r* of *atter*). Onny has been considered to be a pre-English name, but close scrutiny of the early spellings suggests that it is more likely to be an English coinage meaning 'single river', referring to the fact that the main river is a union of two equal-sized head-streams.

As regards hill-names, there is, of course, Mynd, which is the Welsh word *mynydd* 'mountain'. This was perhaps not the specific pre-English name of the Long Mynd (as Wrekin was for the mountain in south-east Shropshire) but rather the word by which English-speaking people heard Welsh speakers referring to the massif. Even so it is a welcome reminder of the indigenous language, and a contrast to Clee, the dominating massif in south-east Shropshire, which has an Old English name (*Cleo*) meaning 'ball'. The most prominent of the Church Stretton hills, Caer Caradoc, was earlier *Cordock*, a name which can be traced back to the thirteenth century. The association with Caratacus is late, as is the addition of Welsh *caer*. *Cordock*, unexplained as yet, may be a pre-English hill-name.

Some overtly Welsh names on the county boundary, Bettws-y-Crwyn, Llanfair and, further north, Llanyblodwel and Llanymynech are not relevant to this discussion, as they are the comparatively late type of Welsh name which is likely to have come into use after most of the English names which will be discussed here. The two Walcots, one in Chirbury parish and the other in Lydbury North, are, however, relevant to the question of Welsh survival after the English takeover. In these names, which mean 'cottages of the Welsh', there is an Old English reference which may be to places where Welsh speech persisted after English had mostly replaced it as the language of the countryside.

Despite their English names most of the settlements whose names appear on Fig. 3 are likely to have been in existence throughout the Roman period and probably for centuries before that. The language of Roman Britain was a Celtic one which philologists call British (from which Welsh and Cornish are descended); so it follows that these ancient settlements once had British names. Clun and Cound were probably applied to settlements as well as rivers: the use of river-names for important places on their courses is well evidenced from Roman Britain. As regards all the others, however, we can unfortunately only speculate. It is perhaps possible to obtain a glimpse of the way in which some of the English names on our map came to replace British ones by looking at the use of the commonest of all Old English place-name words—*tun*.

Old English *tun* was the standard word for a settlement during the middle part of the Anglo-Saxon period, and there is evidence that its overwhelming popularity as the main term in place-name formation developed about 750 A.D. and lasted till the mid-tenth century, by which time it had developed broader meanings such as 'estate', and 'area with a recognised administrative status'. The *-tun* names on the parish map can be divided into three categories according to the defining element (the 'qualifier') in the compounds: *tun* is never used as a simple name. The three categories are:

1. Names with a qualifier which describes the site: here belong Brompton and Rhiston ('broom' and 'rush'), the two Hoptons ('secluded place'), Stanton (probably referring to stony soil) and Stapleton ('steep place').

2. Names which may have a 'functional' significance: the two Actons, Berrington, Eaton, Shipton and Stretton, which refer, respectively, to oak trees, a fort, a river, sheep and a Roman road. Weston can also be loosely placed in this group. There are four Actons in the south-west quarter of Shropshire, the two which are not parishes being in Lydbury and Rushbury.

3. 'Manorial' names, i.e. those which have as qualifier the genitive of an Old English personal name. These are Abdon (earlier *Abbeton*), Bedstone, Cardington, Sibdon (earlier *Sibbeton*) and Woolstaston.

It is categories 2 and 3 which are of special interest in relation to the replacement of Welsh names by English ones. The 'manorial' names record overlordship of the five places listed by Anglo-Saxons called *Abba*, *Bedgeat*, *Carda*, *Sibba* and *Wulfstan*. These individuals are most likely to

Fig. 3 Map of the Parishes of south-west Shropshire

have been thegns in the service of the king of Mercia sometime between the eighth and tenth centuries, and the grant of the estates to them may well have prompted a change of place-name. They would be likely to establish their wives and families there and perhaps to have a new house built.

The first two names in the second category, Acton and Berrington, need to be considered in a countrywide context. A study of all the occurrences in England of 'oak settlement' (Acton) and 'fort settlement' (Burton / Bourton / Berrington) has shown that the distribution pattern is not random, and that

46

both names have a remarkable concentration in Shropshire, where there are eight examples of the first and six of the second. Trebirt in Llanfair Waterdine is a Welsh rendering of Burton, making a seventh instance of that name in the county. It is likely that both names refer to a specialised function which had developed at these places, and here, too, it may be a case of Mercian names replacing earlier Welsh ones. An Acton may have been a settlement which had responsibility for supplying oak timber at a time and in areas where supplies of this were becoming scarce. The nature of a Burton or Berrington is discussed below.

Eaton, 'river settlement', is another recurrent *-tun* name which is common throughout England but especially so in Shropshire where there are six examples. The rivers referred to are usually bigger than the stream at Eaton under Heywood. Eaton is not likely to be a simple statement that this place is beside a river. This would be meaningless, for instance, in the case of Eaton Constantine, which is no more by the Severn than many other settlements to east and west. The name may have been given in recognition of some service (?ferry, ?transport of goods) for which that settlement was responsible. Similarly the Strettons, besides the obvious fact of their position on a Roman road, may have been widely known as places which provided facilities for travellers. Such names may well have been used by Mercian tax collectors and administrators in preference to Welsh names, and this sort of consideration could apply to Shipton ('sheep farm') and perhaps to Weston. The 'directional' *-tun* names, though not well represented on Fig. 3, are especially common in Shropshire. The county has ten Astons, ten Westons, seven Nortons and seven Suttons. Several of the non-parochial Astons are in south-west Shropshire (Aston Munslow, Aston Piggott and Rogers in Worthen, and Aston on Clun), and there is another Weston in Stowe parish. One of the Shropshire Nortons is in Onibury, and Great and Little Sutton are in Diddlebury. These names could have been convenient labels used by Mercian administrators when dealing with large composite estates like Worthen and Diddlebury, but since no record preserves an earlier Welsh name for any Shropshire settlement this can only be speculation.

The two largest categories of Old English settlement-names are the 'habitative' and the 'topographical'. Habitative names are those which have as their main component (the 'generic') a word like *ham*, *tun*, *cot*, *wic*, *worth* which refers directly to a habitation site. Topographical settlement-names do not explicitly mention the farm or village but define it by reference to an outstanding characteristic of its physical setting. This last category, which is well represented in south-west Shropshire, will be discussed after some observations have been made about habitative names with generics other than *tun*.

There is in south-west Shropshire a noteworthy concentration of parish-names ending in -bury: Chirbury, Clunbury, Diddlebury, Lydbury, Onibury, Pontesbury, Rushbury and Westbury. The modern ending -bury derives from Old English *byrig*, which is the dative case of *burh* 'fortified place'. This is the first element of Berrington (earlier *Buritone*), of which more will be said presently. The Anglo-Saxons used *burh* and *byrig* when refer-ring to Iron Age hillforts (Abdon Burf and The Berth in Baschurch both derive from *burh*); but the parish-names listed above are not likely to refer to archaeological remains. They may in some cases refer to the fortified dwellings which are stated in Anglo-Saxon laws to be maintained by men of the social class called thegns. The planting of a manor house with a ditch, a palisade and a gatehouse in countryside not previously charac-terised by such structures might have prompted the coining of new place-names. The large parish of Worthen has a name which simply means 'enclosure', and this also could be an enclosed manor house of Anglo-Saxon origin.

The Burton/Bourton/Berrington names, of which there are about 100 in England, most of them in the Midlands with a heavy concentration on the Welsh border, may refer to yet another type of fortification. A study of the whole corpus has suggested the possibility that the *burhtuns* and *byrigtuns* were defensive centres set up in Mercia and Northumbria in the period before the Danish wars. They could have been mustering places when men were summoned for military service from the surrounding estates, and also places of refuge for people rendered homeless by the sort of raiding which was probably common in the borderlands. An official called *burhweard* 'fort guardian' is referred to in Broseley, Shropshire, and in Burwardsley, Cheshire, and Treverward in Clun is a Welsh rendering of Burwarton.

The category of topographical settlement-names remains to be consid-ered. Despite what has been said earlier, these are names which are likely to have arisen in the speech of Anglo-Saxons who became part of the farming population. Though there is no likelihood of a complete replace-ment of the earlier population there must have been a steady infiltration of Mercian farmers from about the middle of the sixth century onwards, bringing with them the rich topographical vocabulary in which, all over England, they recorded their response to the varied topography of their new homeland. This vocabulary was a subtle code with numerous words for different sorts of hills, valleys and woods, and for settlement-sites in wet and dry areas. By far the commonest landscape word in place-names is *leah*, giving modern names like Leigh, Lee, Lye and innumerable compounds mostly ending in -ley. This is the Old English term for a settlement in a wooded environment. Such names are well represented on the northern part of the south-west Shropshire map, where they form part of a belt of *leah* names which runs east/west across the centre of the county. This woodland term was much used in place-name formation in the period from about 750 A.D. to about 950, the same period in which *tun* was routinely applied to settlements in more open country. Towards the end of the Anglo-Saxon period, however, *leah* lost its association with woodland and came to mean 'pasture', which is probably the sense in Bitterley, 'butter pasture'.

The next commonest topographical word in Old English place-names (though not used with anything like the frequency of *leah*) is *ford*. Ashford, Halford, Ludford, Pitchford and Tugford are parish-names in south-west Shropshire.

The Anglo-Saxons had a particularly rich vocabulary for describing hills and valleys. In hilly country the valleys offer the best settlement sites, so in south-west Shropshire there is frequent use of valley terms. The favourite valley word in south Shropshire and north Herefordshire was *hop*, which means a secluded place. It is wonderfully illustrated in the great landscape feature of south-west Shropshire, Hope Dale, which lies between the parallel ridges of Wenlock Edge and the Aymestrey limestone escarpment, and which has six -hope settlements nestling in the funnel-shaped hollows where springs rise. Easthope, shown on the map (Fig. 3), is the only one of the Hope Dale places to achieve parish status. Others in south-west Shropshire which have become parishes are Hope Bowdler, Hope Bagot, Hopesay (with medieval owners' names added) and Ratlinghope. The two Hoptons have already been mentioned. Among those which did not become parish centres Hope in Worthen is a noteworthy specimen. Sites designated *hop* are always tucked away, hard to see from nearby roads. The most claustrophobic of all is probably Ratlinghope. Another valley term found frequently in south Shropshire and north Herefordshire is *bæc*, found in Colebatch and Pulverbatch. This denotes a well-marked but not dramatic valley which has a small stream.

The site chosen for the church at Ratlinghope makes an intriguing contrast with that chosen for the church and village in the neighbouring parish of Wentnor. Here the name, Old English *Wentan ofer*, refers to the flat-topped ridge with a gently sloping shoulder which has the village on its end. The word *ofer* is used in place-names throughout England for ridges of precisely this shape. This word is the generic in Condover. (Longnor, however, is a quite different name, *Longan alre*, 'the long alder clump').

This is not an area where hill-top sites are favoured, so the hill term which is commonest in the country as a whole, *dun*, only occurs here in Aldon in Onibury and in the parish-name Edgton, earlier *Eggedune*. (It will be seen from references above to Abdon and Sibdon that -ton and -don are liable to confusion). The term *scelf*, modern *shelf*, from which Shelve derives is used in place-names for a level place in hilly country.

There are some unsolved names. Preen appears to be Old English *preon* 'brooch', but the nature of the reference is obscure. Lydham appears to be the dative plural of *hlid*, modern *lid*, but 'at the lids' is not explicable as a place-name. Caynham is ambiguous. The generic might be *ham* 'village', though this is rarely evidenced west of Birmingham, or it might be *hamm* 'land hemmed in by water', referring to the position between two streams; and the qualifier could be a personal name *Cæga* or a hill-name *Cæge* 'The Key'.

Mainstone and Cressage ('strength stone' and 'oak tree of Christ') are interesting. In the first the reference may be to the boulder now placed by the church pulpit, in the second to a revered oak which was allowed to reproduce itself over centuries, like the Lady Oak half-a-mile from the village.

Wistanstow and Stowe have ecclesiastical connotations. Old English *stow*, 'assembly place' often refers to a holy place, and Wistanstow may have had some association with St Wigstan, the Mercian prince who was murdered about 850 A.D. At Stowe the church of St Michael, the patron saint of high places, is sited at the very top of a valley, unlike the neighbouring churches of Bedstone, Bucknell and Llanfair Waterdine, which are more conveniently sited on lower ground by a road. The name may indicate that this was an ancient holy site.

Some of the assertions made in this chapter may sound dogmatic and arbitrary because there is not space to explain the reasoning underlying them. These matters are, however, discussed in great detail in the books listed below.

Bibliography

Gelling, Margaret in collaboration with H.D.G. Foxall, *The Place-Names of Shropshire*, Part 1, (EPNS LXII/LXIII, 1990)

Gelling, Margaret *The West Midlands in the Early Middle Ages* Leicester University Press, 1992

South-west Shropshire's remote and rugged landscape has probably always been matched by the sturdy independence of its inhabitants, and their resistance to change. Consequently, there is less visual evidence of Saxon settlement than in other parts of the county. Nevertheless, in a number of places it is possible to see buildings which were of pre-Conquest foundation, and to compose a picture of the Saxon era.

CHAPTER 6

Anglo-Saxon Churches & Settlements

by John Saxbee

The Anglo-Saxon Chronicle tells us that, in 1006, Aethelred the Unready 'went across the Thames, into Shropshire and received there his food-rents in the Christmas season'. Less than a century earlier Aethelfleda, the Lady of Mercia, visited the fortified burhs which protected her Kingdom, including Chirbury in south-west Shropshire. Such protective measures were consistent with the grandiose schemes of her Mercian predecessor, King Offa who, towards the end of the eighth century, established the frontier between the English and the Welsh with some of the finest stretches of the Dyke named after him being visible in south-west Shropshire.

To recount these events is virtually to exhaust our reliable knowledge with respect to the Saxon period in south-west Shropshire. Literary and documentary evidence is scant indeed, and such archaeological investigations as there have been provide little of substance on which to build a comprehensive picture. To some extent place-names can help us, and some fairly educated guesses can be made about settlement patterns and ecclesiastical sites. But it is often necessary to argue from silence, or project on to Shropshire features of Anglo-Saxon culture and organisation for which there is more reliable evidence elsewhere. Of course, this is to beg the question as to whether the Marches region actually differed significantly from what was usual in the eastern and southern kingdoms. Proximity to Wales, isolation from the main centres of population and political influence, late arrival of first the Germanic then the Viking invaders, together with the rugged landscape, all have conspired to give this territory a distinctive character and culture which exists even to this day. But this must not be emphasised at the expense of conformity to more general patterns of settlement and organisation, especially as pertaining to the growth and establishment of Christian institutions. Remoteness and sparsity may have resulted in things happening here somewhat later and on a reduced scale, but the Anglo-Saxons left their mark nonetheless.

It is usual to divide the Anglo-Saxon age into three periods beginning about 400 A.D. with the invasion or, more likely, the infiltration of Germanic people into eastern and southern Britain and ending with the Norman conquest in 1066. The first period to about 650 A.D. has been characterised as 'Sub-Roman', the second to 800 A.D. as 'Christian' and the third as 'Late Anglo-Saxon'.

When the Roman legions withdrew from Britain early in the fifth century, Christianity was 'a small, even if expanding, religion',[1] but 'it is abundantly clear that even in the fourth century, Christianity did not oust more traditional forms of religion'.[2] This was especially so in the western Marches, and by the end of the Sub-Roman period it is fair to say that 'a good proportion of the population ... were "Christian" in the sense that they were not actively pagan, but the Christianity so espoused was for the most part shallow and without much personal or corporate conviction'.[3] The Anglo-Saxons brought their gods with them, and Woden, Thor and Frig have left their mark on days of the week. They celebrated festivals such as Lammas and Eostre, and erected shrines. But Romano-British Christianity proved resilient in the face of these infiltrations, and as the British Cornovii people ruled Shropshire throughout this particularly confusing period, it is likely that such Christian allegiance as there was yielded little ground to Germanic custom and habits, whether secular or religious. The relative lack of pagan burial sites suggests that the people of this area remained true to their British Christian heritage, and there is little to suggest that the Anglo-Saxon sphere of settlement and influence extended to the extreme west of Britain to the same degree as in other areas. They held to their own languages, much of their pre-Roman social structure, their settlement patterns and their legal system.

'The Anglo-Saxons were converted to Christianity during the last years of the sixth Century and throughout the seventh, a factor which had more than theological repercussions. Indeed, it is only a slight exaggeration to say that the Conversion created English history, for with Christianity came writing, which led to the setting down of documentary records of contemporary events'.[4]

Whilst Romano-British Christianity had more or less survived the Sub-Roman period, more general conversion from paganism was worked through the kings of the network of kingdoms which evolved out of the smaller warring factions which preceded them. In central England Mercia bordered on Celtic Wales, incorporating the territory of the Wreocensaetan, with the kingdoms of the Magonsaetan and Hwicce controlling the southern Marches. Although the name Mercia means 'boundary people', this kingdom came to play a leading role in eighth-century English politics under the rule of Aethelbald and Offa. They built on the foundations laid by King Penda who was first to lead the English who had settled in the area later defined as Shropshire.

There is not space here to trace the crucial events which culminated in Augustine's mission from Rome to Britain in 597 A.D. and the 'triumph' of Roman Christianity over Celtic Christianity at the Synod of Whitby in 664. Suffice it to say that in the century following the Synod 'Christianity prospered and grew in its coverage of the country, in its organisational efficiency and in the way it became more deeply integrated into the life of society'.[5] This was achieved as much as anything by Archbishop Theodore's re-structuring of the diocesan system. Two guidelines were crucial: all dioceses should relate to the distribution of the population, and there should be a scrupulous regard for political and tribal divisions. Consequently, the Hereford Diocese was created to cover the territory of the Magonsaetan which included what were to become Herefordshire and south Shropshire. These diocesan boundaries remain more or less intact today.

However, even if inhabitants of south-west Shropshire in the seventh and eighth centuries would recognise our diocesan identity, they would not be able to relate to our nucleated villages usually centred on a parish church and with a priest to lead worship and provide pastoral care. Whilst Martin Welch maintains that Anglo-Saxon England possessed most of the characteristics associated with later medieval England, including nucleated villages,[6] H.F. Hamerow argues that 'the traditional image of the stable Anglo-Saxon village as the direct ancestor of the medieval village is no longer tenable in view of growing evidence for settlement mobility in the early and middle Saxon periods'.[7] Sadly, as recently as 1977, J. Graham-

Campbell could comment that 'we still know less about the context and practices of the Anglo-Saxon "village" than we do about the Iron Age farm and the Roman Villa',[8] although Martin Welch believes that, in fact, a good deal of ground was covered in the 1960s and 1970s so that we can claim 'to know the full range of buildings used as houses, stores and workshops, and the organisation and layout of settlements'.[9] However, our knowledge is generally confined to sites to the east and south of this region, so there is a risk in assuming that developments elsewhere were matched by organisation and settlement patterns in the Marches.

Still it is fair to assume that the emerging system of districts ('hundreds') based on a focal community ('*tun*') found some expression in even the westernmost parts of Mercia. The king's deputy was based in the '*tun*' and levied dues based on land occupancy. A 'hide' was the area needed to support a peasant farmer ('*ceorl*') and his family. Indeed, the organisation of labour for building Offa's Dyke was based on the hide-unit so something along these lines must have been in place along the border during the eighth century. The 'hide' had originally been equivalent to 120 acres (about 50 hectares), the amount of arable land deemed sufficient to support a Saxon thane and his family, but by the time the system was applied in the border counties it had come to denote an area of land of recognised value, so that the most fertile land would have the least acres to the hide. Five or ten hides constituted a village for administrative purposes which, in areas of relatively inhospitable land such as south-west Shropshire, would cover an extensive area of land. These would have hardly been nucleated villages in the later sense of the term, and it is likely that such nucleated settlements would have been few and far between on the English-Welsh border. Numerous settlements carry the 'ton' suffix that may indicate origins as a focal community in the middle Saxon period, but this is dealt with more fully in the previous chapter.

Christopher Train points out that: 'the Old English place-name suffixes of "tun" - a settlement - and "bury" - a fortified place or, more probably hereabouts, a manor house - trace the English advance up the Clun and Kemp valleys. Sibdon - the settlement of Sibba (a person's name); Aston - the settlement to the East; Brampton - the settlement where the broom grows; Clunbury - the manor house on the Clun; Clunton - the settlement on the Clun; Kempton - the settlement of Cempa (a personal name) ...'[10]

This is in contrast to the persistence of Welsh names such as Llan and Llanhowell on the higher ground above the Clun Valley. Similarly Clun, as a British pre-Saxon river name, also persisted so if place names are anything to go on we must assume a multi-cultural mix of Welsh, British and English influences in the hills and valleys of the Marches.

When it comes to ecclesiastical sites dating back to the Anglo-Saxon age the evidence is, once again, hard to come by. Kenneth Hylson-Smith's assertion that 'even by the late eighth century many communities with a large population of professing Christians lacked a purpose-built place of worship'[11] is, if anything, a gross understatement. In this area there is little to suggest that there were many communities of Christians sufficient to warrant a church building. David Hill's map of the Church in the West Midlands[12] shows only Lydbury North, and as this 18,000 acre Manor (including what is now Bishop's Castle) was given by its Saxon Lord, Egwin Shakehead, to the Bishop of Hereford in the eighth century, we may safely assume that this was indeed the site of a significant church. Elsewhere in England at this time there were a number of Minster Churches which serviced the surrounding area by providing pastoral care, mission and opportunities for worship. Theodore allowed priests to say Mass 'in the field' with standing crosses marking where such services would be held. A flimsy wooden 'field church' may have been erected in some places but it is more likely that worship took place in the open-air. However, it is far from clear that such Minsters were to be found in all the Anglo-Saxon king-doms and, as in other things, the peculiar remoteness and ruggedness of far-west Mercia warrants a degree of caution. Whilst many churches in south-west Shropshire can make a reasonable case to stand on Saxon sites, and Wentnor can lay claim to some record of earlier Saxon foundations, and More to both a circular churchyard and the proximity of a Roman Villa (both indicators of possible early church building locations), most rely on mere speculation in seeking to establish their Saxon credentials. Whether any such sites date back to before 800 A.D. is doubtful, although the Lydbury North connection and the proximity of Wenlock Priory founded in 690, may give credence to the idea of an early Mother-Church with daughters scattered across the surrounding territory.

Domesday is a valuable guide to how things were soon after the Conquest with its naming of Saxon Manors and their Lords, together with a tally of Mother-Churches and their affiliated Chapelries. Whilst this data must be treated with a degree of caution, such of these as there were are likely to belong to the third and last of the Anglo-Saxon periods.

Mercian power did not long survive after the death of King Offa in 796. The West Saxons became dominant, and in 829 Egbert of Wessex annexed

Mercia as a client kingdom. But the greatest threat came from beyond English shores. The *Anglo-Saxon Chronicle* ominously records:

> In the year [787] Beorhric, King of Wessex, took to wife Eadburgh, daughter of King Offa ... came first three ships from Horthaland: and the reeve rode hither and tried to compel them to go to the royal manor, for he did not know what they were; and then they slew him. These were the first ships of the Danes to come to England.

It was another generation before this Danish nuisance became a major threat. But Alfred emerged as the great Saxon hope at the end of the ninth century by defeating the Danish warlord Guthrun, securing his baptism, and driving him out of Wessex to occupy lands above a line running north-westwards from London to Chester—the Danelaw. Whilst Mercia was invaded by the Danes, it seems their influence was minimal in the west-ernmost parts. It is to be noted, however, that in *Domesday Book*, a man called Swein, a Danish name, held the manors of Clunbury, Kempton, Sibdon, Coston and Edgton in 1066.

Eventually, an alliance between Alfred and Aethelred, King of Mercia, resulted in Alfred's son Edward and daughter Aethelfleda combining to defeat the Danelaw so that by mid-century Wessex and Mercia merged to form a united Southern Britain. This heralded a golden age for art and literature, and it also saw the revival of monasticism under Dunstan, Aethelwold and Oswald. However, the Danes were soon back during the disastrous reign of Aethelred the Unready (978 - 1013) and the Danish King Cnut was soon ruling over lands stretching from the Baltic to the Irish Sea. But his son was unable to keep the empire intact, and in 1042 Aethelred's son Edward was brought back from exile in Normandy to rule as Edward the Confessor. He had no heir, and in the ensuing struggle which followed his death William of Normandy took control in 1066, and the rest, as they say, is history!

Whatever may have been the nature and extent of settlements and church buildings at the end of the eighth century, these suffered grievously at the hands of the Danes and Vikings. But by the early tenth century Aethelfleda was busy constructing fortresses known as '*burhs*' to protect her Mercian borders, and Chirbury provides a good example of such a forti-fied enclosure in what, following the establishment of one of the new shires around the 'city' of Shrewsbury, can now be safely referred to as south-west Shropshire. A little further north the village of Westbury grew up around another *burh* sited on the line of the principal Roman road running from Montgomery to Wroxeter. The *Anglo-Saxon Chronicle* records that in 1053 a number of English soldiers were killed by Welshmen at *Waestbyrig* — probably Westbury village.

It is worth noting that the creation of Shropshire represents what Sir Frank Stenton calls 'an artificial union of lands which had once been divided between the Magonsaetan and the Wreocensaetan',[13] and he notes that old loyalties died hard with the Magonsaetan still referred to in the *Anglo-Saxon Chronicle* of the eleventh century. From this it may be concluded that south Shropshire still retained something of its Magonsaetan tribal identity right up to the Conquest, and beyond.

During the tenth century the basic structure of the English village was confirmed, consisting of slaves, *ceorls* (free peasants with their own land), *gesiths* or *ealdormen* or thanes (lords owning land for at least five cattle), and the great lords, local kings or *eorls* under the king himself.[14] *Domesday* indicates that most Shropshire parishes contained a number of hamlets each with their group of two, three or four open fields with *ceorls* cultivating their allotted strips. Field maps around, for example, the south Shropshire village of

Pl. 4 Saxon herringbone work at Diddlebury church, Corvedale

Wistanstow contain names going back to these original open fields, whilst terms such as ridges, furlongs, headlands and butts have Saxon origins. The best preserved evidence of this system is at the hamlet of Lawton in the Corvedale, but David Hill's map of medieval open fields in England shows that large areas remained uncultivated including Clun Forest and the Long Mynd.[15]

So although about one-tenth of the approximately two million inhabitants of eleventh century England lived in towns, still the vast majority lived in the countryside with its more than 13,000 named 'vills'. Some of these 'vills' were large settlements, but in parts of the country dispersed farms and small hamlets of similar size to those found in the early Anglo-Saxon period continued to exist.[16] In south-west Shropshire this was almost certainly the case with river-crossings, *burhs* and even religious communities attracting settlers whilst most of the population lived and worked in isolation from one another. Such isolation may have had its downside, but it probably ensured greater freedom for the south-west Shropshire *ceorl* than was generally the case for peasantry elsewhere in England in the late Anglo-Saxon period. The size of estates being granted in tenth century charters is smaller than those being given 200 years previously, so it was necessary for lords of manors to make their land more productive by bringing their peasants into subjection and

Pl. 5 Saxon doorway at Diddlebury

working them harder. This was less likely to happen where open fields were less common.

This also impacted on the development of the parochial system. Manorial estates came complete with a church building for the use of the landowner and his labourers. These often became parish churches as the Middle Ages progressed. There is little or no evidence to suggest that such manorial churches proliferated in south-west Shropshire. It is far more likely that Mother-Churches, Minster Churches and Monasteries such as those at Chirbury (*caput* or chief centre of Witenstreu Hundred with Chapelries at Church Stoke and Montgomery), Minsterley (Mother-Church of Westbury), Clun (probably the *caput* of Rinlau Hundred with Chapelries at Clunbury, Sibdon, Edgton and Hopton Castle), Wenlock, Bromfield and Wigmore continued to provide for the spiritual needs of

south-west Shropshire well into the late Anglo-Saxon period. Diddlebury and especially Stanton Lacy just to the east of the area show how wealthy lords provided fine stone churches from the proceeds of their increasingly efficient manorial estates. No such buildings have survived to the west, and even if wooden purpose-built churches did stand on the site of post-Conquest edifices, little or nothing is now left of them. Dean Cranage records that 'at least 70 Churches [in Shropshire] still remaining were founded before Domesday book was completed in 1086'.[17] but these tend to be located in the more easily cultivated lands to the north and east

Pl. 6 Saxon north doorway at Stanton Lacy, near Ludlow

of the county. This fact reflects the geographical and topographical character of south-west Shropshire which governed the extent to which this area reflected general trends elsewhere during the long centuries of Anglo-Saxon influence, and which continues to govern our socio-economic circumstances today. But the Saxons left their mark even this far west, and if England is only what it is because of cultural aspects the Anglo-Saxons brought to our shores, then this is also true with respect to our corner of this ancient County—give or take a degree or two of Salopian stubbornness and determination in the face of unwanted change and in defence of a hard-won and rugged independence.

References

1. Hylson-Smith, K. *Christianity in England from Roman Times to the Reformation* Vol. 1. SCM, 1999, p. 64
2. Henig, M. 'Religion in Roman Britain' in Todd (Ed.) *Research on Roman Britain* p.230
3. Hylson-Smith, *op.cit.* p.132-3
4. Laing, Lloyd & Jennifer Laing *Anglo-Saxon England* Routledge, 1979, pp.89-90
5. Hylson-Smith, *op.cit.* p.183
6. Welch, M. *Anglo-Saxon England* Batsford,1992, p.120
7. Hamerow, H.F. 'Settlement, Mobility and the "Middle Saxon Shift": Rural Settlements and Settlement Patterns in Anglo-Saxon England', *Anglo-Saxon England 20*, 1991, pp.7-8
8. Graham-Campbell, J. 'British Antiquity - Western British, Irish and later Anglo-Saxon', *Archaeology* 134
9. Welch, *op.cit* p.14
10. Train, C. *Quietest Under the Sun* Scenesetters, 1996, p.20
11. Hylson-Smith, *op.cit.* p.205
12. Hill, D. *An Atlas of Anglo-Saxon England* Blackwell, 1981, p.160
13. Stenton, F.M. *Anglo-Saxon England* OUP, 1971, p.337
14. Service, A. *The Buildings of Britain - Anglo-Saxon and Norman* 1982, p.28
15. D. Hill, *op. cit.* p.112.
16. M. Welch, *op.cit.* p.120.
17. D.H.S. Cranage, *The Churches of Shropshire*, 1912, p.1019.

The following chapter sketches the history of a small corner of England over one dark century. It charts the wide-ranging campaigns and battles of two cultures, at a time when the history of the area is central to the history of England. Most remarkable is the presence of Offa's Dyke, the massive eighth century earthwork which offers us insights into the Early Middle Ages.

CHAPTER 7

A Frontier in Flames: The Eighth Century
by David Hill

The Anglo-Saxon written sources for the eighth century are poor: Mercia is mainly ignored by the great record of the years, the *Anglo-Saxon Chronicle*, the land-charters are few and far between, and the area is a remote part of the country. However there is a little more Welsh material in the *Annales Cambriae*—the *Chronicle of Wales*—and a unique inscription relating the situation on the frontier from the Pillar of Eliseg. There is above all the monument known as Offa's Dyke, a complex source in itself. There are no architectural, numismatic or ceramic sources. From these fragile materials an attempt is made to construct a coherent story.

In his work on Offa's Dyke Sir Cyril Fox gave a picture of an agreed frontier between peoples, though with the conquering Saxons gaining the high ground and associated commanding views to the west. The dyke system was seen by Fox and Stenton as the product of Offa's final years of power, but this model is now questioned because much more evidence has been brought to light, both by excavation and through reconsideration of the limited texts, in the 60 years since Fox's fieldwork. A new model can be formulated.

Shropshire did not exist until the early tenth century, when it appears as a result of the shiring of Mercia, probably in the 920s. The present-day county results from the south-west boundary being extended under the Act of Union of 1536 and subsequent Acts to include, in particular, the lordship of Clun. The territorial divisions of the area can probably be suggested with the area of present day northern Shropshire being the territory of the Wreocensaetan and the southern area being the northern part of the territory of the Magonsaetan. The Anglo-Saxon kingdom of Mercia certainly lay in the basin of the middle Severn in the eighth century and to its west lay Welsh Powys and its administrative sub-divisions, the cantrefs.

In the *Life* of Beuno, a saint who belongs to the beginning of the seventh century, it is said that, after having been for some time settled at Berriew, near the Severn, Beuno one day heard an Englishman's voice on the further side of the river, egging on his dogs to the chase of a hare (the huntsman was shouting 'Charge! Charge!', *Kergia, Kergia*). Beuno turned upon his heels and without delay went back to his followers, bidding them to make up their baggage and prepare for instant removal. 'For,' he said, 'the kinsmen of yonder strange-tongued man whose voice I heard across the river setting on his dogs will obtain possession of this place, and it will be theirs, and they will hold it in ownership'. The *Life* is late and the incident may be fictitious, but the spirit breathed in those words was most certainly that which possessed the British church in St. Beuno's day.

It should be noted that Berriew was, and still is, on the frontier of Wales. On the Saxon side of the border, it is believed that the area around Much Wenlock was sufficiently settled for Milburga to found a nunnery, or a double monastery, there in the third quarter of the seventh century. It is possible to envisage, therefore, an area of British occupation and one of Welsh divided by an area of disputed land used only for hunting by each side (as was the Vale of Powys in 1066). However, this frontier was neither static nor was it peaceful for long.

The sequence of events revealed by the sources is complex as stroke was followed by counterstroke, with first the Welsh and then the Mercians dominant, the *de facto* frontier moving with the tide of warfare. The *Annales Cambriae* record that in 721 '... the battle of Heilyn took place in Cornwall, and the battle of Garthmaelog and the battle of Pencoed in Deheubarth, and in those three battles the Britons prevailed ... Seven hundred and thirty was the year of Christ when there was a battle on Mynydd Cam.'

Sir Frank Stenton believed that there was evidence from the *Life* of Guthlac that 'in the reign of King Cenred, that is between 705 and 709, the Welsh were carrying out a series of devastating raids over Mercia', whilst Finberg mentions that Much Wenlock may 'have suffered in the Welsh incursions of Ceolred's reign' (709-716).

66

According to the *Annales Cambriae*, in 754 'Rhodri, king of the Britons' died, and this was followed in 756, as noted in the *Anglo-Saxon Chronicle*, by the murder of 'Ethelbald, King of the Saxons'. Æthelbald was king of Mercia and overlord of all England south of the Humber, and his death was followed by civil war from which Offa eventually emerged as the Mercian king. In 760 the *Chronicle* records that 'an encounter took place between the Britons and Saxons in the battle of Hereford.' As Hereford lay within the Mercian kingdom, albeit towards its western edge, it appears that the British resurgence continued in the early years of Offa's reign, a version of events corroborated by the ancient cross now known as the 'Pillar of Eliseg'.

This pillar, which stands in Valle Crucis, Powys, became a famous landmark and gave its name to the valley and later to the nearby abbey. The cross was thrown down in the Civil War, and lay in two pieces when recorded by Edward Lhuyd in 1696. The original inscription, now worn and indecipherable, was exceptionally long (at least 32 lines), and modern research is based on Lhuyd's record. This records the inscription as:

+   CONCENN FILIUS CATTELL CATTELL
+   Concenn being great-grandson of Eliseg
EDIFICAUIT HUNC LAPIDEM PRO AUO
erected this stone to his great-grandfather
SUO ELISEG
Eliseg

Other information on the pillar records that Eliseg and Concenn who, according to the *Annales Cambriae*, died in 854 were kings of Powys. Fox calculates Eliseg's reign to have been from 765 to 773, thereby occupying the throne during Offa's reign, between 757 and 796, in Mercia. The important information on the pillar is as follows:

+   IPSE EST ELISEG QUI NEC(?)
+   It was Eliseg who annexed
XIT HEREDITATEM POUO(I)S
[...the inheritance of Powys....]
PERVIIII [ANNOS(?)] E POTESTATE ANGLO
throughout nine (years?) from the power of the English,
RUM IN GLADIO SUO PARTE IN IGNE
which he made into a sword-land by fire
(or partly by the sword and by fire)

Fig. 4 Map of Powys with schematic eighth-century national boundaries chain dotted, and Offa's Dyke in heavy line. High ground stippled. Mold *and* Glasbury *are the* traditional *boundaries of the eighth-century kingdom of Powys*

In places the meaning is obscure, but the inscription appears to point to the restoration of the frontier after a period in which the Mercian king Aethelbald had overrun parts of Powys. Raid and counter-raid appear to have followed the murder of Aethelbald, the resulting Civil War in Mercia providing the chance for the British/Welsh to recapture 'the inheritance of Powys ... throughout nine years from the power of the English'. These areas included, in the north, the Vale of Llangollen, Yale, Valle Crucis and, in south-west Shropshire, parts of the Vale of Powys and of Montgomery—in other words those areas that were attractive to Saxon farmers.

When Offa had secured his kingdom, his reaction was originally to build Offa's Dyke and later to invade Wales. The idea that the dyke ran from sea to sea is now doubted and Offa's Dyke can be seen as a response to constant and damaging raids from Powys. The other principalities in Wales do not seem to have been involved. It should be noted in this context that recent work by Gloucestershire County Council has thrown doubt on the theory, fully accepted only since 1932, that the anomalous earthworks on the lower Wye are part of Offa's Dyke; a theory with which we also do not agree. The events can be followed in the entries in the *Annales Cambriae*. (The first dates given in each annal are those calculated from a variety of sources; there is a systemic error in the dates perceived by the medieval annalists, which accounts for the second, incorrect, calculation.)

777 And then was the harrying of the men of Deheubarth by king Offa
783 Seven hundred and eighty was the year of Christ when king Offa ravaged the Britons in the season of summer
793 Seven hundred and ninety was the year of Christ when the Pagans first came to Ireland
796 And king Offa and Maredudd, king of Dyfed, died. And there was a battle at Rhuddlan
798 800 the Saxons slew Caradog, king of Gwynedd

In the ninth and tenth centuries active warfare is recorded. The battle of the Conway, and the foundation of the Anglo-Saxon fortification of *Cledemutha* deep within Welsh territory, near present-day Rhuddlan, are two late occurrences in a fluctuating tide of events. The deep impression that Welsh border affairs could leave on English national history can be demonstrated by an obscure reference by a medieval chronicler known as Ingulph, quoted by Riley. Alfred the Great and the last Saxon kingdoms were in desperate straits at the battle of Wilton in 871. The question has

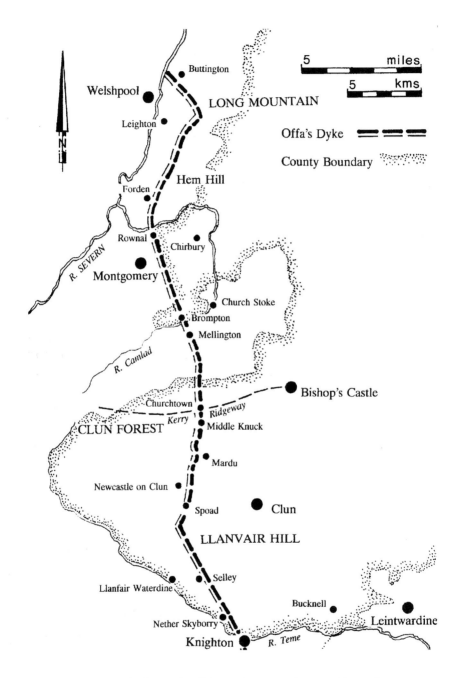

Fig. 5 The line of Offa's Dyke in south-west Shropshire

been asked: Why did not King Burgred of Mercia come to the help of his brothers -in-law, as they had come to help him three years before? Ingulph supplies the answer: Mercia was occupied with a massive invasion by the Welsh. The final result was that Mercia collapsed and Wessex came very close to extinction.

Other evidence that border unrest continued comes in the *Domesday Book* record of the devastation caused by the Welsh before the Conquest in a wide and significant swathe down the frontier. A high proportion of the Marcher region was affected. In addition there were raids deep into Shropshire and the whole of the Vale of Powys was lost as a tax-rendering area, with the owners of the land recognised but the whole area only used for hunting in 1066.

As for Offa's Dyke itself, space does not permit a detailed examination of the evidence accumulated from the 192 archaeological digs in the dyke system, including Wat's Dyke and the valley screen dykes. It would not be relevant to our thesis here to discuss the many 'Short Dykes' in this section of the main Offa's Dyke. These earthworks, which lie both in front of and behind the main dyke, block valleys or ridgeways, and have all been investigated in detail. Suffice to say here that they belong to diverse archaeological periods, none of them can be considered as being contemporary with Offa, and were considered by Sir Cyril Fox as a result of their inclusion in lists supplied by the indefatigable Lily Chitty of linear defences she thought might be relevant to the great survey. The state of Dyke studies can be examined through those articles cited in the bibliography. The section of Dyke in and adjacent to south-west Shropshire can be divided into three sections—river, lowland zone and mountain zone. In the north is the River Severn as an apparently unsupported frontier, borne out for me personally when in 1974 I walked the whole length of the pipeline then being laid behind the line of the Severn. There was nothing that could be interpreted as a Dyke feature; all that could be seen were modern drainage features.

The lowland zone is met at Buttington, and the Dyke climbs the Long Mountain, a strange deviation in the route to the east which exercised Fox's mind and must have something to do with the political or military realities of the time. From Forden, south of Welshpool, the line is set out in a major alignment as far as Hem Hill on the slope north of the River Camlad. (Fox regarded 'major alignments' as the setting-out of the line of the Dyke over several miles so as to deal with major strategic features, whilst 'minor alignments' extend over only a few hundred metres). Another major alignment takes the Dyke to the round hill south of the river Camlad which gives its name to Rownal. The overall alignment is straight but the detailed trace is wavy, as the line passes to the west of the many small drumlins and hillocks of the drift geology. Fox believed the 'wavy' nature of the line at this section was evidence of the Dyke having been built through woodland, the builders not being able to see where they were going. However, the line of the Dyke in fact utilises the topography for additional strength.

This area of the Vale of Powys, where the present-day frontier and Offa's Dyke coincide, has been the principal research area of the Offa's Dyke Project over a number of years. The excavations carried out by the Project on the 'gateways' postulated by Fox have shown that none of these exist. This has important implications for the idea of an agreed frontier. Similarly in the research area, in the Vale of Powys and on the present Shropshire/Powys border there are no original simple gateways. Frank Noble had suggested a model for Offa's Dyke where there was continual movement across the earthwork to fields on the Welsh side. But this does not appear to have happened because no original farmers' gateways have been discovered.

The one thing which is clear both from the detailed surveys carried out over many years and also from the many excavations is that the Dyke was built *against* Wales. Both the bank and the ditch were designed against attack from the west. The line was also carefully placed so that the land to the west was dominated. The Dyke was not simply a marker, an 'agreed frontier'.

In the history of the south-west of Shropshire and its surrounding area the constant threat of the Welsh must have been a dominant theme for a thousand years. The work of the past two decades has been one mainly of delineation of the lines of the Dykes, but my late colleague and friend, Tony Clark, believed that earthworks such as these should also have evidence of people—camps for the builders, and ancillary works such as beacons, garrisons, support roads and bridges. The mechanics of the construction of the Dyke are discussed in some detail in my 1985b note, where it is suggested that, in line with eighth-century practice both in Britain and on the continent, the Dyke was built by a *levée en masse* in a short season, each peasant being responsible (within his group) for a length of, perhaps four feet. The peasant groups would have provided their own provisions and tools and worked on a pre-determined line.

Perhaps the effort for the coming years should be the discovery of some of these works.

Bibliography

Annales Cambriae. There are three inter-linked sets of annals for Wales, the *Annales Cambriae*, the *Brut y Tywysogyon* — 'The Chronicle of the Princes' (in two versions, the Red Book of Hergest and the Peniarth 20 MSS; the former is used here, see under Jones T. below) — and the *Brenhinedd y Saeson*, 'The Kings of the Saxons'. The last two sets of annals are later medieval Welsh translations of the *Annales*. They have some additions. What is offered above is the *Annales Cambriae* in the original together with the translation of the *Brut*.

Finberg, H.P.R. *Early Charters of the West Midlands* 1961

Fox, C. *Offa's Dyke: A field survey of the Western Frontier-works of Mercia in the seventh and eighth centuries A.D.* 1955

Hill, D.H. and Wilson, D.M. 'Frontier Dykes in the Wrexham Area, Recent Work, 1972', *Journal of the Chester Archaeol. Soc.*, pp.58, 93-96, 1974

Hill, D.H. 'Offa's and Wat's Dykes: Some aspects of recent work 1972-76', *Trans. Lancs. Ches. Antiq. Soc.* pp.79, 21-33. 1977a

Hill, D.H. 'The Construction of Offa's Dyke', *The Antiquaries Journal*, Vol. LXV, Part 1, pp.140-2, 1985b

Hill, D.H. 'Offa's and Wat's Dykes', *The Archaeology of Clwyd,* Edited John Manley, Stephen Grenter and Fiona Gale, pp.142-156. Clwyd, 1991

Hill, D.H. (forthcoming) 'Offa's Dyke: Pattern and Purpose', *Antiquaries Journal*

Hooke, Della *The Landscape of Anglo-Saxon England* Leicester, 1998

Hoyle, J. 'Offa's Dyke Management Survey, 1995-6', *Glevensis* 29, 29-33

Jones, T. *Brut y Tywysogyon* or *The Chronicle of the Princes, Red Book of Hergest Version* Critical Text and Translation, Cardiff, 1955

Jones, T. *Brenhinedd y Saesson* or *The Kings of the Saxons* Text and Translation, Cardiff, 1971

Lloyd, J.E. *History of Wales, Volume 1* third edition, London, 1939

Noble, F. (ed. Gelling, M.) *Offa's Dyke Reviewed* British Archaeological Reports British Series 114, Oxford, 1983

Riley H.T. (trns.) *Ingulfs Chronicle of the Abbey of Croyland with the Continuations by Peter of Blois and Anonymous Writers* Henry G. Bohn, London, 1854

Stenton, Sir F.M. quoted in Fox 1955 above

At the end of the first Christian millennium, Saxon England was transformed by the coming of the Normans. The *Domesday Book*, their great analysis of land-ownership, reveals the complexity of the relationships between the Saxon incumbents, their Norman conquerors, and their volatile Welsh neighbours.

CHAPTER 8

From Saxon to Norman Rule:
Domesday Book and the Ownership of Land
by Alan Hurley

When William the Conqueror seized the English throne, it was not his intention to overthrow the established order. As one who had been promised the succession both by the late king, his childless half-Norman cousin Edward the Confessor, and by Harold, the most powerful Saxon earl, and whose campaign had the blessing of the Pope, he was claiming a crown which he saw as rightfully his and with it England's long established administrative and fiscal systems.

William's initial demand in 1066 was only for the surrender of the lands of 'all who stood against me in battle and were killed there'. He needed to reward his principal companions and deploy his forces so as to secure the kingdom, but most Saxon thanes retained their status both as land owners and as Counsellors. However, for several years rebels defied the new regime, men such as Edric 'the Wild', who had been a prominent landowner in Shropshire and Herefordshire, and became the Marcher country's equivalent of Hereward the Wake. In alliance with Welsh princes he devastated a swathe of Herefordshire, then burned Shrewsbury and laid siege to its newly built castle. Three years of guerilla warfare ended in defeat by a force led by the Conqueror himself. Remarkably, William accepted Edric's submission and he is last recorded accompanying the king on a campaign against the Scots.

This widespread insurrection sapped the Conqueror's toleration of Saxons in positions of authority, and by 1070 most former landowners had been replaced by William's 200 leading warlords and by the numerous Norman knights who had fought at Hastings or had subsequently been brought over from France. William abolished the great Saxon earldoms except that of Northumbria, which provided a vital buffer against the Scots, and created three of his right-hand men Earls of Chester, Shrewsbury and Hereford, with unlimited powers to control the Welsh borders. The Earldom of Hereford was, however, suppressed in 1075 after the second earl's involvement in one of the last attempts at rebellion.

Large tracts of the country, including much of eastern Shropshire, were ravaged in revenge attacks, houses and crops were burned and livestock slaughtered, and many thousands of Saxon thanes were killed, exiled or reduced to the status of landless villagers. Some had owned lands scattered throughout England, and their properties were often transferred *en bloc*. This is how Nigel the Doctor, the king's wealthy physician and a substantial landowner in other areas, came to own just one manor in Shropshire — that of Wistanstow. A manor (*manerium*: a holding) could range from a single farmstead to a group of villages: the farm at Coston, near Broome in the Clun valley and worked by just three men, ranked as a manor in its own right, whilst the manor at Lydbury North encompassed several villages and contained about 18,000 acres including the future site of Bishop's Castle.

The passing of the ownership of land, and with it control of the sources of wealth, from one ruling class to another had little impact on the lives of the mass of the people. Feudalism, the system whereby the stronger inhabitants of a locality protected the weak and allowed them to occupy land in exchange for services rendered, was already flourishing in England long before King Edgar decreed in the tenth century that 'every landless man should have a lord'. The customary rights and duties already subsisting between Lords of the Manor and the occupiers of their lands were unaffected by the Conquest, the principal difference between the Saxon and Norman systems being that Saxon landowners held land directly from the king, on terms which might or might not include martial duties, whereas the Normans granted ownership of land specifically in exchange for an obligation to supply military services. The duty to provide a quota of armed knights was then fragmented within ever smaller sub-tenancies, each tenant being sworn to serve his immediate lord and so directing his loyalty primarily towards him.

This is the background against which the Domesday Survey of 1086 may be set.

After a decade of comparative calm William responded to a renewed threat of Scandinavian invasion by hiring French mercenaries whom he billeted on his principal vassals, and by raising a land tax at three times the usual rate to pay their wages. The collection of this swingeing impost must have resulted in discontent and accordingly, in the words of the *Anglo-Saxon Chronicle*, the king 'held very deep discussion with his Council about this country and how it was occupied and with what sort of people ... what dues he ought to have in 12 months from each Shire; also what or how much everybody had who was occupying land in England, in land or cattle, and how much money it was worth'.

The findings of the resultant investigation were compiled into the *Domesday Book*, the most comprehensive survey of its kind made in medieval times anywhere in Europe. It provides an invaluable insight into the structure of society and the effects upon it of the events of the previous 20 years. The basic information listed for each manor included the identities of the owners 'in the time of King Edward' (pre-1066), and in 1086; how many taxable 'hides' it contained; how much land there was for ploughs and how many ploughs there actually were; how many people of various categories comprised the work force; and the manor's annual value to its lord in 1066, at the time the present owner received it (generally assumed to be 1070), and in 1086. The livestock statistics were, however, omitted from the final transcript.

The 'hide' was a unit of assessment for national taxation. It had originally been equivalent to 120 acres (about 50 hectares), the amount of arable land deemed sufficient to support a Saxon thane and his family, but by the time the system was applied in the border counties it had come to denote an area of land of recognised value, so that the most fertile land would have the least acres to the hide. A few manors, although under cultivation, were recorded as never having been hidated, making them virtual tax havens. Clunbury was one of only two Shropshire manors enjoying this exemption.

The main classes of worker were the villager, occupying for life a cottage and perhaps 30 acres, and the smallholder with less than five acres, both of whom worked a customary number of days on the Lord's own land and rendered to him customary dues in the form of produce from the land they themselves occupied. There were also 'riders', former mounted escorts or messengers now settled on the land, whose duties were less onerous. In the early years after the Conquest much of the heaviest work on the lordship land, such as ploughing with teams of eight oxen, was still done by 'serfs', servants of lowly status whose lord could buy and sell them at will.

In Shropshire, where Roger de Montgomery had vice-regal powers as Earl of Shrewsbury, King William retained no land of his own. The earl kept Shrewsbury for his own profit, together with 40 manors, most of which had previously been owned by Edward the Confessor, such as Chirbury and Minsterley, or by the Earls of Mercia (Church Stretton). Sixty Shropshire manors were ecclesiastical fiefs whose ownership was undisturbed; those included, in the south-west, Lydbury North and Onibury, which both belonged to the Bishops of Hereford (the former since the eighth century), Marton, held by St. Chad's Church, Shrewsbury, and Bromfield, owned by Bromfield Priory itself.

A further 45 manors in the south of the county were held directly from the king by five barons who were also substantial landowners in Herefordshire, having profited from the abolition of the Earldom of Hereford. Amongst these was Roger de Lacy, whose properties included Stokesay and Stanton Lacy. It was at about the time of the Domesday survey that he began to build one of the first stone castles in England on a craggy outcrop above the confluence of the Teme and the Corve. Ludlow was to grow up around this stronghold, but *Domesday Book* contains no reference to a settlement there, nor indeed to any at the future sites of Bishop's Castle or Craven Arms. Church Stretton alone of the four largest present day communities in south-west Shropshire qualified as a manor in 1086. Any dwellings in those other localities were outlying farmsteads belonging to the manors of Stanton Lacy, Lydbury North and Stokesay.

Roger de Montgomery divided the remaining 340 Shropshire manors among some 50 undertenants, ten of whom held 250 estates between them. These were the trusted associates upon whom the earl could rely for men and arms in time of war, warriors such as Robert de Say (known as Picot) who had fought at Hastings and controlled most of the Clun Valley, and the brothers Roger and Robert FitzCorbet, whose holdings included Wentnor and Priest Weston.

Almost all the south-west Shropshire manors named in *Domesday Book* are still identifiable on the current 1:50,000 map, as marked, with their modern names, on the map opposite. About a third of them comprise only a single farm or homestead often still called 'Hall Farm' or 'Manor Farm'. The high rate of continuous occupation throughout the last millennium reflects our forefathers' persistence with suitable locations, once established.

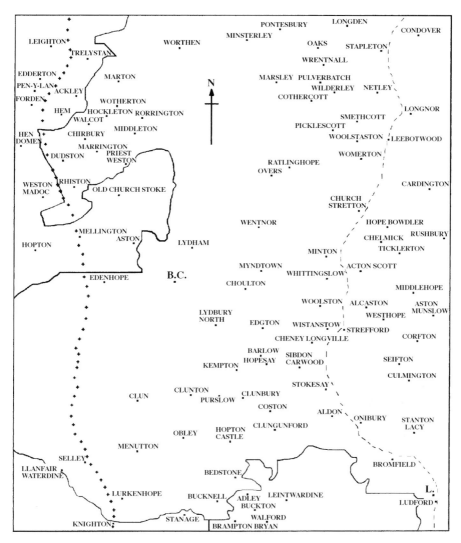

KEY: • • • • •   **Offa's Dyke**
        – – – –   **The modern A49 Shrewsbury to Ludlow road**
        ———   **The present day County boundary**
      **The sites of post-Domesday Ludlow and Bishop's Castle
are marked by their initials**

Fig. 6 The Domesday Manors of South-west Shropshire

Despite the radical transition to Norman rule around 1070, Saxon thanes still remained in control of the Saxon workforce in some places. *Domesday Book* records about a dozen Saxons in occupation of south-west Shropshire manors, several possessing the lands which they themselves held from Edward the Confessor. Ernwy still held Pontesbury; Aldred held Smethcott; and Leofric held Myndtown at the foot of the Long Mynd, north of Plowden. Siward, a kinsman of King Edward who had once been known as 'the rich man of Shropshire', remained lord of Cheney Longville. He had originally surrendered that manor with all his others, but by 1086 had regained it in exchange for the wooden chapel of St. Peter whose site was needed by the earl for the construction of Shrewsbury Abbey.

Most of the 50 references to 'Edric' as the pre-conquest owner of a Shropshire manor seem likely to relate to Edric the Wild. Clun, Hopesay and Wentnor had all been held by an Edric and were probably his, whilst Lydham had definitely belonged to him, being one of six Shropshire manors where the scribe interlined after that name the word 'Salvage' ('the Wild'). Others were Hope Bowdler, and Middleton, north of Priest Weston, where Ertein who had owned the land jointly with Edric retained his own half share in 1086.

An assessment of the total number of individual pre-conquest landowners is hampered by the omission in other cases of their descriptive nicknames, though some inferences may be drawn. The name Swein occurs five times in the Clun Valley or close by, but only twice elsewhere in Shropshire, so one may reasonably assume that the same man had owned Clunbury, Coston, Kempton, Edgton and Sibdon Carwood. Perhaps twice as many individual Saxons had held land in south-west Shropshire before the Conquest, as the 20 Normans, most of whom possessed multiple holdings, and the scattering of Saxons, who were in occupation in 1086. What is certain is that during those 20 years men with such names as Einulf, Oslac and Ulfketel had been superseded by such as Fulk, Gislold and Walter, these latter being men-at-arms settled in Clun and Clungunford to protect them against Welsh raiders, a precaution also taken in a number of other border communities. Instead of being garrisoned in the newly built frontier castles these soldiers were granted sub-tenancies of parts of the manorial lands together with a proportion of the workforce.

Welshmen were resident in some manors, occupying land together with the other villagers but mentioned separately in *Domesday Book* as they usually paid rent instead of rendering services. Four Welshmen in Clun paid 2s. 4d. to Picot, whilst two others worked for the men-at-arms; two more at Kempton paid 1s. 2d., so it seems that the going rate for a Welsh tenancy in the Clun Valley was 7d. *per annum*. Despite ongoing border raids and the taking and retaking of land which was to continue for many years it was evidently no longer the case that a Welshman caught east of Offa's Dyke would forfeit his hand on the first occasion and, on the second, his head. A Welshman in Kinnerley paid one hawk as annual rent, a valuable render indeed, comparable with Rushbury in Apedale where de Lacy's assets included a hawk's eyrie as the source of a regular supply of hunting birds.

Stanton Lacy with a working population of 130 and Lydbury North with 83 were far the largest manors in south-west Shropshire, followed by Stokesay and Clun (both 47), Worthen (46), Leintwardine (43), Bromfield (39), Clungunford (36) and Church Stretton (35). Leintwardine was then in Shropshire, as were the settlements in the hill country west of Wigmore between the Teme and the Lugg. It was at Leintwardine that the mounted guard provided by the citizens of Shrewsbury for a visiting Saxon king would have handed over to their counterparts from Hereford. *Domesday Book* contains considerable details about these larger manors, and locally Lydbury North and Clun are good examples.

Lydbury included a number of settlements—Eyton, Plowden, Walcot, Brockton, Linley and Colebatch. The 'North' distinguished the manor from the Bishops of Herefords' Ledbury estate 50 miles to the south-east. The manor contained 53 hides, of which 32 were 'waste', and its annual value had fallen from £35 in 1066 to £10 in 1070 and was still only £12 in 1086. Land was described as 'waste' if it had at one time been arable but had returned to the wild; references to potential ploughlands far in excess of the number of ploughs at work are commonplace in the border counties. Forty-five Shropshire manors had been wholly waste in 1066, mostly near the borders where settlements such as Bucknell, Knighton and further north Chirbury had been devastated by the Welsh under Gruffyd ap Llewellyn some ten years earlier. The Saxons had long since settled in the Camlad valley around Chirbury, their homesteads reaching westwards beyond Offa's Dyke with northern and southern outposts at Edderton and Edenhope, but Welsh depredations resulted in this group of 20 manors being listed by the Survey as having been used in 1066 only for hunting. By 1086, following the building of Earl Roger's castle at Hen Domen (Montgomery), half of them, including Forden and Hem, were, like Chirbury itself, restored to cultivation, though others such as Hockleton and Mellington remained waste. The number of 'wastes' in Shropshire as a whole had by 1070 increased temporarily to 120, a quarter of all Shropshire manors, reflecting not only the earlier Welsh incursions but also the extent of the revenge taken by the Normans upon the rebels' homelands. Some, such as Purslow, whose annual value in 1066 was 15s., but was later wasted, remained so in 1086.

The manor of Lydbury North had enough land for 120 ploughs, but only 28 were in use. The workforce consisted of 38 villagers, 32 smallholders, 8 riders and 2 serfs, together with the priests at the church who had their own plough. There was a mill and enough woodland for fattening 160 pigs. Few serfs worked on this ecclesiastical manor compared with such as the combined manors of Clunbury and Kempton, where serfs comprised half the 24 strong work force, as they did among the 30 at Wentnor. Within another 20 years Archbishop Anselm achieved the abolition of serfdom. Simultaneously, though, the lot of the ordinary villager moved closer to servitude; having previously been entitled to leave the village provided he forfeited his land, he became liable under the Normans to apprehension and return to his Lord's service unless he could remain undetected in a town for a year and a day.

Clun was a 15 hide manor, worth £25 in 1066, only £3 in 1070 but £10 in 1086. There was land for 60 ploughs but only 12 were working. As well as 3 soldiers and 6 Welshmen, there were 20 villagers, 8 small-holders, 7 serfs and 2 riders, the latter each tendering a cow as annual rent. Clun also had a mill, 'serving the Lord's Hall'. Millers' rentals varied widely. Earl Roger, as owner of Lydham, received one pig each year from the miller there, whilst at Wotherton near Chirbury the Saxon Alward had a mill yielding him 24 measures of corn, compared with 5 packloads for Nigel the Doctor at Wistanstow. The miller at Clungunford paid 2s. 8d., whilst at Leintwardine the dues were 6s. 8d. plus 6 'sticks' of eels at 25 to the stick.

The possession of woodland adjacent to a village has always been a valuable resource, and its existence is frequently mentioned in *Domesday Book*. In this area the manors of Church Stoke, Kempton and Sibdon Carwood, as well as Lydbury North, had woodlands, each with enough to support 100 pigs, whilst at Lydham its extent was expressed in linear terms—two leagues, equivalent to a three mile stretch of woodland, in which pigs could forage for acorns and beech mast. Another woodland feature was the '*haye*' or hedged enclosure in which deer were trapped ready to be released for hunting. Clunton had five *hayes*, and there were others at Kempton, Hopesay and Wentnor.

Stokesay was the only Shropshire manor where mention was made of a bee-keeper, though there must have been many others not distinguished from the general category of 'villager', just as two smiths at Stanton Lacy and a smith working alongside 14 villagers and 6 serfs at Hopesay will have had their counterparts in other manors. Most communities would have relied on itinerant pedlars for such items as metal tools and salt, though the manorial dues at Caynham, south-east of Ludlow, included four packloads of salt from Droitwich.

In addition to Lydbury North and Clun the map shows a dozen smaller manors within six miles of present-day Bishop's Castle. Whilst these two large manors had a combined workforce of 130, the aggregate working population of the remainder was only 160. In south-west Shropshire there were less than three workers per square mile, with villagers making up 40% of the workforce, smallholders 25%, and 20% serfs. The citizens of Shrewsbury had complained to the Domesday Commissioners that they still paid tax on a 100 hide assessment, although 50 of the 250 pre-Conquest houses had been demolished to make way for the castle, 50 more were unoccupied, 40 had been taken over by Frenchmen, and another 40 which the earl had given to the abbey were exempt from tax. From these figures it has been estimated that the total population of Shrewsbury can hardly have exceeded 1,500—equivalent to that of Bishop's Castle today. The whole of Shropshire with a workforce of nearly 5,000 was probably occupied by some 20,000 to 25,000 people. The rural areas of Shropshire, quiet as they may still appear, are some eight times more densely populated today than they were in the late eleventh century.

Yet, despite having the lowest densities of manpower and cultivated land in Shropshire, the annual values recorded for the south-west Shropshire manors in 1086 equalled those for the fertile arable lands south and east of Shrewsbury. This is accounted for by an asset not revealed in *Domesday Book*—the flocks of sheep which had long been established on the open moorlands such as Clun Forest and the Long Mynd, and which supported a thriving trade in wool and sheepskins. The post-Conquest settlement of Newcastle-on-Clun supported 21 tenants sharing only 75 acres and a meadow. Their primary activity would have been tending their flocks on the adjacent uplands, and their communal occupation of the land reflected the old Welsh tribal system which still survived in the Welshry of the Marcher Lordships, under which some land was shared equally by all adult '*Cymry*' (comrades) and such land as was owned individually devolved jointly to the sons in each generation.

The Earldom of Shrewsbury was forfeited in 1102, and power devolved upon the principal Baronies. But the pattern of land tenure reflected in *Domesday Book* provided the basis for life in south-west Shropshire until the Act of Union of 1536 whereby the counties of eastern Wales were created and the Marcher Lordships abolished.

Bibliography

Darby, H. and Terrett, L. (eds.) *Domesday Geography of Midland England* Cambridge, 1954

Douglas, D.C. and Greenaway, G.W. (eds.) *English Historical Documents, Vol. II* London, 1955

Eyton, Rev. R.W. *Antiquities of Shropshire, Vol. XI* London, 1860

Lloyd, Sir John *A History of Wales* London, 1954

Poole, A.L. *Domesday Book to Magna Carta* Oxford, 1955

Stenton, Sir F. *Anglo-Saxon England* Oxford, 1955

Thorn, F. and C. (eds.) *Domesday Book - Shropshire* Phillimore, 1986

Trinder, B. *A History of Shropshire* Phillimore, 1983

Victoria County History – Shropshire Vols. I, III and IV

If south-west Shropshire is among the richest areas in Britain for Iron Age hillforts, it can also claim a remarkable concentration of the small Norman castles described as 'motte-and-bailey'. The nature and probable function of these can be admirably studied by a survey of the clusters of forts in the Vale of Montgomery and around the Camlad, Onny, and Clun valleys.

CHAPTER 9

Mottes and Baileys
by John Smyth

At the end of the second millennium the turf-clad earthworks of timber castles blend seamlessly into the rolling pastoral landscapes of the Welsh Borders. Unlike their stone-built counterparts which still, even in ruinous state, dominate their settings and capture popular imagination, mottes, with or without baileys, can elude all but the observant eye. Nine hundred years ago they would have been centres of considerable activity and conspicuous reminders of Norman military power and presence.

One region of the borderland that played a significant part in the politics of the early Medieval period was the Vale of Montgomery and the valleys to the east that connect with it. The north-western end of the Vale gives access to the ford of Rhydwhyman, an important River Severn crossing point until recent times. Moving eastwards from the Vale, the valleys of the Camlad, Rea Brook and Onny open up routes that lead from mid-Wales into the heart of the English Midlands. Although Offa's Dyke had defined the Welsh-Mercian frontier in the eighth century there is evidence of considerable fluctuation in Welsh and Anglo-Saxon influence over the following 200years (see Chapter 7). A period of Mercian influence in the area is indicated by their establishment of the fortified '*burh*' of Chirbury in 915, and traces of Anglo-Saxon field systems west of the Dyke and close to the Severn re-iterate Mercian presence. However by 1066 there had been significant Welsh incursions to the east of the Dyke and much of the area was described as having been 'waste' by *Domesday Book* 20 years later.

The unstable situation in this and other parts of the borders resulted in a response by the Norman government which was to shape the social and political life of the area for the next 300 years or so and to leave its mark on the landscape for a great deal longer.

The sequence of events began in 1069 when the Saxon thegn, Edric the Wild, along with Welsh allies, laid siege to the Norman motte and bailey castle of Shrewsbury. Although the siege was soon relieved, the turbulent situation on the borders made it essential for the new government to replace English earls with Norman ones and to settle Norman families who would resist the Welsh. In the meantime the revolt was crushed and much devastation caused, though possibly on a lesser scale in Shropshire than in some more northerly counties.

William I's serious concern about the problem of the Welsh frontier is shown by the arrangements that were made for the governing of the area. He appointed his cousin, Roger of Montgomery, as Earl of Shrewsbury and virtual direct ruler of most of Shropshire. This grant carried the duty of defending the area against the Welsh. An essential part of the Norman government's policy for the area was the establishment of castles, initially of the timber and earth variety.

The origin of motte and bailey castles is obscure as neither documentary nor archaeological evidence has established where or when the prototypes were built. What seems certain is that they emerged in unsettled times where powerful men were trying to establish themselves and their followers in defensible bases inside hostile territory. Clearly there was nothing new in fortification through enclosure, a practice dating from ancient times and occurring in many different forms. The new factor in Norman times was the motte, or fortified mound, a phenomenon that seems to have appeared in a variety of shapes, sizes and places during the eleventh century, becoming more widespread over the following 100 years.

Generally mottes were completed by the construction of base-courts or baileys beneath the mounds, fortified with ditches, banks and palisades to provide security for garrisons and equipment. Some of the smaller, or perhaps more temporary, mottes lacked elaborately constructed baileys and may have been completed with more simple fenced or palisaded enclosures.

The best known early illustrations of motte and bailey type castles are those in the Bayeux Tapestry. As well as showing four similar but separate mottes in Normandy, the tapestry depicts the building of a castle at Hastings. Workmen are shown using spades, shovels and mattocks, digging a ditch and throwing the soil upwards to form a mound. Also depicted is a structure, apparently wooden, rising from the summit of the mound.

Although what little evidence there is points towards a Norman origin of motte and bailey castles, the English contribution to this piece of military technology should not be underestimated, both in terms of woodworking and soil-construction. Apart from the proven working skills of Englishmen in both these areas, there existed, in 1066 a well-established obligation to produce forced-labour on defended towns, so the existing obligations and skills could have been adapted by the new rulers to build the castles that were to strengthen their hold over the country.

The mottes and baileys in the Camlad Valley, and areas adjacent, played an important part in the Normans' consolidation of their position in southwest Shropshire. Other roles of these castles were to reduce the influence of the Welsh princes on the area and to act as springboards for an advance into the heart of Wales.

The key to Roger of Montgomery's policy in the area was the ancient River Severn ford of Rhydwhyman. The crossing, a meeting place for diplomatic negotiations throughout the early period of the Welsh Wars, (and the site where the Treaty of Montgomery was signed in 1267) could well be used as a ford today. The river at this point flows over a ridge of gravel, with deep water up and downstream. Earl Roger recognised the importance of Rhydwhyman and chose a site for his castle (which he named after his home town in Normandy) on the ridge overlooking the ford just over a kilometre to the east. This, the original Montgomery Castle, was to be the westernmost point in a defensive system that encompassed the Vale of Montgomery and the valleys of the Camlad, Onny and Rea Brook.

Examples of castles positioned to control river valley routes are those at Gwarthlow, Brompton and further east, Lydham and More, within about half a kilometre of each other between the headwaters of the Camlad and the West Onny. A third fortification was situated at Hardwick, just over two kilometres further east and near to the East Onny. These three castles between them would have been in a position to control the natural valley routeways, north to south and east to west, that converge in this area. In similar fashion the small motte at Colebatch, sited some six kilometres further south is at another valley junction. Additional examples of castles built to control valley routes are those at Bicton on the River Unk, and Newcastle and Clun, both on the River Clun, the last rebuilt as a stone castle in the early thirteenth century.

Where high-level routes existed castles were built to control them, hence the motte and bailey built by the Bishop of Hereford at a western extremity of his Lydbury estate on Yr Hen Fford (Old Road) guarding the ridgeway and overlooking the Camlad Valley. The Bishop's Moat was later

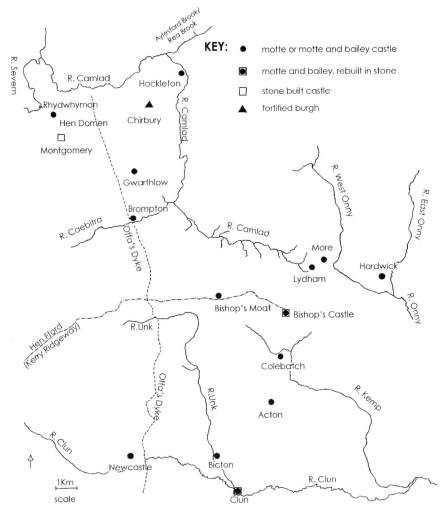

Fig. 7 Castles between the Camlad and Clun valleys

replaced by a motte and bailey, subsequently rebuilt as a stone castle, further east, where it could control not only the ridgeway but also the north-south valley routes and where a planned town was established taking its name from the Bishop's Castle.

Apart from their strategic purposes, the Normans built timber castles to dominate people in the vicinity, as secure residences, and for administering justice and local government. Some, like the motte at Hockleton near Chirbury, could have been fortified farmhouses during the colonising period.

Although mottes without any apparent baileys are not uncommon in the area under consideration, the greatest number of timber castles built were of the motte and bailey type. However, there are examples of mottes with more than one bailey, and some within earlier earthworks. The situation is often further confused as a result of damage caused by fallen trees, agriculture and erosion.

Damage to the earthworks of motte and bailey castles is insignificant in comparison with that suffered by their wooden structures. Although we have very little idea of how the towers on mottes might have been built it is possible that some indication of their shape and construction could be gained by looking at twelfth- and thirteenth-century bell towers such as those at Yarpole and Pembridge in Herefordshire. Their tapering outline and diagonal braces would have made them suitable as motte towers and there is every probability that eleventh-century carpenters would have worked on both types of tower.

If knowledge about the structure of timber castles was based solely on bell towers and contemporary recorded evidence, what is known about the subject would be minimal, but archaeological investigation has increased the sum of our understanding significantly. The most intensive study has been carried out on the site of Roger of Montgomery's castle near the ford of Rhydwhyman. Hen Domen (Welsh for old mound) was built in the 1070s and was to be occupied for 200 years. The motte as it is today stands eight metres high and measures 40 metres in diameter at the base. The bailey is relatively small, covering one third of an acre, but was heavily defended by double ramparts and ditches. Traces of early structures in the bailey suggest some buildings and ramparts built on a massive scale complete with a fighting platform. Some of the structures were evidently constructed using large base plates of timber, set in trenches with uprights morticed into them at intervals.

Among the features revealed in the excavations were a water cistern and what was apparently a granary with access underneath it. There is evidence also of a two-storey building, possibly a first-floor hall which could have been the major residence, screened off from other buildings by a fence. It apparently gave access to the motte via a bridge which crossed the surrounding ditch. Strong though this phase of the castle was, its strength did not make it impregnable, as in 1095 it was sacked by the Welsh and its garrison massacred.

After the fall from grace of the Montgomery family in 1102 the Earldom of Shrewsbury became a royal shire and the castle of Hen Domen, together with its lordship passed into the hands of the de Boulers family who held it until their demise in 1207. The castle continued as a military stronghold but acquired domestic and administrative roles in addition, and these are reflected, not just in the defences but also in the bailey, which the investigation showed to have been crowded with buildings.

Investigations also uncovered evidence of a palisade surrounding the bailey. This was reinforced with post and wattle framework daubed with clay and presumed to have been four metres high. Some slight evidence suggests a palisade around the motte. The cistern and granary seem to have survived from the castle's first stage and there are some indications of a chapel. Among the many buildings in the bailey there would appear to have been two designed or adapted for domestic use and, on the site of another, scraps of metal suggest an industrial role. Although no view of the surrounding countryside would have been obtained from most of the buildings crowded into the bailey, some structures were two or three storeys high, and from these, as well as the towers on the motte and by the gate, an effective watch could have been kept.

The castle was strongly protected by huge concentric defences and deep and, at times, wet and muddy ditches, and it is estimated that ten metres in height separated the bottom of the inner ditch from the top of the bailey palisade.

Most of the evidence uncovered from the motte appears to date from the de Boulers phase of the castle's life. Some indications of a series of towers have been found on the heavily eroded top platform, for instance, remnants of timber uprights set in a trench and daubed with clay to a thickness of over half a metre. Some signs of habitation, for example fragments of pottery and of metalwork, also animal bones, suggest a dual role of residence, as well as watch-keeping for the motte tower.

Hen Domen in its second phase, as home and castle of the de Boulers family, although larger and more significant than most of the timber castles lying in the triangle to the east, probably provides a model for all but the smallest of them.

The last years of Hen Domen's life as a working castle saw it reverting to the status of military outpost again, although it appears to have been abandoned for a spell after 1215 while the area was under Welsh control. When in 1223 Henry III renewed the Welsh War he chose the rock of Montgomery as the site for a new stone castle. Rhydwhyman, the ford and meeting place, was not visible from the new castle, so Hen Domen was re-fortified and appears to have had a role as front-line outpost for about 50 years until the end of the wars.

As well as uncovering evidence about the construction and functioning of a motte and bailey castle, the excavations at Hen Domen have provided valuable information about the mix of military and domestic life within the bailey. The fullest record is from the period between 1102 and 1207 when the castle was in the hands of the de Boulers family. The picture that emerges is one of simplicity, most of the pottery finds being from coarse cooking pots and simple glazed jugs, similar to other material found widely up and down the Welsh Border counties. What little metal uncovered was in the form of fragments from tools, arrowheads, locks and horseshoe nails. The finds point towards a community living frugally and probably recycling metal waste. Many bits of unworked wood and a stave-built tub made of eleventh-century oak were found preserved by wet conditions in a ditch. Material recovered from a latrine pit showed traces of weeds, hedgerow plants and trees of varieties that are still widely found in the area. The pit seems to have been used as both a latrine and a waste disposal area, and material such as wood shavings and bracken were apparently used to compost the contents.

The remnants of bones found in ditches, the cistern and the latrine pit provide evidence about domestic animals, cats and dogs and those kept for meat, as well as animals that were hunted. The bones of cattle, pigs and red deer were plentiful, those of sheep were less so, probably because they were largely kept for their wool.

Further material in the latrine pit established the presence of the dung beetle and the stable fly and, by extension, of horses in the bailey. It is safe to assume that knights were present at Hen Domen, and in the baileys of other castles as well, and that alongside them there would have been the specialists needed to maintain both mounts and their harness in good condition: vets, farriers, saddlers and the like. It is also safe to assume the presence of fletchers, surgeons, and priests to cater for the needs of knights, archers and, particularly during the de Boulers phase, of women and children as well. The need for fodder, for both human and equine inhabitants of baileys would have necessitated the re-population of the areas designated by *Domesday Book* as waste in 1066, but which had recovered by 1086. This could account for the fact that in many instances villages grew up in open countryside near to timber castles. Homes would have been needed for the workers that grew the fodder.

The interpreters of the evidence from Hen Domen, which had close ties with the monarchy and aristocracy spanning 200 years, were surprised at the simplicity and peasant-style existence revealed by the finds, which contrasted unfavourably with the very extensive finds from the Roman sites at Wroxeter and Forden Gaer nearby. It is probably safe to assume that if living conditions in the castle of Earl Roger and later the de Boulers family are now thought to have been fairly primitive, the same would probably have been true to an even greater extent in the smaller and less significant timber castles of the area.

Our knowledge about the ultimate fate of the timber castles in and around the Camlad valley is limited. Some of them were rebuilt as, or superseded by, stone castles, while others would have been abandoned when no longer needed, dismantled or burned, perhaps. The Welsh Wars ensured that the most importantly sited of them should continue in use as long as circumstances dictated. Hen Domen was rebuilt several times during its 200 year life, always in timber. Once Edward I's campaigns against the Welsh moved the conflict further west many of the borderland castles that were still in use became redundant. Rhydwhyman was no longer used as a meeting place after 1274 and by 1310 even the new stone-built Montgomery Castle was in a state of disrepair.

Evidence about timber castles is much less available than that on the stone-built variety. As documentary and pictorial sources provide such sparse information and above-ground timber structures have not survived, the best sources are the surviving, if stunted, remains where, as the Hen Domen investigation shows, valuable evidence can be preserved. The mottes and baileys discussed above, as well as other sites which are recognised ancient monuments, are scheduled and listed and therefore in theory have protected status. This should save them from the fate of Brompton Motte by the River Caebitra which has lost its bailey, and Acton, south of Bishop's Castle, where a former motte and bailey is now only visible as a crop-mark, the earthworks having been ploughed out. Even at Acton, below-ground evidence may well exist, but obviously much has been destroyed.

Regrettable though we may find the destruction of mottes and baileys, the scribe who narrated the events of 1066 in the *Anglo-Saxon Chronicle* expressed different sentiments towards them:

> ... Bishop Odo and Earl William stayed behind and built castles, far and wide throughout the country and distressed the wretched folk and always after that it grew much worse. May the end be good when God wills it.

The monk's prayer was answered in due course. More secure and settled times did eventually ease the distress caused by the Norman colonists, and another

200 years or so saw the abandonment and dismantling of the last of their timber castles. Now their remains in and around the Camlad Valley are peaceful places, palisaded with trees and perhaps livestock fences, and garrisoned not by knights and archers but, in all likelihood, by cattle and sheep.

*   *   *

Brief descriptions of some surviving remains of mottes and baileys, in and about the Camlad Valley, and familiar to the writer.

The Bishop's Moat

This fine and well-preserved motte and bailey castle built about 1100 by the Bishop of Hereford is strategically placed at some 370 metres above sea level on the ridge which forms part of Aston Hill, alongside the Kerry Ridgeway (Yr Hen Fford) and overlooking the Camlad Valley. The nine metre high motte is situated to the west of the bailey, half in and half out of it. A well-preserved bank surrounds the oval-shaped bailey that measures 90 metres by 60 metres. A gap in the bailey bank opposite the motte prob- ably marks the original entrance. The summit of the motte commands a fine view across the Camlad Valley towards Corndon Hill and Heath Mynd. It is possible that pre-1270 references to the castle of Lydbury and suchlike, apply to this site.

Lydham

The motte and bailey castle is situated at the head of the Camlad Valley. The oval shaped motte, now crowned with fine oak and ash trees, rises some five metres above the level of a similarly shaped bailey, and its summit is a roughly-rectangular 12 metres by eight metres. On its western side there is a drop of over seven metres to the bottom of the bailey ditch. Entrance to the bailey would appear to have been on the west side where there is a three- metre gap that possibly gave access, via a bridge, to the motte. A second entrance to the bailey was at the south-east corner and there is some evidence of a palisade to guard it. The bailey appears to have been divided into two sections, the smaller inner one showing signs of what could have been a large timber building, possibly a hall, while in the outer bailey there are indications of what might have been small building platforms, perhaps for huts. Holy Trinity Church at the centre of Lydham is 100 metres to the east.

More

Less than a kilometre north-east of Lydham are the low-lying earthworks of More Castle, consisting of a motte two and a half metres high with two rectangular baileys and possible traces of a third. Excavations in 1959 uncovered an earlier ringwork enclosure and fragments of twelfth- and thirteenth-century pottery. The motte is 135 metres in diameter at the base and 20 metres across the summit. The innermost bailey is virtually square with sides of about 58 metres while the outer one is a rectilinear 49 metres by 85, the entrance apparently having been on the outward-curving south side. The possible third bailey, close to the present village, could have contained a medieval settlement but to date no traces of habitation have been located in it.

Colebatch

The impressive motte rises from a base diameter of 22 metres tapering to five metres at the summit that is five and a half metres above ground level. The Douglas firs, which are currently growing on the summit, add visually to the vertical dimension. Although the motte, on the west side of a tributary of the River Kemp, would in all probability have been surrounded by a palisade, no traces of a ditch are visible, except perhaps in the south-west quarter where a slight surface depression can be traced. The owner of the site, Mr. J. Beddoes, believes that the mound is composed of topsoil stripped off the surrounding area. He observes that topsoil around the motte is virtually non-existent whereas some ten metres away, on the north side of the brook and track it is plentiful. If Mr. Beddoes' theory is correct it could explain the lack of any apparent ditch around the motte. There is every likelihood that the Colebatch settlement owes its origin to the motte fort that stands in its midst.

Hardwick

As in the case of Colebatch and many of the smaller castles this would appear to have been a motte without a substantially protected bailey. Situated a kilometre north of the East and West Onny confluence it stands just over six metres high, measures in excess of 15 metres across the summit and is on a base measuring nearly 43 metres across. A surrounding ditch is discernible in all but the south-east quarter where a bailey could have existed.

Bibliography

Barker, P. and Higham, R. *A Timber Castle on the English-Welsh Border, Hen Domen Archaeological Project* Hen Domen Archaeological Project, 1988 *Hen Domen Montgomery* R.A.I., 1982

Higham, R. and Barker, P. *Timber Castles* Batsford, 1992

Jackson, M. *Castles of Shropshire* Shropshire Libraries, 1988

Merlin, R.H.A. *The Motte and Bailey Castles of the Welsh Border* Palmers Press, 1987

Morris, J. *Domesday Book: Shropshire* Phillimore, 1986

Salter, M. *The Castles and Moated Mansions of Shropshire* Folly Publications, 1992

Stanford, S.C. *Archaeology of the Welsh Marches* Collins, 1980

Stenton, Sir F. *Anglo-Saxon England* Oxford, 1943

There is much architectural evidence for the post-Conquest settlement in this area. The small town of Clun, developed by the Normans around a Saxon settlement, boasts two outstanding examples of the building strengths of the Norman and early Medieval period.

CHAPTER 10

Norman Buildings in Clun
by Maurice Young

The Normans took great pains to protect their interests in the new lands that they controlled following the Conquest. The wealth of the heartlands of old Mercia had been clearly shown in the census recorded in the *Domesday Book*. Over many centuries the Welsh had looked at this rich English landscape with some envy and had often set forth raiding and pillaging, burning and looting, taking a share of this wealth.

A buffer zone was needed to keep out the Welsh and to allow the Norman kings to exploit their rich Midlands plains to the full. The creation of the Marcher lordships was seen as a more viable method of protection than a defended boundary such as Offa's Dyke with its inherent weaknesses. Linear features are very costly in terms of manpower, and garrisons are hard on royal purses. A scheme of private enterprise would be more effective while giving trusted Norman noblemen rewards for services rendered in war. These noblemen were made stewards of land in the Marches and were given freedom to rule in those lands and to take their profits in produce and taxes. Thus a buffer zone was in effect created, controlled by tough fighting men looking to protect their own lands and interests. It also helped make secure the hunting in the Clun Forest much prized by the Norman kings.

The first stages of this defensive system are described in the preceding chapter. Within this system, Roger de Montgomery, Earl of Shrewsbury, granted to one of his chief vassals, Robert 'Picot' de Say, 27 manors of which Clun was the most important. It had been the centre of a rich sprawling Saxon parish, whilst its geographical situation enabled it to control the strategic valley and gave it access to the richer lands beyond. It also controlled the Clun-Clee Ridgeway, the ancient drove road along the valley's southern hills. A town had grown up at Clun on the south side of the river, though the age of this settlement can only be surmised. However, the present curved churchyard wall is taken by many to indicate the existence of a pre-Christian worship place on the site. The Saxon town which is revealed by the *Domesday Book* grew up here, and a thriving Saxon town with mills powered by the waters of the Clun seems quite conceivable since there were still, within present living memory, eight weirs on the river between Clun and Purslow, though traces of some have since vanished. In the 1086 Domesday census a *Molinum serviens curiae* was noted, which can be taken to be a mill serving a manorial hall or court. As this is so early in the Norman occupation it would seem to have been of Saxon origin, or possibly even earlier.

Protection of so valuable a site would be more than prudent. Indeed the Saxon manor had been held by one Edric, probably the Edric the Wild noted in previous chapters, a reknowned warrior. The effects of his activity and counter-measures taken by the Normans reduced the value of Clun at the Conquest from £25 to a mere £3 at Domesday.

Though the first record of a castle in Clun is not till 1140, it is inconceivable that Picot de Say should not have taken very early steps to secure his lordship over the area and indeed provide a safe haven for himself and his retinue in a hostile environment. A timber castle (motte and bailey) could be erected very quickly and would suffice until a more permanent structure was built.

The site south of the river was already occupied by the Saxon town. North of the river below its junction with the River Unk the River Clun looped round a large mound, partly rock but overlaid with morainic deposit from the last ice age. This was fashioned to provide a splendid steep-sided defensible position comprising a motte and eventually two outer baileys surrounded by moats and a fish pond. A bridge or drawbridge gave access to the motte from the southern bailey. On the Welsh side the river loop gave extra protection. The military advantages of the location would not be lost on Norman lords who were well accustomed to using such features in Normandy to protect themselves there from the aggressive attentions of the French.

That such a site had been ignored by the Saxons seems unlikely though the Normans would very quickly have cleared the area for their own development. The Fitzalans who came from Cotentin in France acquired the lordship of Clun about 1155 through William Fitzalan's marriage to Isabel de Say. They are credited with the establishment of a town here in the late twelfth or early thirteenth century, and the layout of the present town shows clearly the straight streets of the planned settlement with the burgage plots still just discernible today. One street, Kidd Lane, curves through this tidy development, which may indicate that the Saxons had some buildings which the Normans decided not to move—Kidd Lane leads directly to the present (ancient?) road to Bishop's Castle.

No trace of any Norman town buildings is evident today. Such houses as were built would not have been of great substance. It is also unlikely that the town was walled. The steep scarp on the north side of the town and the river on the south would have made it comparatively easy to develop defences. In 1277 a murage grant was given to the town allowing the town council to levy taxes on items sold at Clun Market for a period of two years for the purpose of building town walls. No trace of town walls has survived, but it is possible that ditches were dug instead to the north and east of the town. One local historian has suggested that the houses on Trinity Lane at the east of the town were all unstable (*vide* cracking walls and metal wall braces) due to their being built along the edge of 'le Towne Dytche' mentioned in a document of 1589.

Speculation on the town buildings does not alter the fact of the building of the castle by de Say. The effect on the local population can be imagined. Here were foreign invaders demonstrating their intention to stay and to manage the land to their own advantage.

The area remained turbulent and incursions by the Welsh were part of the life of the Marches. Prior to the Battle of Radnor in 1196 Prince Rhys of South Wales attacked Clun Castle and after a long and bitter siege reduced it to 'ashes'. While this may be a victor's liberty with the truth it is not impossible, since at that time the castle was probably a wooden structure. The ruins which are still so striking today are of a later period.

It is not certain at what date the castle was reconstructed in stone. It would seem likely that the process started after the sacking by Prince Rhys. An inventory was made of the castle in 1272 on the death of the owner John Fitzalan III, Earl of Arundel, which records that the castle was 'competently built' but in need of repairs to the tower and bridge. A grange, bakehouse and stable in one of the baileys were in a decaying state. The indication was that there were parts of a structure of more permanent material than wood. Hard times were never far away and an inquest of 1302 found the castle to be worth little more than the annual cost of its maintenance, at £20. There were repairs being carried out, for at this time there was an obligation on the township of Obley to cart timbers to the castle, presumably for maintenance work.

At about this time the nature of the castle started to change. The Fitzalans spent most of their time in their castle and estates in Arundel but the call of the hunt was strong and Clun Forest offered fine prospects for sport. Even royal guests may have come for the chase, one source suggesting that Edward III visited the castle and hunted in the Forest in 1362.

Recent restoration of the castle by English Heritage enabled the City of Hereford Archaeology Unit (now Archaeological Investigations Ltd.) to take a detailed look at the buildings still standing. They were able to offer new theories about the castle, in particular the large building which had been known for many years as the keep because of its imposing size and similarity to Norman keeps elsewhere. Clun was different; it was physically indefensible since the building was let into the side of the motte either to make more stable foundations on the bedrock or because the top of the motte was even then crowded with buildings. There would already have been a keep, a chapel, kitchens and accommodation for troops. A dig may eventually reveal the true nature of the buildings hinted at by the uneven surface of the motte.

The great tower standing some 28 metres in height had a basement and three floors each progressively more grand than the floor below, each with an undivided great hall. This was not military architecture, though some features of the design suggested that. The archers' loops were blank and therefore ornamental only. Also the building was not round but square, which meant that it could more easily be undermined. A fire in a tunnel under a corner of the tower would crack the stone and bring down the building (as happened at Rochester Castle in 1215). Despite this the castle was still considered quite secure, for in 1371 the auditors of the Earl of Arundel reported that £3,267 were held in Clun, a vast fortune for those days.

The two bastions which remain facing west up the Clun valley towards Wales look very imposing. Military architecture would suggest them to be points from which enfilading fire could be brought to bear on the western curtain wall and west face of the tower. They are, however, solid and thus

Pl. 7 Clun Castle from the air, showing the medieval pleasance

do not provide any fire points. It must be concluded that their purpose was more ornamental than military.

Aerial photography has revealed a number of features on the west side of the River Clun which can be interpreted as a water garden and associated pavilions, a medieval pleasance. This confirms that, after its early warlike years of defence against Saxons and Welsh, it became a grand hunting lodge where the Earls of Arundel could take their ease and entertain their guests and their ladies in style while enjoying the pleasures of the chase in the hills of the Clun Forest.

By the time of the Civil War the castle had fallen on hard times. It was so degraded, probably by being robbed of its stone by local people for their own houses, that its owners, now the Howards, Dukes of Norfolk as well as Earls of Arundel, found it impracticable to repair and defend it. The church, which was being used as a defensive position in its stead, took the brunt of attacks and suffered considerable damage.

It is likely that the Normans set about the construction of a church early in their occupation of the site, although no mention is made of it in the *Domesday Book*. Such an omission was not unusual, for in Shropshire only 50 churches are recorded in a total of 631 entries; it seems unlikely that only 10%of places had churches. *Domesday* also mentions many priests without reference to their churches, which may imply the existence other churches or chapels.

The plan of the Norman church is not clear. However, it would have followed the pattern of those in their native Norman towns and been on a grand scale, though without a tower at first. This can be assumed because the west window now looks into the tower, a solid Norman construction only a little higher than the nave. The church has a medieval double pyramid wooden roof typical of others in the area, giving it a squat appearance.

The church now has north and south aisles and a chancel in addition to the nave, but it may not always have been so. The four bays on each side of the nave have pointed arches decorated with zig zags, except for the north-east arch which is round and plain. A similar round arch now gives access to the organ from the south side of the chancel. These plain arches are puzzling; they may have come from some other part of the church at a later reordering, one may even have been the chancel arch at some time. A possible explanation is that the church was originally cruciform in shape with the arches giving access to transepts from a plain nave. The pointed arches with their large supporting pillars could have been inserted at a later date. At the same time the north and south aisles could have been built incorporating the original transepts. This may explain why the clerestory windows on the south of the nave are over the pillars and not, as is more usual, over the arches where there was insufficient room for them.

The Norman arch over the main door is unusual in that it is in the north-west corner of the church. This is presumably so that it lined up with the main street leading up from the river. This fine feature may have been added when the north aisle was built, but the porch is a later addition, mostly of the nineteenth century.

Two factors make it difficult to trace in detail other Norman elements of the present grand building. The first was the disastrous damage and fire caused by the fighting in the Civil War of 1642-6. The townsfolk of Clun were so incensed by the depredations of both parties to the conflict that they formed a band of Clubmen to defend themselves and their property against both armies (*vide* Chapter 15). The second was the radical restoration in 1877. The work was directed by the eminent Victorian architect, G.E. Street, and was far-reaching, including, as it did, the rebuilding of the chancel. The Norman pillars were carefully restored showing both old and new stone. The south aisle was reduced in width, which permitted the

Pl. 8 Clun Church

lowering of the roof line. This allowed the Norman clerestory windows to be seen once more. A plaster ceiling which had covered the roof of the north aisle was removed to expose the splendid collared roof whose 11 trusses are supported by 22 winged angels. These cannot be older than the thirteenth century, dating at the earliest from when the aisle was enlarged.

What is left to this present day is an impressive building giving a clear indication of the size and grandeur of the original Norman church which once served a large parish (now much reduced since Saxon and Norman times, being now the mother-church only to the three small churches of Newcastle, Bettws-y-Crwyn and the Bryn). While Clun residents may today take their church for granted, their predecessors cannot fail to have been impressed by so grand a symbol of their occupiers' intent to remain and exercise their religious traditions and impose them on a subject people.

The present church and remains of the castle, imposing though they are, demand the exercise of some imagination to visualise the original buildings and to appreciate the impression these must have made on our Saxon and Welsh ancestors. Clun can boast of its pre-Norman ancestry and rejoice in its history traced in these fine edifices. As modern non-destructive techniques are developed it may become possible for archaeologists to examine the structure of these impressive buildings to determine their history in more detail.

Bibliography

Baker, F.E.S. *A Brief history of Clun*

City of Hereford Achaeology Unit *Clun Castle – Interim Report*, June 1993

Cranage, D.H.S. *The Churches of Shropshire* Shropshire Archaeol. & Nat. Hist. Soc., 1901

Morriss, Richard K. *Clun Castle - An Outline History* City of Hereford Archaeology Unit, January 1990

Pevsner, N. *The Buildings of England – Shropshire* Penguin Books, 1958

Rowley, T. *The Shropshire Landscape* Hodder & Stoughton, 1972
　　　　The Landscape of the Welsh Marches Michael Joseph, 1986

Trinder, B. *A History of Shropshire* Phillimore, 1983

Watson, M. and Musson, C. *Shropshire from the Air* Shropshire Books, 1993

In the early Medieval period, a number of 'planned towns' were established in south Shropshire, based around Norman strongholds and earlier settlements or religious sites. Bishop's Castle is a good example of this development: its settlement pattern, laid down around 1280, remains remarkably intact to the present day.

CHAPTER 11

Bishop's Castle: A Medieval Planned Town

by Sally Chappell & Anne Lawrence

Between the making of the *Domesday Book* in 1086 and the catastrophe of the Black Death in 1349, a tremendous transition took place that changed the Domesday world of the Saxons into the medieval world of the Normans and their successors. The metamorphosis was expressed in an explosive building and development programme of which the establishment and building of planned or planted towns can be recognised as a part. The evolution of Bishop's Castle is part of this metamorphosis.

Reading between the lines, the *Domesday Book* reveals life in early Norman England as barely above subsistence level for the majority of the mainly rural population. Vast areas of England were still only thinly populated. Settlements were centred on cleared areas of arable land, surrounded by a combination of forest and often impenetrable woodland and, in low-lying districts, fen and marsh. Travel and communication were difficult and had been barely improved in the 20 years since 1066, despite the innovatory Norman network of raised mottes, timber towers and baileys—the 'castles' so vociferously complained of in the *Anglo-Saxon Chronicles*. The main crops, providing food for man and beast, were grains and pulses. All available man and draught animal power was directed towards cultivation, towards productive labour aimed at sustaining life. The only animal mentioned as being herded in any number, because it took little supervision and could forage for itself in the woodlands, was the small, barely domesticated black pig, although there must also have been flocks of sheep. The Domesday world was a hand-made world, a slow world, dependent—except for the occasional water-powered mill—on human and animal muscular power. This was the world in which the Bishops of Hereford had their Manor of Lydbury.

The Manor of Lydbury, held by the Bishops of Hereford since before 1066, was extensive. Still dominating the landscape today is the feature that may have given the Manor lying due north of it a name: the massive hill fort crowning the summit of Tangley Hill, '... one of the finest British encampments on the Shropshire Borders.' Now called Bury Ditches, it was possibly more familiarly known to Egwin Shakehead, Saxon lord of Lydbury North, and the Saxon Bishops of Hereford as the *Hlithburg* or *Hlithburig*, the 'Fortified Height' or 'Stronghold on the Hill'. The great tracts of land lying between this and the dyke built by Offa to define and defend his kingdom from the Welsh became known, on this interpretation, as the lands lying north of the *Hlithburig—Hlithburig Nord*—Lydbury North. Here were the hard-won tracts of farmland, the Novers, Leasowes and Wintles, named by the Saxons who ploughed and harvested them; the long strip fields divided by the banks created by ploughing and planted with protective hedges—a great many of them recorded as waste and under-utilised by 1085/6. Near these fields were the small settlements that comprised the Manor, whose extent the *Domesday Book* gave as 53 hides. Some of these were possibly clustered round small churches, surrounded by their fields and occupied by the villagers, riders, smallholders and slaves listed in the *Domesday Book*—settlements isolated by woodland and forest and continuously at the mercy of the unpredictable elements and their Norman overlords.

But more important than the quantity of land recorded was the quality and its value. This had dropped since 1066 because it was 'waste' or was under-worked. The Domesday assessment lists $32^{1/2}$ hides as waste—approximately 5,000 acres—which was a great amount of taxable, unproductive land to possess at a point when the Crown was about to instigate an ambitious church and castle building programme particularly in an area where the king was to demand that the Marches be significantly defended against Welsh incursion. But Bishop Robert Losinga was an educated, versatile and astute Norman. He was to develop his own interests as well as protecting those of his king. It was probably during his episcopate (1079-1095) that the first motte and bailey castles were built to defend the small settlements that comprised the Manor of Lydbury. These constructions were probably erected sometime during the 15 years between 1085 and 1100. This period takes in the flurry of castle building on the Welsh Borders commanded by the king after intense and unsuccessful skirmishing in the Border hinterland.

Some 30 years later a small town had also been established or 'planted', which was to take its name from one or other of these defences—Bishop's Castle. The intriguing question is whether the town recorded as established by 1127 was actually a 'plantation', a deliberately planned Norman town and part of the twelfth-century speculative boom in town development, or whether it was an enhancement, a solidification of an already existing settlement which the Bishops of Hereford found it advantageous to develop and defend.

Like the speculative building of modern housing estates and new towns, Norman planned towns assumed particular patterns. To maximise land use, order was necessary; and enterprising, entrepreneurial landowners—particularly those with unproductive land—used two distinctive approaches to town layouts in the hope that their unremunerative acres could be turned to profit. The rectilinear or, 'chequer' system, was utilised on flat sites which were often confined within defensive walls. The rectilinear plots of the chequer design made economic use of all available building space within the limits of these town walls. Prime examples of this approach are the Edwardian plantation towns in North Wales. On sites planted along an existing road system or hillside sites developed from top to bottom of the hill, a 'grid' pattern was developed. This consisted of a main, central thoroughfare with back lanes defining the rear perimeter of the burgage plots that ran between the lanes and the main street. The choice of site, then, helped to define the layout of the town. The town developed by the Bishops of Hereford in their Manor of Lydbury appears to conform to the grid pattern, the main thoroughfare running from top to bottom of the hill and the burgage plots running horizontally across the hillside from the main thoroughfare to the back lanes.

This appears simple enough. The conformity of the town to the grid-pattern layout used by the Normans, particularly in the development of hill-sites, would support the contention that Bishop's Castle was—like 80% of similar towns—planted between 1066 and 1100 in the immediate vicinity of its guardian castle. But the history of any town, even one as small as Bishop's Castle, should not be considered separately from the conditions that may have modified its individual development. There have to be adequate reasons for the development of this particular site, which is recorded as an established town, possibly contained within bank and ditch defences by 1127, rather than other possible sites within the Manor.

These reasons are several. In general, the development of towns, small towns included, provided a great education for Norman landowners in the facts of life when very explicit revenue was due to the Crown. The lesson was learned relatively quickly that an unprofitable rural estate which could be organised to produce for a market paid the taxes and made a profit. The establishment of a town with a market on a site central to the whole Manor as well as with easy accessibility to the Welsh border can be seen as part of a deliberate policy. Not only did the town market provide the Manor with somewhere to sell its own surplus produce, it may also have provided the native Welsh just a few miles away across the border with a window of opportunity for trade and a share in the increasing prosperity, so making them less of a continuing threat. Towns also stabilised communities. The bishop's main concerns may have extended beyond his wish to profit from the town; he may also have been seeking to stabilise an existing community with the alluring promise of legal status as free men for the burgesses. This would prevent the migration of the Manor's population to a rival town. Ludlow was near enough and during this period, competition was fierce for skilled labour to create goods for an ever-expanding market policy.

But the development of the town and its market may have been connected with two more immediate features; the existence of an important roadway (or, in this case, roadways) and the siting of the church. The dominant roadway at this time was the long-established trade-route between Wales and England which passed through the Manor at this point, alongside the church-site and, since no church existed in isolation, its possible cluster of dwellings. Although undated and unrecorded, a church in some form undoubtedly existed prior to the building recorded in 1291, since no church was, it appears, ever built in the vicinity of the castle—the obvious Norman location for a place of worship. This would give some credence to the existence of an earlier settlement in the area of the church and the established roadway prior to any later development, enhancement, planting or planning. The burgage strips were consequently aligned with the main thoroughfare running from the castle at the top of the town to the site of the present church at the bottom. Roadway, church and small settlement were well within the proximity and overview of the prominent rocky spur where the bishops chose to build their castle. And the castle, of course, was strategically placed to over-look the second roadway. This climbed steeply up to the Bishop's Motte, the real defensive structure, on a summit of the Kerry Ridgeway overlooking the Camlad valley.

The castle, from which the town was to take its name, was probably built before any development of the proposed town and market site. The rocky spur site would seem to provide little scope for the erection of a wooden posted building since there appears to be an insubstantial soil-layer to provide adequate depth for stable anchorage, unless it was supplemented by the addition of a false, earthen motte. This would have been a time-consuming and labour-intensive project on an site already suitably elevated. It may be possible that from establishment, perhaps about 1097/98, the Bishop's castle was built of stone for which the bed-rock would have provided a satisfactory foundation. If this is the case, the castle may have been intended, from its inception, to be more of an imposing episcopal dwelling, '... a prominent feature of the new feudal administrative order', rather than an overt, defensive device. For some authorities, the positioning of a castle on a site with no recognised name—but central to the geography of the Manor—was intended as a focal point for urban development. The real defence for the area, already mentioned, was Bishop's Motte, now called Bishop's Moat.

There can be little doubt, however, that whatever did exist was regularly formalised or laid out and possibly defended by bank and ditch constructions along the line of the back lanes, now Station and Union Streets. The bank and ditch defences may even have curved round at the points which were to become Pig Fair and Horse Fair to enclose completely the small town (see map on following page). A market place, extending from the outer bailey walls of the castle and possibly comprising at least half of the present High Street—which would have been considerably wider at this time—certainly existed by the mid-thirteenth century. In April 1249, the first market charter regularising trade in the town was granted by King Henry III to Bishop Peter d'Aigueblanche, for the holding of a weekly market on Fridays and a yearly fair on the Decollation (beheading) of St John the Baptist on 29th August. The first known reference to Bishop's Castle, albeit in the Latin form of *Castrum Episcopi*, is in a document of 1255. Its first appearance in the records as 'Bissopescastel' came in 1282. The development of the town, surrounded by its outlying areas of town fields which provided the substance for the market, would have been gradual. The burgage plots nearest to the castle and the market place would have undoubtedly been developed first, since they were near to the protection of the castle and had easy access to the market place.

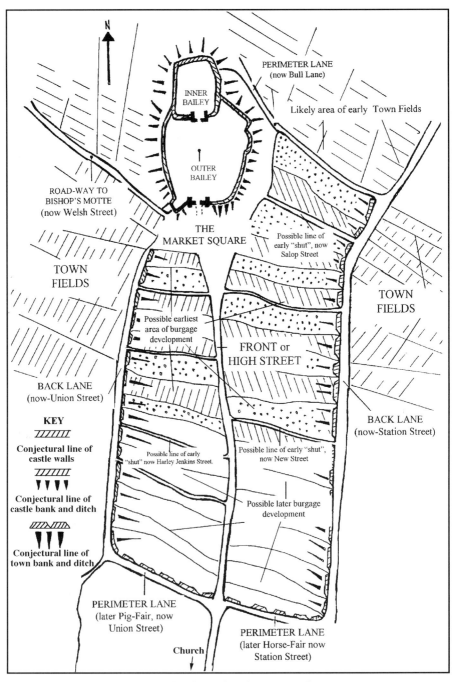

Fig. 8 Plan of Bishop's Castle

The clear identification of a 'plantation' town, the written evidence of the deliberate laying out of burgage plots with the intention of attracting settlement, lies in documents specifically drawn up for the purpose of establishing or registering the town, the Charters of Incorporation. These charters were granted by the Crown only to either well-established towns or to the new towns founded by the monarch during this period. Such charters gave towns a form of self-government, with an elected council of bailiffs or bailiffs and burgesses. However, small or minor plantations like Bishop's Castle, founded by the Lord of the Manor, are classed as seigneurial, mesne, or prescriptive boroughs. The rights and privileges of Bishop's Castle were granted directly to the Bishops of Hereford as the proprietors of the town. In 1203, Bishop Giles de Braose was granted considerable powers by King John, particularly in the administration of justice within various Manors, including Lydbury North. This brought his into line with the almost autonomous powers granted to other Marcher Lords at the time. The exercise of such power and privilege in the manor remained within the discretion of the bishops, and what actual rights, apart from holding markets and fairs, the burgesses of the town enjoyed cannot be ascertained, since none of the original charters has survived.

There are rumours and references to the charters being withheld and even deliberately sequestered by the bishops. But the town was always a prescriptive or proprietory borough and the property of Hereford Cathedral, managed by its powerful bishops. The Church as overlord tended to be the most restrictive in stopping boroughs gaining their corporate independence, since such independence would challenge its fiscal control. The bishop had a great deal to gain from taxes, market tolls, and the profits from any courts held within his jurisdiction. It was not until after the Bishops of Hereford lost the Manor to the Crown in the sixteenth century that Bishop's Castle was able to obtain a Charter of Incorporation from Queen Elizabeth I in 1573. The charter at last defined the town as a borough, and clarified the rights of the burgesses who by 1584 had the additional privilege of electing two Members of Parliament. The borough's powers were further increased in 1617 by the charter of James I.

The town of Bishop's Castle was never large. By the late thirteenth century, in the survey of the property held by the bishops, recorded in the *Red Book* only 46 burgages were noted. There were certainly burgesses as there are some references to their somewhat arcane duties which included finding a man to act as deer-beater, at the bishop's pleasure, and to the amount the burgesses had to pay for the repair of ploughs, shares and coulters at the election of the Bishop's Bailiffs at Pentecost and Michaelmas—no doubt a beneficial addition to the bishop's income from the Manor. But, despite its size and however it may have been planned, planted or enhanced, the town survived.

It survived for several reasons. There was, in all probability, an already established settlement with sufficient population to produce the surplus necessary for a market economy. This population may have been enticed to remain resident, and was probably supplemented and expanded by the bait of burgage plots and the opportunity to become freeholders with the supposed rights and privileges this gave. Failure to recruit a population early and quickly would have damaged the revenue of the profit-seeking planner as well as the livelihood and morale of the burgage holders, and would inevitably have led to the demise of the town. But, perhaps more important, survival may have been ensured by the combination of the town's size and the continual, heavy shadow of the bishops, symbolised by the castle overlooking and protecting the town. There is evidence that small villages or settlements elevated to the status of 'towns' by the establishment of a market, the attraction of trade and the stabilisation and even expansion of their populations by whatever means, could survive under the sheltering monopoly of a powerful seigneurial overlord, while officially planted towns with officially documented charters withered and decayed. There is also evidence that the granting of markets and fairs did not always ensure expansion and advancement. Shelve and Lydham are local examples, despite the latter being given a borough charter by its lord, Adam de Montgomery. While a majority of town plantations were successful, one in seven folded—and this is usually attributable to poor siting and failure to attract trade. Caus Borough is a notable example in south-west Shropshire.

By the late sixteenth century, as the remaining oak timber-framed buildings show, Bishop's Castle had become prosperous and had probably extended beyond the confines of its early bank and ditch defences down towards the church. The town never grew to the size of neighbouring Ludlow, which was more strategically placed and always more politically powerful. It was probably hoped that the granting of charters from the thirteenth to the early seventeenth century would make the town more attractive to new-comers and increase its size and prosperity. In an area of such sparse population, however, this was not to be until the late nineteenth and early twentieth centuries. But that is another chapter in Bishop's Castle's intriguing and ever colourful history.

Bibliography

Beresford, M. *New Towns of the Middle Ages* London, 1967

Cheesewright, M. *Bishop's Castle Town Guide* 1986

Dalwood, H. et al. *Archaeological Assessment of Bishop's Castle, Shropshire* Project 945, Report 299 Field Section County Archaeological Services, May 1996

Douglas, D.C. and Greenaway, G.W. (eds.) *English Historical Documents Vol 2 1042-1189* London, 1955

Gelling, M. *Place Names in the English Language* Penguin, 1984

Griffiths, E.G. 'Places of Interest in the Neighbourhood' (locally published 1901), in *Documents Concerning the Parishes of Bishop's Castle and Colebatch* Local Studies Publication, 1987

Hayward, L.H. 'Ancient Land Tenures', *Transactions of Shropshire Archaeological Society (TSAS), Vol XLIX* 1937-38

Hoskin, W.G. *The Making of the English Landscape* Penguin, 1985

Ingram, Rev. J. (trns.) *The Anglo-Saxon Chronicle* Everyman, 1917

Lavender, F. 'Charters of the Borough of Bishop's Castle' *TSAS, Vol LIII* 1949-50

In spite of Roman forts, Offa's Dyke and a chain of Norman castles, the Welsh Border remained for many centuries unsettled and disputed territory. In the fourteenth and fifteenth centuries there is evidence of a considerable number of Welsh incursions into Shropshire and Herefordshire, which reflect the most complex cross-border politics.

CHAPTER 12

Unrest in the Marches 1280-1485
by Robin Howard

Asa Briggs picked out a comment by a fifteenth-century gentleman on his times that all Europe was 'Right Wild'. The specific uncontrollable wildness of Wales and the Marches led Edward I to the immensely expensive campaigns of the 1270s and 1280s, to extend and strengthen Marcher Lordships particularly in the northern Marches, and to a vast castle-building programme — nine state-of-the-art royal castles were added to the large numbers already built by the occupying power that included Shrewsbury, Caus, Montgomery, Welshpool, Bishop's Castle, Clun, Knighton, Wigmore, and Ludlow. The castles can be seen as shameful memorials to the subjugation of the Welsh by the English — 'the magnificent badges of our subjection' was how the eighteenth-century antiquarian Thomas Pennant put it. The Welsh historian R.R. Davies suggests that the castles can also be seen as a tribute to the tenacity of the resistance of the Welsh to their conquerors, 'eloquent testimony to the task of uprooting from Wales the rule of the Welsh'.

After his conquest Edward I aimed to 'end the malice of the Welsh'. The Archbishop of Canterbury instructed the clergy to undertake a campaign for the political re-education of the Welsh 'in order to wean them from the Trojan fantasies and from their messianic hopes of recovering the mastery of Britain'. Geoffrey of Monmouth's *History of the Kings of Britain*, completed in 1136, and the accepted history of Britain at this time, traced Welsh origins back to Troy and in particular to the founding of Britain by

Brutus. This history was a vital part of national consciousness, and not easily erased. The Welsh looked for a saviour in some descendant of their heroes Cadwaladr (d.682) and of the Llewellyns (d.1240 and 1282), one who could be acknowledged both by achievement and by genealogical descent. The hopes were kept alive by the clergy, by the influential Cistercian order and by peripatetic poets who were sustained by the Welsh gentry and the churches, as well as rhymers and storytellers in public places, who were heard by the common people. The poetic tradition flowered in these centuries. The fulfilment of Welsh hopes failed under Glyndwr, but were perceived to find a fulfilment with Henry Tudor's seizure of the throne of England after the Battle of Bosworth Field in 1485.

Conflicts and unrest were widespread through these centuries in the lordships which comprise south-west Shropshire: in Clun under the Fitzalan Earls of Arundel, in royal Montgomery, Bishop's Castle under the Bishops of Hereford, Caus under the Corbets, and, in the surrounding areas, the Charltons at Welshpool, and the mighty Mortimers at Wigmore. The unrest was between Welsh and English in each area, with a peak in the national revolt of Owain Glyndwr in 1400. But there were also continuing struggles between kings and Marcher lords, notably in the 1390s; and between Marcher lords, struggles which culminated in the rivalries of the Houses of Lancaster and York and the Wars of the Roses. The battles were largely waged by Welsh archers, the mercenaries of their time, prepared to fight for anyone, who formed the bulk of all the fighting forces. The skills of the Welsh archers, honed in the Hundred Years' War in France, inevitably spilled over into continuing violence in the Marches.

Much complaint of violence was recorded. Two Welshmen, Owen ap Maradoc and Mareddud ap Madoc, petitioned the king around the year 1300 that they were 'the rightful heirs of the cantref of Kedeweyn until Sir Edmund de Mortymer came by force and dispossessed them completely of the land between Severn and Kerry'. But the king had no means to enforce any remedy. In 1306-8 five vills including Horderley on the Onny were 'burnt plundered and destroyed' by the Welsh. (They sought relief from one of Edward's tax impositions, for his Welsh activities had cost ten times his annual income and he had already borrowed heavily from his Italian bankers, a debt he had to service. In addition he was very short of money for his Scottish campaigns.) In 1318-19 the Bishop of Hereford petitioned that 'Hugh de Audeley, keeper of the castle and lands of Montgomery took into his hands ... three vills (including Church Stoke) belonging to the Bishop's Castle to the loss of the king and the disinheritance of the said bishop and his church'.

There are cases of friction between royal Montgomery and episcopal Bishop's Castle. In the first of these John Says from Montgomery petitioned, in 1383, that 'a certain Ieuan, a tenant of the bishop of Hereford, with several men at arms with him, tortuously took John Says on the high road within the Lordship of the Bishop, without cause or blow. Ieuan brought John Says as far as the castle of the Earl of Arundel which is called Clunne, outside the lordship of the Bishop, and there imprisoned him for eight days'. In the same year, the people of Halcestre in Montgomery complained that 'certain tenants of the Lordship of the Bishop of Hereford of Bysshopes Castelle which is parcel of the lordship of Montgomery ... feloniously killed one W(illi)am ap Howell, tenant of the king. Certain tenants of Halcestre suddenly with hue and cry took one of the felons and brought him to the king's castle at Montgomery'. They petitioned that 'the Bishop sued to the king by untrue suggestion to have delivery of the felon unto his castle at Bysshops castell ... against the custom and usages, for the Lordship of Montgomery is parcel of the Crown and never yet made March...'

Nor was this the only way in which Crown and Church came into conflict. The Cistercians had an important abbey at Strata Marcella, on Severnside north-west of Welshpool (SO 103251). Early in the fourteenth century it was claimed that 'unlawful assemblies' were held there 'to excite contentions between the English and the Welsh'. The Abbot of Strata Marcella was not popular with his English Lord, John Charlton at Welshpool, and Edward II was subjected to a barrage of complaints. First, John Charlton petitioned the king about the bad keeping of the abbey's rules. The abbot counter-petitioned that Charlton kept soldiers at his gate which prevented him from carrying out divine service. The Abbot of Cîteaux now sent a commissary, one Peter, who complained that Charlton would not let him enter his land, threatening loss of life and limb. 'Sir John says "Je suis Papes; Je suis R(oy)s et Abbes en ma terre"'. Pope, king, abbot; an absolute claim characteristic of a Marcher Lord at that time. Peter asked that the abbey be put under royal protection. The king made elliptical comment: ' Let the Chancellor provide a remedy'. What remedy might the Chancellor of England, based in Westminster, effectively supply?

Abbots of Strata Marcella were neither meek nor mild; at about this time the Prior of Chirbury petitioned that the abbot 'came against the king's peace with horses and arms and banners ... and took the tithes' which produced a comment on the roll that 'it would be difficult for the prior and his men to fight with an established house where there is established a convent of 140 monks and the son of Sir Griffin and his power'. The

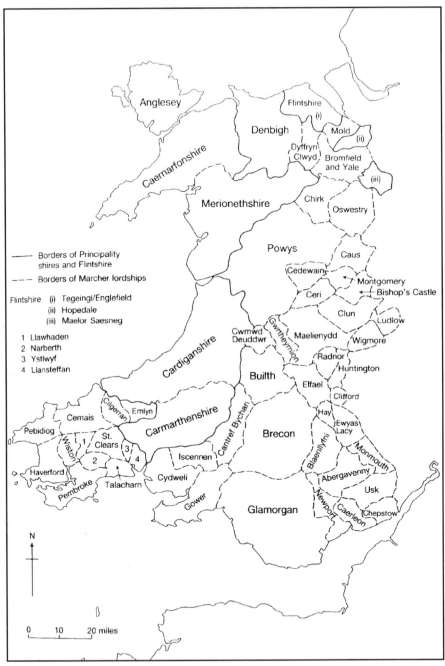

Fig. 9 The Major Administrative and Lordship Divisions of Wales and the Marches in the Fourteenth Century

inability of the king to have much influence without mustering a major force is again striking.

There is a further vignette from Chirbury. In 1393 Richard II wrote to Richard Arundel asking him to establish what had happened in a dispute. Arundel reported 'Unlawful words were spoken; Robert Modelton called the prior a peasant; the prior said he lied; Robert drew his sword; Richard, sergeant of the prior, drew his bow in defence of the prior, whereupon several ran in, so that no injury resulted'. The sense that the king was personally interested in your grievances and distresses and could and would take some action to address them is an abiding feature of the cases reported in Rees' *Calendar of Ancient Petitions relating to Wales.*

Conflict between King and Marcher Lords came to a head in the 1390s with the high-handed behaviour of Richard II, eliminating by other means what death by war and natural causes had failed to cull. In 1397 Thomas, Duke of Gloucester was murdered in Calais (he had held the lordships of Caldicot and Huntington). Thomas Beauchamp, Earl of Warwick was disgraced and his lands, Elfael and Gower, confiscated in 1396. Richard Arundel was beheaded in London, and Clun, Oswestry, Chirk, Bromfield and Yale were confiscated and re-allocated. Thomas Mowbray, Duke of Norfolk, was exiled for life, losing Gower and Chepstow. The Earl of March died in battle in Ireland. He held 16 lordships and was next in line for the throne. John of Gaunt died a natural death but his exiled heir, Bolingbroke, was disinherited of Monmouth and Cydweli.

All this, taking place inside two years, transformed the pattern of Lordship in the Marches. R.R. Davies comments 'The excitement in Wales must have been intense. Old loyalties and certainties were undermined, men cast adrift from established allegiances'.

It soon changed again. Returning from exile Bolingbroke raised an army and moved through the Marches from Bristol to Chester via Leominster, Ludlow and Shrewsbury. A delegation met Richard II at Conway where the king was taken captive; thence to the Tower of London via North Wales and Chester; to deposition and subsequently death. Bolingbroke took the crown as Henry IV, but his claim was not universally recognised. In North Wales and Chester there was continuing loyalty to Richard II. These sparks added fire to the subsequent national revolt of Glyndwr.

Owain Glyndwr claimed his descent from the great houses of Wales; the poets, notably Iolo Goch, agreed. He was, said the poet, 'of the stock of the Lord Rhys'. Rhys was ruler of Deheubarth or south-west Wales, dying in 1197. He was also 'of the stock of Bleddyn ap Cynfyn' who was regarded as the founder of the ruling dynasty of Powys, dying in 1075. These were two prestigious princely dynasties: Glyndwr was the senior surviving representative of both. He also claimed the blood of the third princely dynasty, Gwynedd, adopting the arms of the first and last formally acknowledged native prince of Wales, Llywelyn ap Gruffydd (1267-83) on his great seal. In September 1400 Glyndwr boldly announced himself Prince of Wales.

Between 18th and 23rd September Owain's supporters attacked a string of English towns in the Marches: Ruthin, Denbigh, Rhuddlan, Flint, Holt, Oswestry and Welshpool. North-west Wales rose simultaneously. By mid-1401 the revolt had flared across the length and breadth of Wales. Glyndwr's charisma carried all before him; he denounced 'the madness of the Saxon barbarians who have usurped the land of Wales'; hope and deliverance, hatred and revenge were all in the air. The poets' war-cry 'Rout the English' (*rhuthro Eingl*) seemed to be on the verge of achievement.

In east central Wales the battle of Bryn Glas took place to the west of Pilleth, a small village south of Knighton, on 22nd June 1402. (SO 680252). 'Owen arose with a great host from Gwynedd, Powys and the South and made for Maelienydd; where the knights of Herefordshire gathered against him'. The Monk of Evesham recorded that 'the Welshmen of Maelienydd, not of the tribe of Judah, but born to be similar traitors, traitorously turned their faces and weapons against their own lords'. Perhaps half the English army was killed. Walsingham reported the subsequent mutilations of the English, particularly their genitalia, by Welshwomen; tales which lost nothing in the telling. Shakespeare echoed the English dismay;

> ....the noble Mortimer,
> Leading the men of Hereford to fight
> Against the irregular and wild Glendower,
> Was by the rude hands of that Welshman taken,
> A thousand of his people butchered;
> Upon whose corpse there was such misuse,
> Such beastly, shameless transformation,
> By those Welshwomen done, as may not be
> Without much shame re-told or spoken of..
>
> *Henry IV Pt.1* - Act 1; Scene 1

Bryn Glas was the signal for massive defections to Glyndwr from the border lordships. In three vills at Bishop's Castle, 77 Welshmen were to forfeit their lands.

By the high summer of 1403 no part of Wales was immune from the virus of rebellion. Henry IV had given a very prominent part in Wales to the Percy family in appreciation of their support in his bid for the throne—Henry Percy Earl of Northumberland, his son Henry called Hotspur, and the senior Henry's brother Thomas Percy Earl of Worcester. Hotspur as chief governor of North Wales, of Cheshire and Flintshire was given a prominent role in dealing with Glyndwr's revolt. But the Percys were disillusioned with the king and in July Hotspur changed sides, only to be defeated and killed at the Battle of Shrewsbury eleven days later, on 22nd July 1403—a battle in which some prominent Welshmen also fell. But the momentum of the revolt was not halted. 'Indeed it was then that the men of the County of Flint became rebels', and joined Owain Glyndwr.

The king and parliament responded to Glyndwr's uprising with a succession of measures. In July 1401 there had been 'appointments for the good governance of the marches of north Wales ... to punish all sending victuals to the rebels ... and for the resistance of the malice of the Welsh rebels'. The castles were in disrepair, and poorly supplied with men, arms and food. The Commons required the Marcher Lords to reside in their lordships, to put supplies into their castles, and to act against the rebels. Eighty-two castles in Wales were placed in a state of defence. Montgomery Castle acquired a force of 20 men-at-arms and 100 archers, later increased to 50 men at arms and 150 archers, to defend Montgomery itself and also the associated castles at Caus and Bishop's Castle, and to secure border districts from raids of Welshmen by making forays into north Wales.

Glyndwr's revolt also involved attacks on Welshpool and Montgomery. The town by the castle at Welshpool was devastated, and 'Montgomericke was deflorischid by Owen Glindour'. The *Arundel Estate Accounts* for Ruyton, Sandford and Aston, west of Shrewsbury, show a trail of burnt and empty villages and mills. The situation became so desperate that several communities in Shropshire and Powys were allowed to conclude local treaties with the Welsh.

In 1403 the king instructed knights and esquires with land to the value of 100 shillings to 'go home and there continually abide to resist the malice of the rebels, in case they shall attack'. This applied to Gloucestershire, Salop, Worcestershire and Herefordshire where, 'For lack of victuals Owen Glyndowdy and other rebels are purposing to come suddenly to the marches to seek victuals and waste those parts'.

Shropshire records of breaches of the peace between 1400 and 1414 give a range of illustrations of the unrest, some, though not necessarily all, directly associated with the Welsh uprising. In the Hundred of Purslow 'Tocke the Miller of Clunbury commonly receives Welsh rebels; he guided certain rebels to the town of Pusselowe (Purslow) where they took John Bloke captive and carried him off to Wales'.

'Yewekes Duy of Bishopscastle received three men who were Welsh rebels knowing that they had broken into the house of William Hicks of Hardwick and Richard Mayns of Hardwick and stolen four coverlets and four pairs of sheets valued at 40s; he gave them food and other necessities'.

Walter and William Ionkyn were accused of 'unjustly taking 47 oxen and cows price £29 from Thomas Bondeleres at Winsbury [near Chirbury] and driving them into Wales'.

Howell ap Cadwaladour and Howell ap Madogyn feloniously murdered at Bishop's Castle and burned houses at Norbury; 'They were notorious thieves and despoilers of fields'. John Thomason of Kempton 'feloniously stole three oxen price 40s at Little Brampton from Hugo son of Thomas of Brampton'. John son of Margery Godmon of Edgton 'feloniously stole a mare price 13s 4d'.

The Hundred of Ford is particularly open geographically to external raids. John Dod of Pontesbury had bullocks stolen by Welshmen in 1411 and at Moorwood 24 oxen and cows. Minsterley, Whitton and the Borough of Caus were burnt; and the townships of Caus, Marsh, Vennington, Westbury and Yockleton were excused taxation. In 1416 the Bishop of Hereford, incensed at the theft of cattle from his lordship at Bishop's Castle, excommunicated William Knight of Norbury, John Fernour of Egdon, John Fewtrere of Munslow, Roger Aldon of Braston and William Kynton of Cressage.

All in all, the physical damage of the years of and following Glyndwr's rebellion can be seen as 'the most devastating experience of destruction that Wales (and the Marches) has suffered as a country'. This is vividly illustrated in a return to the Exchequer early in 1406 from Robert Mascall, Bishop of Hereford, naming 52 churches so badly damaged that the benefices should be exempt from king's-aid, a tax the king was levying for the French wars. Charted on a map, the list shows as a band of territory some ten miles wide stretching from the Severn in the north to the Monnow in the south. Half the churches are in two deaneries in the Archdeaconry of Shropshire.

In the Deanery of Clun Forest, according to Bishop Mascall's report, the following churches were damaged: Clun, with the vicar's glebe land;

Ashton; Wentnor; Leodone (Lydham?); Stowe with the adjacent chapel; Moore; 'Wantenovere' (probably Wentnor, repeated); Bromptone; Bishop's Castle with the vicar's glebe land; Lydbury North, with the vicar's glebe land and Bokenhulle (Bucknell). In the Deanery of Pontesbury: Montgomery; Worthen; Westbury; Pulverbatch; Shrawardine; Pontesbury, with the glebe land ; Alburbury, with the vicar's glebe land and the '*temporalia*' (worldly possessions) and '*mobilia*' (moveables) of its prior; Hawood (Hanwood?); Meole Brace, with the vicar's glebe land; Ford; Chirbury, with the glebe lands of the precentor of Wenlock and Newton, with the '*temporalia*' of the Abbot of Wigmore. The Bishop's own temporalities were destroyed at Bishop's Castle and Lydbury North.

The Glyndwr uprising led to a tide of anti-Welsh ordinances unleashed by Parliament in 1401-02. It was the 'right and duty of the king to repress the insolence of his rebellious subjects'. They were not to hold assemblies; their minstrels and rhymers were to be starved into silence; no Welshman was to serve in English garrisons in Wales: arms and victuals were not to reach the Welsh rebels.

Ethnic barriers were raised; no Welshman could buy land in England or in eight English towns in Wales; top posts, down to the level of chief forester, were closed both to Welshmen and also to English persons married to a Welsh man or woman 'of the friendship of the alliance of Owen de Glyndowdy, traitor ...'. The Commons confirmed these oppressive measures in 1406/7 and the king commented in 1430/31 'Let the statutes be firmly kept and held'. It was crudely racist. R.R. Davies suggests that these measures 'held back the process of social reconciliation for several generations, delayed the birth of modern Wales, and gave a new and vindictive lease of life to the past'.

But Glyndwr's revolt faded and lost its power; individuals and communities returned to obedience, Clun perhaps as early as 1406. However, huge and daunting indemnities were imposed and official rhetoric would remain, for generations, that of cold war.

The bewildering lawlessness was not merely the work of irresponsible hordes of outlaws, hardened ruffians and soldiers out-of-work. Substantial numbers of English and Welsh 'became the retainers of a depraved nobility whose predatory habits they aped'. John Talbot, a valiant soldier, was Constable of Montgomery Castle in 1424 when the king summoned him to France. Talbot refused to go until he had indemnified himself for the arrears of his wages, and launched a profitable raid on the prosperous farmers and citizens of Herefordshire. More than 20 accomplices were named to the Privy

Council, an even mix of English and Welsh. Sir Reginald Grey and Hugh Wenlok, who were on the sharp end of Talbot's activities, petitioned Parliament to compel Talbot to give security that henceforth he would keep the peace. It did him no long-term harm; he later became Earl of Shrewsbury.

Talbot's activities were surely behind the more general complaint in the same year, from the church, when Henry VI's Council were seeking funds for the French wars. The church complained that these were 'heavy and insupportable burdens; there is wasting of crops through dryness of the air; destruction of cattle by murrain through failure of pastures, and unwonted violence of manifold hostile raids'. The distress continued at least until 1440.

Following Glyndwr's revolt, the flood of prophetic poetry and Messianic hope looked to others. The poets sang now to Yorkists, now to Lancastrians, seeking among the various leaders a man fitting in terms of ancestry and credible in terms of power to be the second Cadwaladr.

At length, in August 1485, Henry Tudor marched from Milford Haven through Wales to Mynydd Digoll (Long Mountain), near Welshpool, a strategic meeting point, where substantial contingents from all parts of Wales joined him. He went on to triumph on Bosworth Field, with the help of his Welsh archers. Future generations decided that Henry Tudor had proved to be the one who was to come; he could be seen to be the true descendant of Brutus, of Cadwaladr and the Welsh princes, and to rule all Britain. He carried the Red Dragon of Cadwaladr in the Battle of Bosworth, to St. Paul's Cathedral and at his Coronation afterwards. Arthur Kelton, a Welshman from Shrewsbury, referred with immense pride to Henry VII being of Cadwaladr's line, 'rightful King of Britain called England' and assured his readers in 1546 of the meaning of Henry's triumph:

> thus God above
> of very love
> His kingdom hath assured.

Sixteenth- and seventeenth-century Welshmen regarded Henry VII as a heaven-sent, historic deliverer of his people, a man of epic, scriptural proportions; a Moses, a second Solomon, a noble David, who graciously eased their pains.

Under his son, the Wildness eased. Welshmen became equal under the law with Englishmen. The monasteries were dissolved. Marcher Lordships were abolished. Modern Wales was born.

Bibliography

The Shropshire Records & Research Centre has printed translated Calendars on which I have particularly drawn; the king's own letters, and a variety of rolls from government sources and *The Arundel Estate Accounts*. Anyone could make petitions concerning grievances, and expect a reply; *The Calendar of Ancient Petitions relating to Wales* (ed. W. Rees Cardiff 1975) was particularly helpful.

The Shropshire Peace Rolls 1400-1414 (ed. Elisabeth G. Kimball 1959) illuminate the detailed concerns of the period of Glyndwr's revolt and its aftermath.

The Register of Robert Mascall, Bishop of Hereford 1404-1416 (Parry J.H., 1916), printed in Latin, includes his account of churches burnt.

The Victoria History of Shropshire Vol. VIII covers the Hundred of Ford.

Briggs, Asa *A Social History of England* BCA, 1994

Cowan, A. *The Penguin Book of Welsh Verse* (in translation) Penguin, 1967

Davies, John *History of Wales*, Penguin, 1990 ET 1993

Davies, R.R. *The Age of Conquest 1063-1415* OUP, 1987

Davies, R.R. *The Revolt of Owain Glyndwr* OUP, 1995

Evans, H.T. *The Wars of the Roses* CUP, 1915 republished Alan Sutton, 1998

Geoffrey of Monmouth *The History of the Kings of Britain* c.*1150*
    (ed. L. Thorpe) Penguin, 1966

Hodges, Geoffrey *Owain Glyndwr and the War of Independence in the Welsh Borders* Logaston, 1995

Jenkins, Philip *A History of Modern Wales 1536-1990* Longman, 1992

Williams, Glanmor *Renewal and Reformation; Wales c.1415-1462* OUP, 1987

A striking feature of south Shropshire hill-country is the network of small hamlets which comprise isolated farms and homesteads. They have no village nucleus, and yet maintain a strong identity and sense of community, often centred around an ancient church. One such community is Bettws-y-Crwyn, with its church nearly 1,300 feet above sea level which must be one of the highest in the land.

CHAPTER 13

Bettws-y-Crwyn
by John Leonard and Alan Wilson

Everything about Bettws-y-Crwyn is improbable. Even the name is odd—
bettws is said to be Welsh for 'chapel' from OE *bed-hus* (oratory) but *crwyn*
may be Welsh for 'pigsty'. An alternative explanation is that *crwynwr*
(Welsh for a skinner) may relate to fleeces, reflecting the local preponder-
ance of sheep. The very situation of the church is bizarre—not comfortably
in the Clun valley at Duffryn in the centre of the parish, but isolated on a
wind-swept hillside. It commands glorious views indeed (this scarcely
mattered to medieval parishioners), but is difficult of access, especially in
inclement weather. At 1,253 feet above sea level, it may well be the highest
parish church in England. Why, indeed, was it built *there*? For remoteness
of situation it is unrivalled in Shropshire, possibly in all England. The
church is seven miles west of Clun, on high ground between the valleys of
the Clun and the Teme, still in Shropshire but west of Offa's Dyke. And not
only is Bettws remote: it is very thinly populated. The area of the parish is
about 15 square miles, and with a present-day population of *c.*210, this
gives a density of population of just 14 persons per square mile—surely
one of the lowest in the country.

The history of Bettws goes back a long way before the Middle Ages.
Human activity in the area was dominated by two ridgeways used by the
cattle drovers which cross at Kerry Pole. One is the Kerry Ridgeway which
connected mid-Wales to the English Midlands, and which now forms the

northern boundary of the parish. The other is a ridgeway from Onibury to Anchor and extending into Wales; before the Romans, this was a route to distant chalk lands in southern England. Hundreds of flints found in Bettws and along the ridgeway to Clunbury, now in the Clun Museum, originated in Wiltshire, indicating that in the hills around Kerry Pole dwelt a community who used flints as tools and arrow-heads. It may be significant that a field east of Cefn Vron hill is known as the Knapps, perhaps referring to the chippings found locally and indicating an area where rough flint was shaped for use. In exchange, Wiltshire might have received picrite for axe-heads from Brithdir, south of Corndon Hill. Prehistoric activity is also shown by a glance at Ordnance Survey maps which show two stone circles, half a dozen tumuli and several prehistoric settlements within two miles of Kerry Pole.

The Romans also came to this remote area. A Roman pot was found on Cefn Vron in 1927, whilst the shortest way from Caersws (where there was a Roman fort) to Leintwardine (*Bravonium*) was along the two ridgeways. Soldiers from the lead mines south of Felindre used the present route from Anchor to Sarn.

In Anglo-Saxon times, Welsh marauders were a constant threat. Three defensive earthworks across the Kerry Ridgeway were established before King Offa built his dyke—these now end ineffectually in fields, but would originally have finished in marshes. The middle of the three, the Upper Short Ditch, is still plain to see. When Offa's Dyke was built in the eighth

Pl. 9 Castell Bryn Amlwg

century east of Bettws, these subsidiary defences may have ensured that Bettws remained English.

The Normans sustained these defences with several strongholds. The most impressive was a motte and later a castle built at Bryn Amlwg ('the hill with a view'), about half a mile south-west of the Anchor Inn and which could dominate both ridgeways. The name has not been traced earlier than the sixteenth century. Mounds indicating the former motte and bailey are still standing (Plate 9). When the site was excavated in 1963 five stages of construction were revealed. In the early twelfth century, a ditch was dug and a bank thrown up to form an oval ringwork around a knoll. Later that century a timber pallisade and a circular stone keep were constructed, the walls of the latter being eight feet thick. A stone revetment or curtain wall was then added to the front of the ring-bank, abutting the keep. In the next century two towers were added to the curtain, and finally a twin-towered gateway was added on the north, facing the easiest approach to the castle. In the nineteenth century a Bronze Age axe and spearhead were found here and are now in the Powysland Museum. The position of the castle above the Rhyddwr brook defined the western limit of the Honour of Clun. Another motte and bailey, known as the Moat, is found at Beguildy in the Teme Valley just north of Brookhouse Farm (then in the Maelinydd lord-ship), whilst yet another was built at Bettws Grange, close to the ridgeway in the north of the parish.

The origin of St. Mary's church is lost in antiquity, but it is known that at some stage it was appropriated to Abbey Cwmhir. This was a Cistercian monastery in mid-Wales founded in 1143 by Maredudd, son of Madoc ap Idwerth (according to the *Chronicle of Chester Abbey*), and re-founded in 1176 by Maredudd's brothers. It had a grange farm in Beguildy in the Teme valley, just south of Bettws.

Only occasional glimpses of light illumine the medieval history of the parish. On 5th August, 1276, the Bishop of Hereford (Thomas Cantilupe) wrote to the Dean of Pontesbury; he instructed him to excommunicate those who, contrary to the immunities of the church of Hereford, had committed depredation and sacrilege in respect of the goods of the Prior of Alberbury and in respect of the chapel of Betteus, which at that time belonged in part to the Prior of Chirbury. In 1331, the chapel of *Bechous* was recognised as a dependency of the church of Clun, and therefore belonged to the Prior of Wenlock. After the Reformation, in 1587, the Visitation-book of Bishop Westfaling mentions that Bettws is in the diocese of Hereford, and ranked as a united curacy with Llanfair Waterdine.

Pl. 10 Bettws-y-Crwyn Church: Perpendicular Screen

The church today is basically medieval, but so thorough was the Victorian restoration of 1860 that little remains to help in dating the building. The windows are mostly lancets, but all are Victorian, whilst the bell-turret dates from this restoration. The church has, however, several excellent attractions. The finest is the late Perpendicular screen of Spanish chestnut (Plate 10), with round arches, mullions running up into their apices, and small and intricate panel tracery. There is a frieze of heavy pierced quatrefoils above the dado. The roof is also good, and may be late-medieval (Plate 11); it has collar-beams on arched braces, and two lateral tiers of wind-braces carved into quatrefoils. The communion rail is simple and rustic, and may be Jacobean. The benches (Plate 12) are of rude crafts-manship—an unusual feature is that they are inscribed with the names of the farms in the parish. The church possesses a marvellous silver chalice with repoussé ornament (ornament raised in relief), hallmarked 1665.

The names on the pews are as follows: Rydycwm; Vron; Parsonage; Crosshouses; Moate; Hall Forest; Lower Duffryn; New House and Black Mountain; Tyn y Vron and Foesyrow; Lloyds Anchor and Croseysarney; Anchor and Cefn Vron; Amblecote; Pentiken and Clark; Moor Hall; Upper Duffryn; Trebodier; Llanllwyd; Black House and Bettws; Brook House and Upper Ho.; Cwm and Travelly; Upper Lawn. One bench was reserved for

Pl. 11 Bettws-y-Crwyn Church: Medieval Roof

the singers, and five benches were free. The owners of these pews were the major tithe contributors, the free benches being for the poor and for visitors. Almost all the named farms can be identified on the 1:25000 Ordnance Survey maps, and the parish records contain the names of the holders of these farms who were overseers of the parish in the 1860s, at the time of the restoration of the church. None of these properties is held today by a family with the same name.

No village ever grew up around the church. The parish remained (and remains) a scattered accumulation of farmsteads without any recognisable focus apart from the church. The only neighbours of the church are Church Farm and the old mid-Victorian vicarage. There are no traces of a lost village.

It may be that the situation of the church preserves a pre-Christian site; there is a derelict farm nearby called Temple, and a few hundred yards north-east of the church is an ancient well, known as the Ladywell, associated with the early history of the church. At one time, this chalybeate spring was said to have healing properties. In more recent times, congregations used to go to the spring after a service and drink a glass of water; possibly prehistoric travellers on the Ridgeway paused there for refreshment too. If so, a shrine may have marked the spot, which later may have become a local focus of devotion important enough to be turned into a chapel by the

Pl. 12 Bettws-y-Crwyn Church: Benches

earliest Christians in the area. The Ladywell is about 300 yards north-east of the church. Is this the reason for the unusual siting of the building?

Vincent Waite relates the unedifying story of the travelling pedlar who collapsed and died near Crossways. The surrounding parishes disputed which of them should incur the cost of burying the stranger, but finally Bettws-y-Crwyn gave him a resting-place. At the site of the pedlar's death, the Cantlin Stone (possibly named after the victim) was erected, with the inscription 'W.C. decsd here buried 1691 at Betvs'. By an ironic turn of events, 200 years later this act of charity paid off for the parish; for when the Clun Forest Enclosure Act was passed in 1875, parish boundaries were readjusted; on the evidence of the Cantlin Stone Bettws obtained several hundred acres on the northern boundary of the parish.

Some insight into ecclesiastical conditions at the end of the eighteenth century is provided by the visitation of Archdeacon Plimley on 23rd May, 1793. The incumbent, Edward Woollaston minister of Llanfair Waterdine, lived in London, being one of the masters of the Charter House school. The curate, Price James, had an annual salary of £15, but also received £15 for the curacy of Llanfair Waterdine and £20 for the curacy of Beguildy. He had nine children, and worked as a labourer, mowing hay from the glebe lands. He took services at Bettws every Sunday, alternately at 9 a.m. and 2 p.m.

Holy Communion was celebrated four times a year; at Easter there were about 30 communicants, and at other times from 12 to 15 (the population in 1801 was 308). The archdeacon reported that the size of the congregations depended much on the weather; sometimes snow barred all access to the church. He continued that the nave contained 30 pews, irregular and dirty; the floor was bad, the pulpit cushion 'indecent'.

The parish has always been sparsely populated, the earliest firm figure coming with the first census in 1801 which gives the population as 308. Successive censuses recorded a steadily increasing population which peaked at 561 in 1871; this is in marked contrast to Mainstone, where the population remained between 217 and 296 throughout the nineteenth century (see Chapter 18). After 1871, the population recorded at each succeeding census steadily declined until in 1961 it was only 247; today it is just under 200.

The expanding population at Bettws doubtless encouraged the erection of dissenting chapels. Primitive Methodism first came into the Clun area around 1828, and the earliest missionaries in the area were often insulted and abused. Nevertheless, by 1832 the chapel at Bishop's Castle was the head of a wide-ranging circuit, and yet the town had earned for itself the title of 'Little Sodom', such was its reputation for debauchery. In Bettws, a Primitive Methodist chapel was built on Black Mountain about 1850, but in 1868 the Methodists moved downhill to a chapel at Lower Rose Grove, close to Anchor Bridge. This chapel remained in use for 103 years, and then the building became a private dwelling. The original chapel on Black Mountain was taken over by the Baptists and remained in use until very recently. Unusually for a non-conformist chapel, it has its own burial ground. In view of the declining population, it is not surprising that both chapels are now closed, but the parish church survives and still has a service every Sunday—no mean achievement in this area. The number of Easter communicants is about the same today as in 1793.

Education was not overlooked in Victorian England. In 1880, the Earl of Powis built a school at Weals Bridge, and this provided both primary and secondary education until 1951, the children leaving school at the age of 14. At its peak, the school roll had about 40 pupils, but in the first half of the twentieth century numbers were falling; and when Bishop's Castle provided secondary education in 1951, the Weals Bridge school was closed, primary educational needs being met at Newcastle-on-Clun. Today, children travel from as far as Anchor Bridge to the Community College at Bishop's Castle, a journey of around 17 miles each way.

The community has never had a shop or a post office, but in the nineteenth century ale-houses were apparently numerous. There was one, for instance, at Ale Oak Grange, and others are recalled by local people. Today, just one public house remains at the head of the Clun valley, the Anchor Inn on the road from Newcastle to Newtown.

Bettws-y-Crwyn remains a very special place—remote and wild, with roads almost free of traffic, and sheep outnumbering the human population many times over, an increasingly rare and precious survival in the England of today.

Bibliography

Alcock, King, Putnam & Spurgeon *Excavations at Castell Bryn Amlwg* (see below)

Bird, A.J. *History on the Ground* University of Wales Press, 1977

Ekwall, E. *The Concise Oxford Dictionary of English Place-names* Clarendon Press, Oxford, 1960

Montgomeryshire Collections Vol 23 (Roman period), 24 (Abbey Cwm Hir) and 60 (Bryn Amlyg)

Morgan, R. *Welsh Place Names in Shropshire* Cyhoeddwd Gan, R.M., 1997

Ordnance Survey map *South Wales & The Border in the Fourteenth Century*

Waite, V. *Shropshire Hill Country* Dent, 1970

Timber-framed houses are synonymous with the Welsh Border. In south-west Shropshire, 'black-and-white' houses begin to give way to Welsh stone, but there are still some fine examples, of national significance, from small cottages to large manor houses. Remarkable buildings are sometimes concealed behind their later façades. In the following chapter, Madge Moran, the leading authority on Shropshire Vernacular Architecture, has provided a most detailed account of these buildings.

CHAPTER 14

Early Vernacular Architecture
by Madge Moran

The surviving medieval and early modern houses within the parishes of south-west Shropshire show a variety in size, form and, to a certain extent, the building materials used. There is not much evidence of brick building among the older houses, but otherwise the area can be said to reflect the county as a whole. Timber-framing is robust and well-carpentered, cruck-building is favoured, decorative detail is not lacking, local stone is skilfully worked and thatch, where it survives, demonstrates its indigenous origins. Plan-forms, with one exception in Clun, also produce no exotic surprises, and although numerically the harvest may be small compared with some areas of England, south-west Shropshire has some remarkable examples of vernacular architecture at its best, as these brief descriptions of some of the houses will show.

One of the finest cruck-built hall-houses in the county and arguably in England, is the Manor Farm, Bedstone (SO 368756). It is H-shaped and consists of a two-bay cruck hall flanked on one side by a contemporary box-framed solar crosswing and on the other by a later crosswing which probably replaced an original service end. The crucks of the central truss are dendro-dated to 1448, measure nearly 3ft (0.91m) at the elbow, and are moulded with a series of rolls and hollows, seven to face the dais end of the hall and five to face the service end. The spurs are shaped like butterfly hinges and the soffit of the collar has a fine ogee form. Though less elabo-

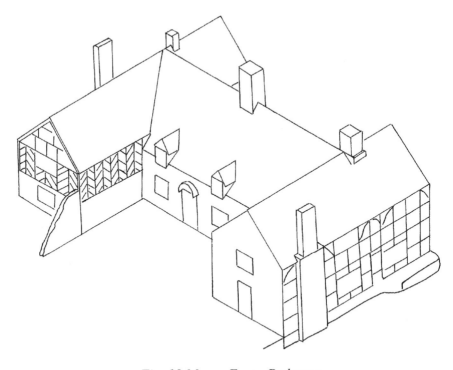

Fig. 10 Manor Farm, Bedstone

rate, the solar crosswing is divided into six half-bays, two of the trusses having open arch-braced collar construction. Fragments of floral wall-paintings were found in the solar. The lower end crosswing is dendro-dated to 1560/1 and includes cable-moulding and herringbone work in its external features. It also has an interesting trap-door arrangement in which joists could be removed to enable goods to be hoisted upstairs. The joists are triangular in section and are similar to those of the inserted chequer-board ceiling of the hall. The names of Jay, Ireland and Bennett are associated with the tenurial history and it was probably Sir Rowland Jay who built the house.[1]

Blunden Hall in Bishop's Castle (SO 325884) is another fully developed H-plan house, but all box-framed and of a contemporaneous date, possibly *c*.1600. As such it represents the zenith of vernacular plan development. The hall is jettied at the front, the parlour crosswing is jettied at the front and the side and the service crosswing is jettied at the front only. Each wing projects. Originally the house had a porch entrance with an upper room in the re-entrant angle of the hall and service wing. There is elaborate moulding on the beams of the hall and the parlour crosswing, and an interesting carved male bracket figure which supports the corner of the jettied parlour crosswing. The sash windows are an insertion of the early eighteenth century, ovolo-moulded on the inside, with the top half fixed and with wide glazing bars and flush frames. There is later slate-hanging on some of the outer walls, a feature which, with jettying, seems to be popular in Bishop's Castle.

There are a number of other timber-framed houses in Bishop's Castle town. Among them is Harp House, Church Street (SO 323885). The house takes its name from its use as an inn. It was licensed in 1642 and de-licensed in 1907, but its origins are much older. Basically it is a T-shaped timber-framed house in which the stem of the T is set parallel to the street. This unit is probably of fifteenth century date and contains a cruck truss in which the blades are fashioned from whole trees. A cambered collar-beam is present on the truss which, if the house occupies its original plot, is likely to have been part of a three-bay building. The crosswing is box-framed and jettied and represents partial replacement of the earlier house. In the crosswing there is a moulded bressumer and some herringbone work in the upper storey. The northern corner post has traces of cable-moulding. These features suggest a date perhaps in the late sixteenth century, and this is supported by the remains of wall-paintings in the ground-floor room. Here five panels are known to have paintings, but only one is exposed. It depicts a man and a woman in Elizabethan costume. The panel also has flower-heads and is surrounded by a border with a scalloped edge. The art work is carried out in black distemper outlines on a thin plaster skim over the wattle-and-daub infilling which, in places, shows through. Another town house is 27 High Street (SO 324888). Now in commercial use, this property incorporates the remains of a box-framed hall-house which is set gable-end on to the street. It has a gable jetty with herringbone work in the gable, but this is not visible from the street because an encroachment has been built up against it. The original framing appears to be of c.1550 and the plan consists of a great chamber towards the street with a single-bayed open hall behind it. These two units have threaded purlins and plain curved windbraces. The hall has smoke-blackened timbers and the great chamber has an intermediate truss. There is, at present, no evidence of an original upper floor in the great chamber, but it may have been removed. Beyond the hall is an added bay.

Another box-framed house in the High Street is The Porch House (SO 324889). This takes its name from the distinctive porch which bears a date of 161? (last number defaced), but this is an addition to what was basically a box-framed L-shaped town house consisting of a two-storied hall, a cross-passage and an ambitious crosswing which had its own external staircase. The older part has been dendro-dated to 1564. As elsewhere in Bishop's Castle street encroachment occurred later. The building has some elaborate carvings and also some eccentric features; for example the hall seems to have had no original heating arrangements and was decorated with paintings. Some paintings occur on the plank-and-muntin screen at the low (passage end) of the hall and have a chequer-board design giving a three-dimensional effect. There is evidence that a bench was fixed against the screen, although usually benches were fixed at the high end of the hall. Plank-and-muntin construction continues on to the rear wall, making in effect an external wall of solid wood. It is one of only two examples known in Shropshire, the other fortuitously, is opposite in 25 High Street. Several additions appear at the rear and in one room is a wall painting, a fresco, supposedly of the castle, but it cannot be earlier than the eighteenth century wall on which it appears.

A few doors away from The Porch House is the House on Crutches (SO 324889), so called because the oversailing upper storey is supported on two large moulded oak posts. This arrangement provides a covered passageway for pedestrians on what is the steepest part of the hill, but this is unlikely to have been its prime purpose which was surely to provide an extension to the medieval house, the remains of which form an L-shaped structure behind it. The extension has some unusual heart-lozenge decorative work in the gable and a good series of carpenters' assembly marks on the long side, while the medieval part has eccentric details such as very short queen-struts, foot-jowling to one main post and staggered tenons and mortice housing on another. Now a small museum, the house has many other interesting details and artifacts.

Still within the parish of Bishop's Castle, but at Colebatch, is the house now called Swallow Beck Cottage (SO 319871). Outstanding for its steep stone-flagged roof and huge chimneystack this little cottage is all that remains of a substantial cruck-built hall-house, possibly Colebatch manor house. The original arch-braced central truss of the hall now serves as the gable next to the added stack. Similar situations have been noted at 25 Kempton, Clunbury (SO 357832) and in Frankwell, Shrewsbury. 25 Kempton is all that is left of a much larger medieval cruck-built house, and like Swallow Beck Cottage it is the central truss of the two-bay hall which is exposed. Here, though, the crucks are crow-stepped towards the top and are tied to the posts by means of small spurs shaped like butterfly-hinges. It retains its thatched roof and has been dendro-dated to 1474.

If Manor Farm, Bedstone, is the grandest cruck-built house, the cottage at 28 Brockton in Lydbury North parish (SO 328857) is surely the most picturesque, although the crucks are not visible from the exterior. With its thatched roof, low profile and dormer window its 'chocolate-box' appearance is entirely unintentional.

In Llanfair Waterdine, Trebert (SO 256757) has every appearance of being the surviving manor house but in this case of a deserted medieval village. Some years ago it was in use as two cottages, one of which was derelict, but in which were three cruck trusses. There were probably more, but part of the structure had collapsed. One truss was either the central truss of the hall or the spere truss. It was distinguished by a steeply-cambered collar-beam with cusping on the upper part and there was further cusping on the V-struts above. More cusping appeared below the level of the inserted ceiling and the cruck blade also displayed quarter-round moulding. Smoke blackening from the old open hearth was present on the roof timbers. Such degree of richness in the decoration suggests a high-status house with a date in the first half of the fifteenth century.

Llanfair Waterdine has further examples of cruck building in the parish. A five-bayed barn at Coed-y-Hendre (SO 214786) has two cruck trusses, probably re-used, and a wooden threshing-floor; and a three-bayed road-side barn (SO 268743) employs reused crucks for tie-beams and upper-crucks for the superstructure. This barn has stone walls with timber-framing above first-floor level and weatherboarding, a typical Shropshire mixture of materials and techniques.

A particularly interesting building in the area is Plowden Hall, Lydbury North (SO 375866). The Plowden family has occupied this site since the time of the crusades, and the present house has building phases of each century since the fourteenth. The earliest part is the base-cruck hall which has crown-post roof construction of a superior type, and this is dendro-dated to 1302. The tree which produce that part of the frame was growing in 977. Now the family's private Catholic chapel, a solar wing was added in 1454, and this has lavish cusping in its roof trusses. 'Lawyer Plowden's wing' was added in the late sixteenth century. One of the ablest lawyers of his day, he was treasurer of the Middle Temple, and he has a fine monument in Temple church. Because of the family's faith and the frequent necessity of keeping a 'low profile' the house has never been replaced with a

Pl. 13 Plowden Hall

completely new and up-to-date structure, and so remains an unsurpassed example of English house evolution through the ages.[2]

Another manor house of interest is Abcott Manor in Clungunford parish (SO 392787). The manor house complex is of stone, brick and timber-frame, the framed unit appearing to be a late sixteenth or early seventeenth century parlour wing added to an older house now cased in brick and stone. Clearly the new wing was a status symbol. Externally the framing has four rails to wall-plate level giving a pattern of small rectangles, and there is a huge outbuilt stack in stone with twin brick shafts, ribbed, and with open zigzag brickwork between them. Internally the upper chamber has an elaborate plaster ceiling with a design of pomegranates, scrolls, heraldic beasts, strapwork and plain oval bosses. It was probably commissioned by the Prynce family, of Whitehall, Shrewsbury, fame.[3]

The house known as More Farm, once called 'Manor Farm' in More (SO 340922), though not as elaborate, is similar to Abcott Manor in size, status and framing pattern. Here too the emphasis is on the parlour cross-wing, the hall is losing its importance, becoming in this case merely a two-storied appendage. An unusual feature of More Farm is the timber-framed stair turret which contains a full-length chute, presumably for the purpose of hoisting grain into the attic.

Periods of prosperity in south-west Shropshire seem to be expressed in adding a high-status parlour crosswing to the house. A further example is at

Tudor Cottage in Lydbury North. Here herring-bone work and diagonal strutting in the jettied gable make a positive statement.

Another high status house was Lower Broughton, Lydham (SO 314905) Although the outer walls are rendered this is basically a timber-framed house of the fifteenth century which retains its complete plan of service end, screens passage, spere-truss, open hall and solar end. The hall roof is heavily smoke-blackened and the upper bay of the hall is distinguished by two nail-head/pyramid motifs on the collar-beam, while the lower bay has only one. A very simple post/principal rafter joint gives the impression of being a cruck, but the construction is fully box-framed. The high end of the hall had a canopy over the dais. Clearly this was a high-status house in medieval times, and it is not often possible to find all the components so well preserved.

In Norbury parish a house where at least three major building phases, perhaps four, are identifiable is Hardwick Hall (SO 369906). It is a classic example of piecemeal development. The oldest part is the south-eastern range and this is of cruck construction. Three cruck trusses remain here, one of which has an arch-braced collar beam suggesting that it was the central truss of a two-bay hall. Also discernible is the cross-passage and the service end of buttery and pantry beyond. At right-angles to this range is the earlier of the two added units. This is box-framed with fairly close studding and mid-rails, giving a pattern of rectangular framing. The roof line of this unit has been heightened and two dormer windows have been inserted at the new eaves level. To the north-west of this unit is a further extension with an even higher roof line, the two blocks giving the overall impression of a double-pile plan. At some time a large elaborate two-storied and jettied porch was added to the old cruck range, and this has concave lozenge-work, diagonal strutting and rectangular panels. Hardwick Hall was the home of the Ambler family from the 1580s to the 1900s.

Norbury has a specialised building stone which, in geological terms, is Pentamerus sandstone, but because when it is split the exposed fossils (*Pentamerus oblongus*) resemble the broad arrows of H.M. Prison service it is known locally as 'Government Rock'. Perhaps it is fitting that the broad arrow has roots in south Shropshire: it is included in the coat-of-arms of Sir Henry Sidney (1529-86), one-time President of the Council of the Welsh Marches and Governor of Ludlow Castle. The shield remains over the entrance to the castle. Freehold Farm in Norbury is built from 'Government Rock', as is the church.

Some buildings in the area may be termed yeoman's houses. One of these is The Bryn Cottage, Clun (SO 294854). Basically this house is L-shaped and of hall-and-crosswing plan. It has a two-storied porch and is dated 1653. There is a large central stack which, with the porch, creates a 'lobby-entry' layout. It is stone-walled but some of the internal partitions are timber-framed. It retains its stone-flagged roof and floor and its distinctive chequer-board ceiling in the crosswing. The ceiling supports a large bacon-cratch and the fireplace retains its spit-rack. Also present is the cheese-press; artifacts reflecting a bustling household economy. This house is a text-book example of the level of planning and living pattern that a Shropshire yeoman could expect at that time.

In the same area, set a little to the south of the Clun-Clee Ridgeway, is Pen-y-Wern, an isolated stone-built former farmhouse of three units, which is unusually tall for the area. In 1747 (datestone) it was extended at the front and altered a little internally, but the basic plan is that of a floored 'houseplace' flanked on one side by an unheated room and on the other by a dairy with a heated parlour behind it. As such it conforms in text-book fashion to the plan of many late seventeenth century farmhouses in the Marches. But Pen-y-Wern had a lobby-entry originally, that is, if the dominating stone-built chimneystack is an original feature, which appears to be the case. This and the provision of a 'wet' cellar with access from the dairy suggests a degree of wealth, but this is counter-balanced by some idiosyncratic carpentry in the roof which includes the use of passing-braces in one bay in place of the normal wind-braces. The datestone bears the initials of the Whettall family.

Similar to these in status was 17/19 High Street, Clun (SO 303808), which, though much altered, has a fine central cruck truss incorporating a low beam. This indicates a class of building whose origins lie at wealthy yeoman or manor level. For many years it was the home of the Hamar family who were related to the Likes. John Like was a Shropshire coroner until his death in 1720, and there is a tradition that the property was used as a court house at some time. Opposite, still in the High Street, is the Sun Inn (SO 301808) which may have once been an agricultural range belonging to 17/19 High Street. Inside are the remains of three cruck trusses, but they have been cut off below the apex and the stone walls have been heightened.

There are further houses in Clun parish of considerable interest. One of these is Clun Farm, Clun (SO 304808), an L-shaped farmhouse, basically timber-framed with each unit cruck-trussed. At a later date it was clad with stone and given a brick extension to form a T-shaped plan. The brickwork is carried out in rat-trap bonding which is a little unusual, and the cruck truss at the division of the hall and the crosswing is scarfed at purlin level, with the apex pegged through from the side, a feature which has been noted in other cruck-built houses in the area.

On a smaller scale 'Little Hospital' in Clun contains the remains of a cruck truss in No. 2 and it is possible that at one time the whole range was cruck-built. No. 1, Little Hospital has an unusual canopied bread-oven. Still in Clun parish, but at Newcastle-on-Clun is the remains of the old 'Plough' Inn (SO 247823) which also contains evidence of a cruck building.

One would expect to find longhouses in the Welsh Marches, and an example of this in the Clun area is Lower Spoad (SO 257820). Now an isolated farm, this is reputed to be the 'castle' of Newcastle-on-Clun, but stylistically it is a cruck-built longhouse which has a further two-bay cruck range built at right-angles to the byre. There is a seventeenth century box-framed addition at the western end and this has its own garderobe. The large inserted chimneystack in the main cruck range has a distinctive carved overmantel depicting a hunting scene. This has a sixteenth century appearance and is very skilfully executed.

Timber Croft, Pentre Hodre, Clun (S0 326768) is an isolated upland ex-farmhouse, possibly of longhouse origins, now restored. It contains the remains of a cruck-built open hall of two bays where the central truss is fitted with a low beam in similar fashion to that at 17/19 High Street, Clun. The upper bay of the hall is distinguished from the lower bay by the chamfers and stops on the central strut which rises from the low beam. These do not appear on the low side although the beam itself is chamfered on both sides. The crucks are very substantial measuring nearly 2ft at the elbow. As with Swallow Beck Cottage and 25 Kempton the house has been truncated and a large chimneystack built up against the central truss.

Similarly, Bryncambric, Chapel Lawn, Clun (SO 316758) is an isolated upland ex-farmhouse, cruck-built and with longhouse origins. It is strikingly overlooked by the Iron Age Hillfort of Caer Caradoc. Three cruck trusses remain internally and there is evidence for a fourth. It has recently been re-thatched in reeds, the previous thatch was of gorse. The cruck trusses may not all be of the same date as two are wrought from whole trees and one is from sawn oak. One bay has an inserted framed chequer-board ceiling of good quality of c.1550-1600. A large inserted chimney stack creates a lobby-entry layout.

Old Farm, Bucknell (SO 356740) probably functioned as a longhouse, but at a later date the cattle byre was converted to a parlour. It is still possible to discern the wide communal entrance for humans and cattle. Though partly weatherboarded and rendered over, Old Farm is basically an early seventeenth-century box-framed farmhouse which has had various additions and alterations. The farm complex is entered through a drift house and the farm buildings, which include one with upper-cruck construction, are grouped around a courtyard plan. Clearly the site pre-dates the present buildings. To the south-east of the house is an early motte which has been hollowed out to provide an ice-house.

On the other hand, Nanty Pwlly, Bettws-y-Crywn (SJ 182834), a small upland farm with the house sited on a downhill slope, gives the impression of being a longhouse, but there is no direct access from the house into the adjoining unit which, in any case, is not a byre but a barn. However, the range is self-contained, with a barn, two byres, a calf kit and a granary adjoining the house at the lower end and a stable attached at the upper end. The stable has been converted to a small parlour. Unlike the other houses mentioned so far this house is stone-built, has a slate roof, was probably single-storied originally, and appears to be of eighteenth century date.

Another house which probably had longhouse origins is Cwm Colbatch in Mainstone parish (SO 291866). Stone-built, it is an isolated farmhouse of two bays, two storeys and with end chimneys. It has a large single-storied porch. Angled downhill from the house is an attached unit which appears to have been a byre. Although now stone-walled it is basically cruck-built, one truss remaining reasonably intact and of superior quality. Within the unit a 5ft 6ins (2.87m) wide feeding-walk with cobbled floor remains. This was later modified to accommodate horses, but it is likely to have once provided the communal entrance for people and cattle.

Downhill sitings usually evoke longhouse traditions because of the natural drainage from the animals' quarters, but at Home Farm, Asterton in Myndtown parish (SO 398912) appearances may be deceptive. This is a stone-walled, two-storied former farmhouse of linear plan and four bays. But the bays at either end are additions. There is evidence inside of a two-bayed open cruck hall, the central truss of which remains and is of superior quality with an arch-braced collar-beam and provision for a low beam such as was found at 17-19 High Street, Clun. The cruck is chamfered on both edges as are the arch-braces, and smoke-blackening from the open hearth has left deposits on the roof timbers. When the open hall was given an inserted chimneystack a lobby-entry layout was created, providing further evidence for the superior status of the house. Of course, some longhouses were very well wrought and Home Farm may have been an example in this genre.

Mention has been made above of the 'castle' at Newcastle-on-Clun. One house in the area actually has part of a castle attached to it, namely Lea Castle Farm, Lydham (SO 352893). The house was modernised in the late nineteenth century and incorporates brickwork on the frontage, but there are older stone walls and fragments of timber-framing. The remains of the fourteenth century castle are joined onto the house at the rear, but they form a separate unit. At one time the house had a stone-flagged roof. A datestone of 1560 has been moved to the front of the house. The present kitchen preserves a stair-ladder to the men's room. The farm buildings include good barns, cowsheds and some goosepens.

A good many timber-framed farmhouses have survived in this part of Shropshire. In Clungunford, for example, there is Clungunford Farm (SO 397787), an H-shaped farmhouse, of which the timber-framed northern wing is probably the oldest part. This has a jetty in which the joists are tenoned into the back of the bressumer and are boarded over underneath so that only the spine-beam shows. At first-floor level is a labelled 'Cheese Room.' Low House, Broome, also within the parish (SO 401808) is another such farmhouse consisting of a low hall and crosswing. Probably it was originally H-shaped, the eastern wing being replaced with 'The High House'. The hall has a chequer-board ceiling of good quality and the western wing is jettied in a similar fashion to Clungunford Farm.

26/27 Kempton, Clunbury (SO 357831) is a text-book example of an early seventeenth century box-framed three-bayed farmhouse of one-and-a-half stories with a central stack and a lobby entry. A stone spiral staircase rises from the parlour on the opposite side of the stack from the entrance. The plan consists of a kitchen and dairy on one side of the stack, and a parlour on the other. Beyond the parlour is a small area which may have functioned as a byre with a croglofft above. There is no access from the room over the parlour to the room above the kitchen, suggesting that originally the kitchen or 'houseplace' may have been open to the roof. Like its neighbour, No. 25 (described above), it retains its thatched roof.

Bryndrinog, Clun (SO 256825) is a Clun Valley isolated farm, box-framed and not stone-cased as the majority are now. It is situated on Offa's Dyke, opposite Lower Spoad and is of c.1600. Of 'hall and crosswing' type, it is two-storied and has a lobby-entry, but this may be the result of later alteration, the hall may have been open to the roof originally. Square-framing is predominant throughout.

Two houses show no outward appearance of their timber-frame construction, having been stuccoed over. One of these is Castle Cottage,

Clun (SO 298807), a box-framed house of unusual cruciform plan which incorporates a two-bay open hall, a contemporary three-bayed crosswing and a further bay beyond the hall. Smoke-blackening is evident in the roof over the hall and there are two areas of plank-and-muntin work, one for the infilling of the frame at the upper end of the hall and the other for a frame in the crosswing. These make interesting comparisons with the examples at Bishop's Castle where the technique is used for external and internal walls. Castle Cottage probably dates from *c*.1500 and has the concept of a town house with the solar above the service rooms. Stucco similarly obscures the timber-framed origins of Field Farm, Purlogue, Clun (SO 285771). This complex consists of two-semi-detached smallholdings, the eastern house older than the western. The latter has a three-room plan, one room, now a parlour, may have housed animals originally. The main room has a fine chequer-board ceiling and there is a panelled door with the date 1635 and the initials MW.

In Wentnor parish 'Criftins' (S0 379916) has a roof covering of slates set in what is known sometimes as 'Granary' fashion but often as 'hit and miss'. The slates are spaced out, saving about one-third on the cost of the material.

Finally mention should be made of an early brick house, The Red House, Lydbury North (SO 365860) so called because of its unusual brick construction. It is a single-phase building with a plan of two identical square rooms and a smaller square room leading off on each level. Dating from *c*.1640 it is completely symmetrical and four stories high with the recessed entrance at first-floor level reached by a flight of steps. The original kitchen occupied the whole of the southern side of the lower ground floor and here the well, bake-oven, pump and cooking range survive. At one time it was a coaching inn on the old Craven Arms to Bishop's Castle road and the detached octagonal cockpit with its wood-shingled roof has associations with Clive of India who owned the mansion at Walcot nearby.

This survey has concentrated on domestic housing rather than farm buildings, although there are good examples of barns, dovecotes, ginny-rings, etc. It does not attempt to cover all the early houses in the area, but to provide sufficient examples to give an overview of the varied typology and perhaps emphasise what lies hidden in this very beautiful part of Shropshire.

Glossary

Arch-brace: A curved brace (one of a pair) supporting a main timber.

Bay: The space between two main structural frames.

Box-frame: A framework of posts and beams on which the roof rests. The opposite technique to cruck-building.

Bressumer: The beam which supports the upper story of a jettied building.

Chequer-board ceiling: Where the joists are set at right-angles to each other in squares.

Collar (beam): An important transverse timber connecting rafters or crucks at a point between the apex and the tie-beam.

Croglofft: A raised platform or sleeping shelf. A Welsh term.

Crown-post roof: A form of roof construction where an upright timber is set between the tie-beam and the collar on the main trusses. Usually braced four ways. May be decorative. Usually found without side purlins.

Crucks: A pair of inclined timbers, usually curved to form an arch, rising uninterrupted from ground to apex and supporting the roof. Variations are Base-Cruck: Here the crucks rise to the level of the first transverse member; the roof trusses can then be of various types. Upper-crucks: Here the feet rest on the first-floor ceiling beam. There are others.

Cusp: The point between intersecting curved edges of stone or timber. Used in tracery or as a decorative edge on braces, etc. Cusping in timber helps to resist bending.

Dais: The raised platform at the upper end of the hall, traditionally where the family took meals and business was conducted.

Dendro-dating: The science of dendrochronology, in which samples are taken from timber-framed buildings and the tree-ring growth is analysed to find the felling-date. This is a useful indication of the building date.

Double-pile: Where the plan is of 2-room depth. Achieved by various means and diversity of roof form.

Drift House: The open but roofed over bay between two ranges of farm buildings in which laden wagons could stay overnight.

Fresco: Paintwork applied to damp freshly-laid plaster.

Garderobe: The privy or latrine chute in a medieval house.

Ginny-ring: Also called 'horse-engine house', 'wheelhouse', 'pound house', etc. Single-storied, usually round open-sided building where horse(s) or oxen in circumabulatory motion turned the gearing that powered the threshing machine in the adjacent barn. Also used for apple crushing and rolling oats.

Jetty: Cantilevered overhang of one storey above another, or of a gable.

Jowl: Expansion of the head or foot of a post.

Lobby-entry: Entrance leading into a lobby in front of chimneystack, so that access is possible only to rooms on the right or left.

Longhouse: House and byre under one roof and with direct access between the two. Often with a communal entrance for people and beasts.

Lozenge work: Decorative framing, basically diamond-shaped but often ornamented.

Mortice-and-tenon: A common form of jointing, the mortice is the socket on one timber which received the projection (tenon) from the other.

Motte: The mound upon which a castle is built.

Nail-head (ornament): Resembling the pyramid-shaped heads of early nails.

Ogee: A wave-like moulding formed by a convex and a concave curve joined to present a bracket-shape.

Ovolo moulding: Moulding with an egg shaped profile.

Plank-and-muntin: Partition work formed from studs with vertical planks or panels held in the grooved sides. Usually found as internal partitioning, rarely as exterior walling.

Purlin: A longitudinal timber in a roof which supports the common rafters. They vary in the way they are attached to the principal rafters.

Quarter-round moulding: Where the profile is a quarter of a circle.

Queen-posts: Paired uprights set on a tie-beam and directly supporting the purlins. May be straight or curved.

Queen-struts: Paired uprights set on a tie-beam and directly supporting the collar-beam.

Rail: Horizontal member of a wall-frame between posts or studs.

Rat-trap bond: Where the bricks are set on edge instead of on the flat. Usually used for economy.

Scarf: The term used for joining two lengths of timber together to form a longer length.

Screens passage: Entrance passage with doors at either end and with a partition (spere-truss) on the hall side. Sometimes called a cross-passage or through passage. Movable screens were kept in the passage in medieval times.

Soffit: The lower surface of a horizontal timber.

Solar: The private room of a medieval house, usually found at first-floor level in the upper end or crosswing. The etymology of the word is doubtful.

Spere-truss: The truss at the lower end of the hall which divides the screens passage from the hall proper. 'Spere' is old-English for 'screen'. Often highly decorated. Not a structural truss, more a status symbol.

Spine-beam: The main flooring beam which is set following the plane of the roof. Sometimes called an axial beam.

Spur: A short piece of timber forming a connection between the cruck and the post and often supporting the wall-plate.

Wall-plate: The timber on top of a masonry or framed wall on which the roof trusses rest.

Wattle-and-daub: Twigs or laths woven between staves and plastered over with a mixture of clay or mud (the daub) to form the infilling of framework.

Windbrace: A brace in the plane of a roof usually tying together the purlin and the principal rafter. So called because it helps to resist the pressure of wind on the roof. They vary greatly in their treatment.

References

1. see 'Some Old Shropshire Houses and their Owners: XII Bedstone Manor' by H.E. Forrest in *Transactions of the Shropshire Archaeological Society*, *Vol XLVI.*
2. A fuller account of this house is contained in an article entitled 'The Mediaeval Parts of Plowden Hall' by M. Moran, which can be found in *Transactions of the Shropshire Archaeological Society Vol. LIX.*
3. see 'Old Shropshire Houses and their Owners: XXIV Abcott' by H.E. Forrest in the *Transactions of the Shropshire Archaeological Society Vol. XLI* (4th Series vol. 8).

The English Civil War in Shropshire is best known for the concealment of the fugitive Charles II in the oak-tree at Boscobel after the battle of Worcester in 1651. But the south of the county had its excitements too—political manoeuvres and violent incidents which vividly reflect the confusing and tragic realities of civil strife.

CHAPTER 15

The Civil War
by Peter Bigglestone

In 1642 Charles I faced crises on three fronts. In England an ongoing financial, religious and constitutional crisis was to lead to Civil War with the first major battle fought at Edgehill in Warwickshire on Sunday, 23rd October 1642. In Scotland attempts at religious reform by Charles and William Laud, Archbishop of Canterbury, had brought the Scots in arms to the border in the First Bishop's War of 1638-1639 and across the border in the Second Bishop's War of 1640. In Ireland in October of 1641 the native Catholic Irish of Ulster took advantage of the situation to rebel, their chief target being the Protestant settlers encouraged into Ireland by Elizabeth I and James I, to settle land confiscated from earlier Irish 'rebels'.

On 22nd August 1642 Charles raised his Royal Standard at Nottingham Castle and the First Civil War officially began, but the Corporation of Shrewsbury was preparing for war months before that. On 1st October 1641 the Corporation had ordered that three town gates and the upper gate in St. Mary's Water Lane be repaired and the people of Shrewsbury were to furnish themselves with arms and guard the gates. A little later the ordnance of the town was tested and four new cast-iron cannon were purchased at a cost of £70.

From Nottingham Charles moved on a recruiting drive through Derby to Shropshire. On 19th September he was at Wellington and on the 20th he reviewed his troops below the Wrekin before moving on to Shrewsbury.

From there he could command the other two approaches to Wales through Chester and Hereford.

There were to be no major battles in Shropshire, but of strategic importance was the control of the towns and castles, the routes through the county to North Wales — seen by the King as an important recruiting base — and the industrial resources. In the early part of the twentieth century, when views of the Civil War and its causes were somewhat simpler, Shropshire was seen as part of the rural, rather more feudal, northern and western royalist heartlands. The present view is that civil war was as much a product of local issues as national ones and that local concerns heavily influenced side taking in the war. No area was united in its support for any one faction, and neutralism was rife both in the early months of the war and, in some localities, at later stages. Linked to this was a deep desire to protect people, property and a way of life from the depredations of war and the ravages of both sides in the conflict. Shropshire was no exception to these emerging patterns of thought and action.

In the seventeenth century Shropshire was represented in Parliament by 12 MPs — two Knights of the Shire and two MPs each for Bishop's Castle, Bridgnorth, Ludlow, Much Wenlock and Shrewsbury. Of these, eight were Royalists and four were for Parliament. Sir Richard Lee of Lee Hall and Acton Burnell, Knight of the Shire, was for the King but Sir John Corbet of Stoke and Adderley, the other Knight of the Shire, stood for Parliament and became Colonel-General of Parliamentary forces when war broke out. Thomas Whitmore and Edward Acton, MPs for Bridgnorth, and Ralph Goodwyn and Charles Baldwyn, MPs for Ludlow, all stood out for the King but in other towns there was division. For example, in Bishop's Castle, Sir Robert Howard was a Royalist and Richard More was a Parliamentarian.

On 8th August 1642 a letter had arrived in Shrewsbury from the King explaining his position and his desire to defend and maintain the true religion and soliciting the help of the county. In response a Grand Jury gave expression to their willingness to support the King and explaining they were willing 'to adventure their lives and fortunes in defence of his Royal and Sacred Person.' It was signed by the High Sheriff, Sir John Ward and 45 to 50 other gentlemen. This document was circulated to other local towns and soon grew to number over 100 signatories, including Sir William Craven of Stokesay Castle and William Blunden of Blunden Hall. The latter was elected Mayor of Bishop's Castle a month later in September 1642.

However, on the Parliamentary side were such local worthies as Thomas Mytton of Halston, Robert Wallop of Hopton Castle, Samuel More of

Linley, who eventually became a colonel in the Parliamentary army, Jeremy Powell of Clun and Bucknell and Sir Robert Harley of Brampton Bryan in neighbouring Herefordshire.

This division was not restricted to the gentry. On 24th August 1642 the loyalist clergy of Shrewsbury formed an association for promotion of the King's interest in their parishes, and subsequently produced 'The Resolution of the Clergy of the County of Salop'. From outside Shrewsbury 17 clergy signed this resolution, including clergy from Bishop's Castle, Hopesay, Prees, and Wem. Walker's *Suffering of the Clergy* suggested that after the war 40 Shropshire clergy were removed from their posts as a result of their Royalist sympathies but research in the early twentieth century puts this number nearer to 60. However that was out of 194 parishes in the county at that time. Little is yet known of the true feeling of the clergy in other parishes, unless they came to notice like the Rev. Thomas Fraysell of Clun ('a district of marked Puritan tendencies') who fled to London for safety.

This pattern of division can be seen across the county. Ludlow, Bridgnorth and Whitchurch were Royalist. In Oswestry the main families stood for Parliament but Colonel Edward Lloyd of Llanfordawith eventually held the town for the King with a garrison composed almost entirely of Welshmen. Wem became the main Parliamentary base in the county, a garrison established there in August 1643 by Thomas Mytton of Halston, Humphrey Mackworth, Thomas Hunt and Richard Baxter. South-west Shropshire held several pockets of strong Puritanism and had in the period 1630-1645 several important Puritan gentry families, notably the Mores and the Walcots. C.D. Gilbert suggests south-west Shropshire was influenced in this respect by Sir Robert Harley of Brampton Bryan, a close friend of Richard More and Humphrey Walcot, and Speaker of the House of Commons.

This division in the county and the county town was such that by the time Charles had reached Derby on his way to Shrewsbury he was undecided whether to move on to Shrewsbury or to Chester.

Indecision and mention of Humphrey Walcot of Walcot raise the issue of neutrality. Clarendon wrote in 1644 in reference to the counties of Shropshire, Lancashire and Cheshire '... and it fared in these counties as in all Parliaments of the Kingdom that the number of those who desired to sit still was greater than of those who desired to engage of either party; so that they were generally included in articles of neutrality'. Jonathan Langley, who became Mayor of Shrewsbury in 1663, wrote in a letter from Birmingham on 22nd February 1643 to Sir Francis Ottley, that he fled the county when neutrality was seen as being anti-King but he wished to return home and remain there unmolested. 'I never had an intention nor yet have of taking up arms of neither side; my reason, this my protestation already taken binds me both to King and Parliament'. Humphrey Walcot, one of the wealthiest men in the county, wished to follow suit, though he had an inclination to Puritan simplicity in church. As a result for a while he was imprisoned in Ludlow for disaffection to the King's cause, even though in 1642 he had complied with the demands of Charles when the latter was in Shrewsbury and donated £5,000 to the Royalist cause. (By way of comparison, a little later Rupert demanded of all Birmingham the sum of £2,000.)

The preparation made in Bishop's Castle for war suggests similar neutralist tendencies. On 6th December 1642 the Corporation of Bishop's Castle ordered that:

> In consideration of the imminent dangers wherein the town and the adjacent parts stand by reason of the soldiers remaining in the county, all householders ... shall upon due notice keep the King's Watch during the whole night; that upon the town's charge all persons who keep horses and mares shall be ready upon due notice to ride to such places as the bailiff shall appoint; and that all householders shall at their own cost provide a good and sufficient weapon for the safeguard of their own persons.

This was surely evidence of an attitude that was to lead to the emergence of the Clubmen at a later stage in the war. On 24th December 1642 the Corporation further ordered that:

> Whereas an association has been formed throughout the county of Salop for the preservation of every particular person from plundering, of late too much exercised, and whereas it has been concluded by the several Justices of the Peace for the allotments of Clun and Purslow and most of the inhabitants, gentry and freeholders of the same, that eight horses with able riders ... shall be instantly provided within every allotment [a division of a parish,or hundred], William Blunden esq. shall have power to nominate four able and sufficient inhabitants of the town of Bishop's Castle to provide four horses with riders etc. at the general charge of the town.

The Association referred to was one of 80 landowners in Shropshire who signed an 'Engagement and resolution of the principal gentlemen of the County of Salop for the raising and maintaining of forces at their own charge, for the defence of his Majesty, their country, and more particularly the Fortunes, persons and estates of the Subscribers.' Richard Oakeley of Oakeley near Bishop's Castle was one of the signatories and his accounts show that in January 1643 he paid 10s 8d for a 'levy for the raising of a dragoon and part of his army and pay' and a further 6s on 12th March 1643 towards raising a dragoon at Lydham. Dragoons were equipped with horse, musket and short sword; they fought as cavalry or, dismounted, as muske-teers. The aim of the Association was to raise a regiment of dragoons led by Sir Vincent Corbett.

This Association reflects the gentry's fear of the dreaded apprentice mobs of Parliamentary supporters mentioned in Royalist pamphlets, and the threat posed by a puritanical Parliament to themselves and the country. Clearly the people of Bishop's Castle were concerned to defend the area against looting Royalist soldiers as much as from Parliamentary incursions.

To further the aim of the Association, Richard Oakeley, Walter Waring, William Blunden and H. Bromley sent out warrants to the High Constable of the Hundred of Purslow ordering him to summon all able bodied men between the ages of 16 and 60, with such horses and weapons as they possessed, to assemble at the Town Hall at Bishop's Castle upon 23rd of January 1643 by nine o'clock. Despite the fact the order was accompanied by a threat of fines and imprisonment for those who failed to obey, the inhabitants of the district were reluctant to join the dragoons. The warrant was reissued on 9th February but the response remained poor.

The disruption of authority occasioned by the Civil War obviously led to some unrest in the area. In May 1643 Richard Oakeley and his kinsman Ambrose King and other local burgesses met to protest at the lack of law and order. As a result the more forceful Edward Broughton replaced Henry Wall as Sergeant of Bishop's Castle, and a warrant was issued for the High Constables to search for Royalist deserters who were stealing from local inhabitants.

Despite the war, life continued and with it many of its everyday prob-lems. The papers of Richard Oakeley reveal that in 1643 the burgesses of Bishop's Castle were faced with a levy of £10 each to meet the cost of repairing the Town Hall and the Tower. In July 1644 there was heavy rain and each inhabitant had to contribute £5 for the repair of the Church Bridge and the Town Conduit.

Inevitably the ravages of war did visit the area. Between 1642 and 1651, 22 battles were fought each involving more than 5,000 soldiers. Estimates suggest as many as 80,000 men may have been killed—some of whom would have come from south-west Shropshire. If this figure were accurate it would represent a higher proportion of the population than died during World War One. While no major battles were fought in Shropshire, sieges of town and castle were not uncommon and one such siege reveals the uglier side of warfare.

Brampton Bryan in neighbouring Herefordshire was the property of Sir Robert Harley, a strong Parliamentarian. Many will be familiar with the heroic defence of Brampton Bryan by Lady Brilliana Harley till her tragic death left that duty to her doctor, Lieutenant Wright. Hearing the Royalists planned to fortify Hopton Castle, in February 1644 Wright sent Samuel More and about 20 men to Hopton where they seized the castle without loss. More was installed as commander.

In his diary Samuel More recorded the dramatic events.

> I went to Hopton Castle on the 18th of February, 1643 (old calendar) which was the Sabbath Day, at night. The next night the Royalists came before it who facing us with a body of horse first within an hour sent a body of foot who approached the outer walls. They brought ladders to scale the walls but upon our killing three of them they sent Major Sutton to tell me the Prince demanded the delivery of the castle. I sent word that I understood no message that comes without drum or trumpet. Thereupon they sent a summons by a drum subscribed by Sir Michael Woodhouse who demanded the castle in the name of Prince Rupert. My answer was that I kept it by authority of Parliament and by consent of the owner for King and Parliament.

The garrison held out for a fortnight against a number of sharp sallies and sudden attacks. Then the Royalists brought up two heavy guns and a summons was sent to the castle that if Captain More did not surrender before the first shot from a gun he and his men must expect no quarter in accordance with the accepted rule of war that those who wilfully attempted to hold an indefensible position were punishable by death.

More returned a defiant answer, which infuriated the besiegers who had already lost a number of men killed and had many wounded. They opened

Pl. 14 Hopton Castle

fire and the first shots killed one of the garrison and wounded two more as well as making some impression on the walls, which they then started to mine. It soon became clear More could not hold out much longer.

> Our men, weary of working all night and not out of their clothes for a fortnight's time, it was moved we should desire a parley which being done they bade us send our conditions which Major Phillips and I contrived to this effect, that we should march away with our arms and ammunitions, which they denied. We agreed then to propose to the enemy we should yield the castle upon quarter for our lives. Answer was brought that no other condition could be yielded to, but to be referred to Colonel Woodhouse's mercy. Being brought to this condition it was thought better to yield than be blown up. But indeed we all thought we should only be made prisoners and did not think of such a death as hereafter appears.

Samuel More was taken to Ludlow Castle a prisoner, later to be freed in exchange for Edward Cressett of Upton Cressett. Major Phillips offered

£20 to save his own life. He was taken to Broncroft Castle where he was sworn at and stabbed to death. The rest were stripped, kept naked on a cold winter's day for an hour or more and then clubbed to death by common soldiers. A contemporary (Parliamentary) news-sheet contained this graphic account:

> More was seized upon and carried away prisoner and the twenty-four soldiers tied back to back, and then some of them had their hands cut off; some with a hand, parte of an arme, and the rest cut and mangled both on hands and arms, and then all of them throne into a muddy pit where as often as any of them endeavoured to raise themselves out of the mud, striving to prolong their miserable lives, they were straight by these bloody villains beate down into the mud again with great stones and in this sad manner lamentably perished.

Gradually the war began to turn against the Royalists, nationally and within Shropshire. On 22nd June 1644 Oswestry was taken by Parliament while the Governor and part of garrison were absent taking prisoners to Shrewsbury. This enabled Parliament to gain control of the key routes into North Wales.

In September 1644 Sir Thomas Myddleton took Montgomery for Parliament and exposed western Shropshire to attack. This marked a turning point in the control of Shropshire. On 21st October 1644 Sir Michael Earnley, Governor of Shrewsbury, wrote to Prince Rupert: 'Since the disaster at Montgomery the edge of the gentry is much blunted; the county's loyalty is strangely abated; they begin to warp to the enemy's party'. The royal garrisons at Ludlow and Bridgnorth began to face problems collecting supplies from the surrounding areas. The demands for free quartering of soldiers, free victuals etc. by both sides had always annoyed the ordinary populace. Vincent Waite records a popular saying as:

> I had six oxen t'other day,
> And them the Roundheads got away,
> A mischief to their speed.
> I had six horses in a hale,
> And them the Cavaliers stale;
> I think in this they be agreed.

In south-west Shropshire this issue came to a head with the emergence of the Clubmen Movement. Clubmen were citizens who banded together to resist the depredations of both sides in the war. Such movements were found in the Marches and in the south-west of England, the earliest being in Bishop's Castle and Clun.

In March of 1644 the Corporation of Bishop's Castle had already ordered that 'all inhabitants of the town, upon hearing of a musket or other public notice, shall repair to the aid of any particular house or village, with their best arms, for the defence of the same from plundering or any other violent or wilful breach of his Majesty's peace.'

The earliest reference to the Clubmen appeared in a report from the Parliamentary garrison at Wem, dated 18th December 1644 and printed in *Perfect Occurences* a Parliamentary newspaper, on 20th December. It announced that the countrymen of the Shropshire Hundreds of Clun and Purslow had risen 1,200 strong to resist the plundering of the royalist Colonel Vangeris. They were led by the parson of Bishop's Castle and some very minor gentry called Jeremy Powell, Richard Heath and Francis Harris, and demanded the re-posting of Vangeris, compensation for the goods taken and the evacuation of the local Royalist garrisons of Stokesay Castle and Lea Hall. Another group of local men had collected at nearby Leintwardine and was preparing to join them.

A report in the *Mercurius Britannicus* of the week beginning Monday, 6th January 1645 states: 'Out of Shropshire we hear there are above a thousand in arms about Clun and Bishop's Castle standing out against both sides, neither for the King nor for the Parliament, but standing upon their own guard for the preservation of their own lives and fortunes.' They were resolved not to lay down their arms until three demands were met—to have restitution for the wrongs done by Royal officers, notably Vangeris; the removal of the garrisons from Stokesay and Lea Castle (garrisons set up just prior to this in an area relatively free of garrisons); and to have commanders of their own. (This latter was a reference to the King's 'One and All' proclamation of the late summer of 1644 in which he called for a mass rising in the provinces of men under their own officers and for those men to march on London and compel Parliament to make a peace.) Sir Michael Woodhouse, Governor of Ludlow, had written himself to Prince Rupert in October 1644 complaining about the looting of the area by Vangeris. Vangeris was eventually re-posted and killed in action in Gloucestershire in February 1645.

C.D. Gilbert has tried to identify leaders of the Clubmen. He suggests they were Gervase Needham, Richard Heath, Francis Harris and Jeremy or Jeremiah Powell. Gervase Needham, parson at Bishop's Castle from 1629, was a moderate puritan but loyal to the King in the Civil War. In August 1642 he signed the 'Loyal Address of Shropshire Clergy' to Charles. After Parliament's victory in 1646 he was ejected from living, his 'house and goods were burned, nor was he permitted to keep a private school for the subsistence of his family, in so much that, had they not been relieved by the charity of some relations, they must have wanted for bread'. Needham died on 27th January 1649, three days before the execution of his King. Richard Heath, was possibly the Richard Heath who was curate of Clunbury from 1641 and Rector of Hopesay from 1647. He became Vicar of St. Alkmund's, Shrewsbury, in 1651, but was ejected in 1662 after the Restoration. Francis Harris was probably a landowner with land in Hopesay and Aston and Obley, south-west of Clun. Jeremy or Jeremiah Powell was probably owner of Shadwell in the Parish of Clun. He was one of the Powells of Edenhope near Mainstone, nephew of Erasmus Powell, Vicar of Clun. In March 1645 Sir Charles Gerard was in Newtown, Montgomeryshire with 800 Royalist foot and horse. As he moved through this area he attacked Powell's township. Powell defended himself but his house was taken and he himself made prisoner.

Within the county Royalist fortunes continued to decline. On 3rd February 1645 Parliament captured Shrewsbury. Prince Maurice, who had arrived in the town the previous day, escaped. Governor Earnley refused to surrender and was killed. The garrison surrendered on condition the English soldiers were allowed to march to Ludlow; the Irish troops were left to be taken prisoner.

Bishop's Castle was now in the middle of warring factions based at Shrewsbury and Ludlow. In April 1645 a meeting of the Corporation ordered that all inhabitants over the age of eleven were to form a night guard to watch against looting by soldiers.

In June 1645 a document was published in London, probably quite typical of many reports published at that time. It was:

> Intelligence from Shropshire of three great victories obtained
> by the forces of Shrewsbury Commanded by the Committee
> There viz
> The Taking of Stokesay and Caus castles, places of great
> strength; and a great victory obtained in the fields, with a

Catalogue of the prisoners.
Sent from persons of worth, that were in the Action, to a
Person of Honour, in London.
Printed for Thomas Underhill, and are to be sold at the Bible
in Woodstreet, June 28 1645.

In summary it describes how in early June 1645 a parliamentary force of
500 foot and 300 horse set out from Shrewsbury—part of Col.
Mackworth's Regiment and part of Col. Lloyd's Regiment—to march to
within five miles of Ludlow, with three objectives in view—to secure the
area for Parliament; to place garrisons at nearby castles; and to block up the
Royal forces in Ludlow.

The Parliamentary forces viewed Howgate (Holdgate) and Braincroft
(Broncroft) Castles, both demolished by the Royalists. Lord Calvine was
placed in the latter to repair and fortify it. Lieutenant Col. Riveling (gener-
ally called Reinking) was sent to view Stokesay Castle, garrisoned by the
Royalists. He saw the place as a considerable obstacle. The next day the
Parliamentarians surrounded Stokesay and called for it to surrender, but the
Governor, Captain Daurett (or in other accounts Danet) refused. The
Parliamentarians prepared to storm the castle and then sent a second
summons for the defenders to surrender. After a parley the castle was delivered up to the Parliamentarians without a fight and they garrisoned it. The
battlements were slighted but the rest left.

At this point Sir Michael Woodhouse, Governor of Ludlow, led 2,000
Royalist horse and foot out to engage the Parliamentarians, who immediately moved to Wistanstow where they felt they might be more easily reinforced from Shrewsbury and Montgomery, though no reinforcements
arrived in time. Woodhouse moved towards Stokesay to besiege it and the
Parliamentarians were forced to attack. To their surprise the Royalists were
routed, despite their superiority in number. About 100 were slain, 300
common soldiers were taken and 60 officers, together with all their ordi-
nance and baggage, four barrels of powder a good quantity of match and
bullets and 100 horses. Among the Royalist dead was Sir William Croft of
Croft Castle.

After this great success the Parliamentarians returned to Shrewsbury on
11th June. Three days later they marched out to Caus Castle which appears
to have been defended more stoutly, for the siege was reported to have lasted
seven days before the defending Royalists marched out with single arms and
no baggage, their horses to be made available for service to the public.

As the Royalist cause continued to collapse in Shropshire so Parliament felt in a strong enough position to set up a Committee for Sequestration in Shropshire. The task of the Committee was to sequestrate (seize) the estates of delinquents—those active against Parliament—to raise money for wages, munitions and provisions. The war meant few were able to buy such estates, so owners were given the option of compounding—retrieving their estates for the cost of one-tenth its value, or two years' pre-war income from the estate. Allowance was made for dependant relatives. Delinquents also had to take the 'Negative Oath', a promise not to take up arms against Parliament.

Richard Oakeley of Oakeley was one of the first to be arraigned before the Committee and his case was probably typical of many across the country. Evidence was given against him by William Sayse, including an account of warrants issued, the raising of dragoons and an account of Captain William Blunden's and Lieutenant William Corbett's exploits with the dragoons at Cholmley House in Chester against Parliament. Richard Wooton, once High Constable of Purslow Hundred testified to Richard Oakeley's enthusiasm for the Royalist cause. Esay Thomas, former Mayor and one time Town Clerk of Bishop's Castle testified as to the money raised for the Royalists by Oakeley.

Officers of the Committee went to Richard Oakeley's house, made an inventory of belongings, and seized Oakeley's estates. Richard compounded for part of his estates, paying probably £150 to regain stocks of food and articles of property to settle his dependents in comfort. He then petitioned the Committee for Compounding in London for compounding the rest of his estates. Royalists in Ludlow heard of this and in September 1645 they attacked and pillaged his home leaving it devastated and bare, in revenge for his being involved with Parliament. In November 1645 Royalists seized Richard Oakeley and imprisoned him in Ludlow Castle. He was released later in the month, to continue his attempts to clear his debts in London.

It was at this late state of affairs that Bishop's Castle was attacked. On 25th August 1645 there was a Fair at Bishop's Castle. The garrisons of Ludlow and Bridgnorth saw this as an opportunity to replenish their supplies, especially as Bishop's Castle was regarded by this time as nominally for Parliament. Four hundred dragoons and horse were sent, led by Colonel Devalier. The Parliamentary Committee for Shropshire heard of the plan and sent 80 horse and 80 foot to protect the town, led by a Colonel Fenwick. The two sides met about a mile outside Bishop's Castle. Terence

Bryan proposes that this battle took place at the foot of what is now Stank Lane, where the narrowness of the high-banked road severely hampered the fighting abilities of what should have been the superior Royalist forces. The Royalists were defeated with several killed and 200 taken prisoner. Some of the people of the town (possibly Clubmen) helped the Parliamentarian forces. As a result, a few days later, in September, the Royalist commander Sir William Vaughan (nicknamed The Devil of Shrawardine from the name of one of his Shropshire garrisons) burnt part of the town, including the church, as it had been used for 'the preaching of sedition'. There was such severe damage that the church had to be rebuilt in 1648. Vaughan left troops in the district but they fled at the approach of Sir Thomas Myddleton, who took the opportunity to clear the Royalists out of Lea Castle.

So the First Civil War drew to a close. On 26th April 1646 Bridgnorth surrendered, with many buildings destroyed by fire by the retreating Royalists. On 29th May Ludlow fell to Parliamentary forces led by Sir William Brereton, and Colonel More was made its Governor. However, by that time Charles had already surrendered to the Scots at Southwell.

After a brief and disastrous attempt to regain power by force of arms in the Second Civil War (which did not touch south Shropshire). Charles I paid the ultimate price for failing to resolve the crisis which struck Britain in the mid-seventeenth century, when he was executed at Whitehall in January 1649. His son was proclaimed King Charles II on 5th February 1649 leading to what some call the Third Civil War. Charles' attempt to regain the throne of England by force of arms ended with the Battle of Worcester on 3rd September 1651. South-west Shropshire was not involved in subsequent events.

It is hard to judge just how the war affected the people of Shropshire, especially the 'lower orders' of the more remote south-west corner of the county. Undoubtedly the war brought shortages and hardship, the quartering of troops and the depredations of marauding soldiers and deserters. In towns such as Bishop's Castle and Clun houses were destroyed and in both places the churches were partly burned down, one reason being their castles had already declined in what was thought to have been an age of peace and the church towers had become places of refuge. Similarly in Clun the outer walls of Trinity Hospital were pulled down by the Royalists to prevent the building being used as a strongpoint. For some the war brought honour and glory, excitement and hope, for change, progress, something better. In that respect the end of the Civil Wars was not the end of the story. The Interregnum, the constitutional experiments of Oliver Cromwell, the social and political ideas of radical groups such as the Diggers and the Levellers were all to leave their mark upon the land and the people. In the long term, it was these ideas emerging from a society in crisis which have had a greater impact on the lives of the people than force of arms ever has.

Bibliography

Anderson, A. *The Civil Wars 1640-9* Hodder & Stoughton, 1995

Bryan, T. *A Civil War Trail Through South West Shropshire*

Coward, B. & Durston, C. *The English Revolution* John Murray, 1997

Farrow, Wm. J. *The Great Civil War in Shropshire* Wilding & Son, 1926

Gilbert, C.D. 'Clubmen in South West Shropshire 1644-45' *Transactions of Shropshire Archaeol. Soc., Vol. LXVIII*, 1993, pp.93-98

Kenyon, R. 'Committee for the Sequestration of the Estates of Shropshire Delinquents, 1894' in *Transactions of Shropshire Archaeological Society Vol. VI*, No. 8, p.19-26

Oakeley, H.F. *Richard Oakeley of Oakeley 1590-1653* H.F. Oakeley, 1988

Waite, V. *Shropshire Hill Country* Dent, 1970

The eighteenth century brought to new prominence some of the ancient families which had established residence here after the Norman Conquest. At Lydbury North, Walcot Hall was bought by Clive of India, whose family was later joined by marriage to the Earls of Powis. The great families had much influence on the social and political life of towns like Bishop's Castle.

CHAPTER 16

Clive, Walcot & Bishop's Castle
by David Preshous

Robert Clive was born on 29th September 1725 at Styche Hall in the parish of Moreton Say near Market Drayton in north Shropshire. The family name was perhaps derived from the village of Clive, north of Shrewsbury. Robert's father, Richard, was a respected country gentleman, and the family had held lands in Shropshire from the reign of Henry II. An earlier Robert Clive, a colonel in Cromwell's army, had been a considerable scourge to the Royalists of the county. There was a contemporary jingle, based upon the Royalists' fear of Clive and the Parliamentarian garrisons at Wem and Nantwich:

> From Wem and from Wyche,
> And from Clive of the Styche,
> Good Lord, deliver us!

There are many stories about the wild exploits of young Robert, both in Market Drayton and in the three schools he attended, and although these may well have been embroidered by his early biographers, it seems clear that he was an extrovert, perhaps hyperactive, youth, unlikely to settle in formal education. However, Macaulay's suggestion that he was 'a dunce if not a reprobate' is not borne out by his subsequent cultural and intellectual achievements.

At the age of 19 he was sent to India as a writer (clerk) in the Honourable East India Company, probably not so much because of his behaviour but because this was seen as a promising new career opportunity. Between 1744 and 1767 he spent three periods in India, steadily amassing a considerable fortune much of which he was to use to secure political interest in his later life. In 1760 Clive assessed his own fortune at 'half a million', which would be around £200m in today's money. On a conservative estimate his wealth when he died in 1774 was about twice that amount.

His first period in India was spent in Madras and the Carnatic region of south-east India, the 'Coromandel coast'. He rapidly became very disenchanted with his work and the prospects before him in the Company and even attempted to take his own life. When the pistol failed to fire at the second attempt, he is said to have observed ' I am reserved for something'. He transferred his career from clerical to military, and engaged upon a series of bold actions, first as a volunteer and later as an officer in the British Army. His shrewd tactics brought famous victories, including the Relief of Arcot and Trichinopoly, and won him military promotion and personal acclaim as well as securing British domination over the French in that part of India. He married Margaret, the sister of his close friend and fellow military volunteer, Edmund Maskelyne, and returned with her to England in 1753. One of the first instances of his use of Indian money in Shropshire was in reducing his father's mortgage on Styche Hall by £6,000.

In his second period in India he saw even more distinguished service as a senior officer commanding substantial British and Indian forces in Bengal. At Plassey in 1757 he avenged the 'Black Hole of Calcutta' massacre, when, with a force of only 3,000 men, he defeated Nawab Siraj-ud-daula's Indian army which numbered over 60,000 men supported by French artillery. At this time he received the famous or infamous '*jagir*' from the Indian prince, Mir Jafar—an annual income of 300,000 rupees (£27,000), the customary grant of the revenues of a certain district to a military commander of high status.

His return to England in 1760 was marked by popular acclaim for his imperial achievements: he was elected M.P. for Shrewsbury in 1761, created Baron Clive of Plassey in 1762 (an Irish peerage which enabled him to continue to sit in the House of Commons), and made a Knight of the Bath in 1764. He was soon, however, embroiled in conflicts of interest within the East India Company, and confronted by serious accusations of financial corruption.

174

Clive's third and final visit to India (1765-7) was in response to a deterioration in British fortunes in Bengal. Clive settled the situation quickly and returned to England to build and promote for himself a political career.

In his paper entitled *Robert Clive and Shropshire Politics*, J.F.A. Mason singles out three main objectives for Clive's use of his fortunes in England: 'he wanted to benefit the family he had left back in 1744, to protect his own reputation and his *jagir*, and as part of that ambition to build up a following in the House of Commons.' These objectives were to combine to bring Clive back into Shropshire and in particular into the south-west of the county.

In the middle of the eighteenth century, Shropshire returned two Members of Parliament for the county, not subject to election and both firmly in the grasp of the Tories. In the five parliamentary boroughs, candidacy was also controlled by the most powerful local families: in Shrewsbury and Ludlow by Lord Powis; in Bridgnorth by the Whitmores of Apley Park; in Much Wenlock by the Foresters of Willey Hall; and in Bishop's Castle by the Walcots of Walcot Hall, Lydbury North.

An ambitious gentleman wishing, as Robert Clive now did, to achieve parliamentary power and influence, had to achieve four interdependent objectives. He had to gather around him in the House of Commons a group of members who were his own personal nominations and who could be relied upon to give him loyal support. To do this he needed to purchase properties within or close to the targeted constituencies to enhance his local influence. Having done that, he had to study the particular local electoral scene, its practices and malpractices. And finally, he needed the right friends, in the right places, at the right time. Such a campaign required the deployment of considerable amounts of money.

In the years of his second return to England (1760-65), Clive had begun to secure his parliamentary footing in Shropshire, in rather curious circumstances. His father, Richard Clive, had in 1759 been returned as M.P. for Montgomery with the support of Lord Powis, who was anxious to restore his waning influence in Shropshire. The chief rivals of Powis were the Pulteneys of Bath. The Marquess of Bath, who did in fact replace Powis as Lord Lieutenant of Shropshire in 1761, intended that his son, Lord Pulteney (at that time M.P. for the uninhabited constituency of Old Sarum in Wiltshire), should acquire one of the two Shrewsbury seats. In 1760, a vacancy appeared when Robert More of Linley announced his intention to resign at the dissolution the following year. At the instigation of Lord Powis, Clive came straight to Shrewsbury after his return from India, and successfully convinced the town corporation that he was the right man to join the sitting member, Thomas Hill. At this time, he rented Condover Hall as his Shropshire base, and at some point also occupied the property in College Hill, Shrewsbury, now called Clive House.

In 1763 another set of fortuitous circumstances brought Clive new political opportunities. The Walcot family of Lydbury North, who had for many years nominated the Members of Parliament for the borough of Bishop's Castle, fell heavily into debt.

The Walcots were, with the Oakeleys of Oakeley and the Plowdens of Plowden, the most ancient family in south-west Shropshire. The Walcots are known to have lived here from at least 1462. The family became impoverished following its support for the Royalist side in the Civil War, but its fortunes were restored by John Walcot who had been taken prisoner by the Roundheads at Shrewsbury and subsequently ransomed for £50. The fifth bell in Lydbury North church is inscribed 'Long live John Walcott Esquire, 1660'.

When a later John Walcot inherited the estate in 1726 it was valued at £140,000, and with his gardener, Thomas Dobbs, he set about the improvement of the surrounds of the hall. Both men are listed as subscribers to the monthly periodical *The Practical Husbandman and Gardener* in 1733-34. To judge by the impressive account of materials used in its building between 1703 and 1706, quoted by Paul Stamper, the kitchen gardens were probably among the finest in Shropshire at that time. Sadly, however, within 20 years, electioneering expenses had pushed John heavily into debt. He left the fate of the 6,000 acre estate in the hands of his 23 year old son Charles, a young man greatly under the influence of his uncle, Sir Francis Dashwood, of Hell Fire Club notoriety, and he was persuaded to sell it to Robert Clive in 1763 for £92,000. The Walcot family moved to Bitterley, near Ludlow, and the way was open for Clive to influence the voters of Bishop's Castle.

On 23rd September 1763 one of the sitting members for Bishop's Castle, Francis Child, died suddenly. Clive had not yet taken possession of his new estate, and he remarked with brutal frankness that Child had died 'rather sooner than I would have hoped' since he himself was as yet 'almost an utter stranger to the borough'. Nevertheless Clive took swift and decisive action. He moved into Walcot Hall, secured the support of Charles Walcot by promising him a seat in Parliament at the next General Election, and attempted to buy off the other contestant for the seat, Walter Waring of Owlbury, for £1,000. Although the bribery was unsuccessful, Clive was

Pl. 15 Walcot Hall, Lydbury North

able to get his cousin, George Clive, elected as the new member by 80 votes to 53. In the space of a few months he had been able to strengthen substantially his parliamentary standing and future prospects.

A descriptive article on Walcot Hall by Arthur Oswald in *Country Life* (1939) states that 'When Clive bought it, the house was a brick building with a three-gabled front of Elizabethan or Jacobean date. Such it appears on an estate plan of about 1750, which shows this main front looking north towards the fish-ponds and a formal garden centring in a fountain-pool lying in the east. Clive, it would seem, without entirely rebuilding it, greatly enlarged and transformed the house, giving it new elevations with sashed windows and a parapet'.

Clive employed William Chambers, the eminent architect whom he had already entrusted with work on his father's house at Styche, to redesign Walcot. Chambers appears to have been governed by the height and proportions of the existing building. The elevations are simple and severe, the only new 'feature' being the Doric portico. Much internal embellishment was undertaken by Chambers, introducing elaborately decorated ceilings. Also built at this time was the substantial and elegant stable-block.

Further extensions, including the ball-room, a series of hothouses, and a three-storey tower (since demolished) at the west end of the south front, were added by Clive's son, Edward, who occupied Walcot for over 65 years. Edward was very active in the development and beautification of the park, sending his employee, Robert Gardener, to Kew to 'take dimensions of one of the royal gardens there'. The long curving hothouse, constructed around 1822, was described by the Shrewsbury writer and publisher, Charles Hulbert, as 'the most spacious and costly I ever beheld'. Edward was also responsible for the creation of the magnificent 25 acre arboretum, which still boasts a Douglas Fir planted about 1827 from the first seeds brought back from Canada and the United States by the Scottish botanist, David Douglas.

The noted landscape designer, William Emes, was employed by Edward Clive both at Walcot and at Oakly Park, Ludlow (which he acquired in 1771), from 1774. It is possible that he was responsible for altering the existing fishpools to create the graceful curving lake that still fronts Walcot Hall, although there is an attractive local tradition that the excavations for this were carried out by Napoleonic prisoners of war. The lake and buildings appear on a map of 1827.

One of the features of the Walcot gardens was The Hermitage, an Indian temple, built for Edward Clive between 1802 and 1803 to a design by the celebrated Shrewsbury architect, Thomas Farnolls Pritchard. This was deliberately burned down on the orders of the Estate Office in the middle of the twentieth century, presumably to reduce maintenance costs. Ernest Harris, the unfortunate estate employee despatched to carry out the orders, described The Hermitage as 'a beautiful round thatched building. The floor inside was laid with coloured flagstones. The roof and walls were prettily designed like Chinese wickerwork. It also had a circular verandah with large supporting pillars. It was rather an uncanny place and too beautiful to describe. It stood on a large flat piece of land like a tennis court and was very immaculately kept.'

The Walcot Estate in the mid-eighteenth century included lands in Lydbury North, Mainstone, Kempton, Acton Farm, Owlbury, Lower Down, Clunbury, Colsty Farm, Old Churchstoke, Hyssington, Clun Mill, and Snead Mill. This gave the owner estates almost completely encircling Bishop's Castle. Indeed in a letter to his friend, the former Prime Minister, George Grenville, in 1769, Clive refers to 'the purchase of some estates which I am making ... for the purpose of entirely surrounding the town of B.C. with my own possessions'. Two of these estates were leaseholds in the possession of a Bishop's Castle landowner, Corbyn Morris, and a third was that of the late Charles Mason of Bishop's Castle, purchased by Clive from the new owner, the Irish peer, Lord Catherlough.

Clive bought numerous estates both in Shropshire (Montford 1761, Oakly Park, Ludlow 1771) and in other parts of the country (Usk Castle, Monmouth, 1768, Okehampton, Devon, 1771/2). In 1769 he purchased the great house of Claremont, near Esher in Surrey, which, having earlier acquired a fine London house in Berkeley Square, he probably intended to become his principal country residence. He invited Capability Brown to redesign and rebuild it. In most cases, however, his intention (not always achieved) in the purchase of new estates was to create opportunities for political advancement in these areas. Oakly Park gave him a foothold in the Ludlow political ring, while the purchase of Walcot, and subsequently of the estate of Walter Waring for some £30,000 in 1767, left the way open for Clive and his family to control Bishop's Castle's politics for some 60 years.

Pl. 16 Robert Clive's statue in Shrewsbury

The political history of this tiny borough during the eighteenth century and up to the Reform Act of 1832 is highly intriguing, as it steadily acquired a certain notoriety for its political vagaries. Its elections were frequently contested, and bribery of the voters was an essential component of the exercise of the franchise. Lord Powis, writing to Robert Walpole in 1740, wished his political aspirations in Bishop's Castle kept secret from the voters.

He surmised, probably correctly, that they would fear that 'there would be fewer contests in the future, and less corruption; by which they support themselves. They are very jealous of their liberty (as they call it); which is the liberty of being as corrupt as they please.'

From 1660 until 1695, Bishop's Castle had been represented in Parliament principally by wealthy local landowners. This period of relative calm was broken by the deaths, during the 1690-95 Parliament, of two members of these prominent families, William Oakeley of Oakeley and Richard Mason of Bishop's Castle. Elections for the next 70 years were destined to be contested and their outcomes decided by what was known as *unum necessarium*—'the one necessity'—hard cash.

At the centre of the storm of corruption which now broke over the town was Richard Mason's younger brother, Charles. Between 1695 and 1727, he was elected for the borough eight times, unseated three times for bribery, and once succeeded in unseating another candidate even less principled than himself—Bowater Vernon in 1726. On that celebrated occasion Mason was able to show that 51 of the 52 people who had voted for Vernon had received bribes. The rate had been £12 per voter, with one guinea for each of their wives, making a total expenditure on Vernon's part of over £600. Mason's petition was upheld by the Commons Committee and he was given Vernon's seat. The pot had succeeded in calling the kettle black.

Pl. 17 The Clive Coat of Arms in the Market Square, Bishop's Castle

There are other well-documented examples of Bishop's Castle's opportunist voters in action. The Harley family of Brampton Bryan, when their candidate, Lord Harley, was defeated by Charles Mason in 1714, railed against the 'villainous roguery' of the 'profligate wretches of Bishop's Castle'. Indeed Edward Harley was so outraged that he sold his Bishop's Castle estate, to prevent his son being tempted into 'a great expense upon such mercenary rascals'.

In February 1734, when Robert More of Linley was defending the Bishop's Castle seat he had won in 1727, he was opposed by the Walcot family, who, although Robert's mother was a member of that family, sent servants into the town to provoke trouble. According to More, a drunken mob roamed the streets shouting 'Down with the Roundheads. Damn More. Down with him.' More did retain his seat on this occasion, but retired from the fray before the election of 1739.

In the 1739 election there was further trouble for one of the candidates. Henry Brydges incurred crippling expenses in securing one of the Bishop's Castle seats for himself. He had to relinquish this seat in 1744 when he inherited his father's title of Lord Caernarvon. The debt he had incurred for his electioneering campaign was so severe that he confided to his friend, John Walcot, that he wished he had never seen Bishop's Castle!

It was into this arena that George Clive was propelled in 1763, suitably backed by the Indian wealth of his cousin, Robert. The family tightened their grip on the borough further in 1768 when Robert was able to engineer the election of his brother, William, to the second Bishop's Castle seat. This was in part ensured by paying £1,000 to Charles Walcot, to be released from Clive's earlier promise of a seat.

From 1768 the borough of Bishop's Castle remained under Clive control for over 30 years. William Clive occupied one of the seats continuously for nearly 41 years, eventually becoming Father of the House of Commons. The other seat was held alternately by the other Clive nominees, Scottish lawyer, Alexander Wedderburn, a man of high ability and ambition, who ultimately became Lord Chancellor of England, and the family secretary, Henry Strachey.

In 1802, however, while Edward Clive was in Madras, the electorate saw a new opportunity to increase their political income. The customary price of a vote was raised from £20 to £25 as new money was brought into play. Blunden Hall in Bishop's Castle had been inherited by J.C. Kinchant of Park Hall, Whittington, who put up for election Thomas Clarke of Peplow in north Shropshire. Clarke's considerable wealth had come from involvement in the Liverpool slave-trade, and he began to use it to woo the Bishop's Castle voters. Henry Strachey, who was one of the sitting members at that time, felt apprehensive at facing such a rich and powerful contender and withdrew, to be replaced by Edward Clive's brother-in-law, Colonel John Robinson. Despite the challenge, the Clive candidate held the seat.

The continued fervour of the opposition to the Clive candidates is graphically expressed in an election song from the Bishop's Castle Town Records, dating from January/ February 1818:

> Let Clive and corruption together be driven
> From the Boro' wherein they have hitherto thriven.
> Let Robinson, Clive, and the rest of them know
> That the lads of old Clarke can yet strike ye blow;
> They can send up a member to sit in the house,
> Who cares for the ministers less than a l---e;
> Who'll never support any measures but those
> Which give to the nation content and repose;
> No upholder of Corn bills shall ever succeed,
> For we know, and can prove, that he always was fee'd;
> Or how did he get at a stall, let me know,
> Which he gave to the Bailiff, his worthy H.O.
> But the Bailiff will certainly justice dispense,
> He cannot, he will not, pervert his good sense.
> And therefore my lads let each give a plumper,
> Resist every bribe, like John Bowen, the jumper;
> **Indulge ev'ry hope, dispel ev'ry fear,**
> **Corruption must vanish! Independence is near.**

In the election of 1819, Douglas Kinnaird, a personal friend of Lord Byron and Sheridan, finally ousted one of the Clive candidates, Lord Valentia, by the narrow margin of 87 votes to 83. The veteran member, William Clive, retired before the 1820 General Election and a four-cornered election contest ensued. The Clive family candidates were Edward Rogers, a barrister and son of a Ludlow alderman, and William Holmes, the Tory Chief Whip, opposed by Douglas Kinnaird and Robert Knight, a Warwickshire squire. A vigorous campaign resulted in each of the candidates securing 87 votes. A first Parliamentary scrutiny gave the verdict to Kinnaird and Knight by a single vote, but a subsequent investigation of bribery charges reversed this verdict.

The Clives had regained control, but the end was near. In the Reform Act of 1832, Bishop's Castle, with its population of less than 2,000, was disfranchised. The Members of the House of Commons were no doubt highly amused, in the debates over the Act, to hear one of Bishop's Castle's contemporary MPs, J.L. Knight pleading that the town's electors were 'as free from improper bias as any in the kingdom', and that the only influence they acknowledged was that of 'kindliness'. There is no doubt that, even in the period of Clive control, when there were few contests over seats, the critical political factor had always been the *unum necessarium*.

Lord Robert Clive himself, who had brought his interests and his Indian money to bear on south-west Shropshire in 1763, committed suicide at his Berkeley Square house on 22nd November 1774. He was 49 years old. The reasons for his quite unexpected death remain uncertain. Politically he had achieved a strong presence in Parliament, his fortune remained huge, and he had a happy marriage and a promising 20 year old son and heir. He was, however, always an impulsive and moody personality, and it is probable that his final moment of despair was caused by a debilitating combination of recurrent ill-health and deep disappointment at the apparent lack of honour afforded him for his Indian achievements. He was buried quietly in an unmarked grave in the churchyard at Moreton Say.

In 1804 Edward Clive married the sister and heiress of Lord Powis and was made Governor of Madras. While he was in India, Lord Powis died unmarried and the Herbert estate including Powis Castle passed to Edward's eldest son, Robert Henry Clive. Edward was granted the title of Earl of Powis, and took as a second title, Viscount Clive. The family remained wholly or partly resident at Walcot until the house and part of the estate were sold in 1933.

Until the Second World War necessitated the removal of such landmarks, there was a dramatic local monument to Clive's presence in the area: a plantation beyond the lake at Walcot, which spelt out the name 'Plassey' in different species of trees. Today, there are three physical reminders in Bishop's Castle's of the town's association with the family. The most recent is a mid-twentieth century residential block of flats off Corporation Street named Clive House. At the top of Station Street a plaque on the front of the former Boys' School declares:

National School
Erected by Public Subscription
To commemorate the majority
Of The Viscount Clive.
November 5th 1839.

However, the most imposing is to be found in the square—a large stone-carved coat-of-arms (Pl.17). It is dated MDCCLXXXI and displays an elephant and a griffin with the motto of the Order of the Bath '*Tria Iuncta in Uno*', and once adorned the market hall (demolished in the 1950s).

Bibliography

Bence-Jones, M. *Clive of India* BCA, 1974

Cunningham, R. *Notes on the History of Walcot Hall and the Walcot Family* Bishop's Castle Local History Research Group, 1988

Harris, E.'*Those Good Old Days' – A Lifetime of Service on a large Country Estate* 1981

Mason, J. 'Parliamentary Representation, 1660-1832' *V.C.H. Shropshire ,Vol. III*, OUP, 1979

Mason, J. '"A Nabob worth Half a million" - Robert Clive and Shropshire Politics 1754-74' *TSAS Vol. LXXIII*, 1998

Oswald, A.'Walcot Hall, Shropshire' *Country Life* 14 October 1939

Stamper, P. *Historic Parks and Gardens of Shropshire* Shropshire Books, 1996

Watney, J. *Clive of India* Saxon House, 1974

The Industrial Revolution, with its heart not 30 miles away in Coalbrookdale, may have been slow in affecting south-west Shropshire. But in 1865, the legendary Bishop's Castle Railway opened, an optimistic project designed to bring new prosperity to this remote area. By then the road system had been improved and extended.

CHAPTER 17

'Getting There':
Communications & Transport from *c*.1700
by Robert Anthony

South-west Shropshire is a hilly, somewhat remote agricultural region lacking such natural advantages of access enjoyed in the north and east of the county by the navigable River Severn and the easily traversed terrain of the north Shropshire plain. The principal routes follow a north-east to south-west alignment. The reason is not hard to discover: Wenlock Edge is a product of the Church Stretton fault system and runs as an unbroken escarpment for 30km from Ironbridge in the north-east to Craven Arms in the south-west, and is matched on the western side of the fault valley by the Long Mynd, an equally formidable barrier to communication. Church Stretton lies between, in a gap less than 1 km wide. It was through this gap that the Romans constructed Watling Street; the A49 and main railway line from Shrewsbury follow substantially the same route. The B4368 through Corvedale from Much Wenlock to Craven Arms, on the dip slope side of Wenlock Edge, follows a similar alignment. The west-east routes in south Shropshire and north Herefordshire for the most part follow the river valleys: from Lydham to Cheney Longville, the valley of the Onny (now the A489); from Newcastle and Clun towards Craven Arms, the valley of the Clun (B4368); from Knighton (Powys) to Ludlow, the valley of the Teme (A4113).

The region also lacked, in the eighteenth century, the imperative of large-scale industrial development: towns such as Wellington, Broseley and

187

Madeley in the north-east were obviously concerned to ensure the maintenance of lines of communication, whether road, river, canal or rail, for the movement of raw materials and finished product. Whilst it is true that south-west Shropshire possessed extractive industries of note in the eighteenth and nineteenth centuries (a lead mining industry of national importance in the Stiperstones region; coal mining in the Hanwood and Pontesford areas; coal, iron-ore and the quarrying of dhustone in the Clee Hills) these industries did not have a significant effect on transport systems over the wider region and roads remained the most important mode of travel. The major ones served the main market centres such as Shrewsbury, Bridgnorth and Ludlow, and the minor ones served the villages and their fields. The drovers' roads were also a significant feature of the Shropshire landscape. For centuries Welsh cattle were driven into England by long-recognised routes to markets in Shrewsbury, Gloucester and even further afield. One of the best known was that which the Montgomeryshire drovers took to Shrewsbury: it went by Bishop's Castle and then eastwards to Plowden, over the Long Mynd, using the Portway, and down to Leebotwood. These drove roads remained important until the coming of the railways.

In 1555 and 1563, two Acts of Parliament established what became long-standing arrangements for the maintenance of roads. This was the system of 'statute labour', an obligation on individuals in a parish to work, without payment, for four days a year (subsequently increased to six) on the roads within their parish. Each parish was to appoint a surveyor of highways, who had to view all the roads, highways, watercourses, bridges and pavements in the parish and report to the Justices of the Peace. They, in turn, were given power to 'present' ill-repaired roads in their district and to levy fines if 'statute labour' had failed to bring the roads to a satisfactory standard, and those fines could then be used for road repairs. Although these arrangements, with some modifications, remained the basis of road maintenance until 1835, administratively the system was not a success since there was an inherent unfairness in its operation. In some parishes, where the traffic on the roads was local, it worked quite well; in others the existence of long-distance and well-used main routes meant a heavy burden of repair falling on local inhabitants without contribution from road users. In 1663 the first Turnpike Act was passed and the busy Great North Road (later the A1) was turnpiked.

The aim of the turnpike system was not to create a new system of roads to replace the existing, but to transfer part of the financial burden of repair of the busier main routes from hard pressed local parishioners to those using the roads. This was achieved by collecting tolls from travellers and enforced by means of a network of gates and tollhouses. Maintenance of the lesser roads remained the responsibility of the local parish. Ultimately, after the demise of the turnpikes in the nineteenth century, it was to be development of this arrangement, from the Vestry as the board of management for its roads, through to the creation in 1862 of the highway districts with a wider geographical responsibility, which led to the modern system under which road maintenance is the responsibility of the county and its cost raised by local impost.

After a slow start, the turnpike system spread and in the eighteenth century many local Acts were passed authorising the setting up of trusts charged with the improvement of the road system throughout England and Wales.

Shropshire's roads did not enjoy a high reputation in the early eighteenth century and complaints about their condition and lack of maintenance, and consequent difficulty of travel, were rife. The roads of west Shropshire were particularly bad, evidence for which can be found in the Shropshire Quarter Sessions records and the numerous references there to 'presentments' for non-repair. For example, in April 1755 Bishop's Castle seems almost to be blockaded by the condition of its roads with presentments by one Thomas Browne of 'ruinous' roads between Bishop's Castle and Ludlow in the parishes of Edgton, Stokesay, Onibury and Bromfield. Repairs, if done, appear not to have been very effective, as proceedings were frequently initiated in respect of the same roads, although, as noted, 'presentments' could be used as a means of levying fines to supplement 'statute labour'.

The coming of the turnpikes marked the start of a process of gradual improvement. In south-west Shropshire turnpike trusts were established from 1751 with the setting up of the Ludlow First Trust, followed by the Ludlow Second in 1756 and the Bishop's Castle Trust in 1768. Edward Knight was a major investor in the Ludlow Second Trust, with two turnpiked roads (including the later A4113) running close to his ironworks at Bringewood (Herefordshire) and then east to the river port at Bewdley (Worcestershire). Between 1756 and 1759, he advanced £1,700 on loan to the Trust on the security of the tolls, and the money was invested in improving the two roads. This was the normal practice. The Trust did not just level the road surfaces and improve drainage, but often constructed new lines (the old lines usually being stopped up to wheeled traffic), removed bends and eased gradients. Most of the modern 'A' and 'B' roads were turnpiked, whilst minor roads were formed into through routes: examples include the unclassified roads from Bishop's Castle through Bridges to Pulverbatch and thence to Shrewsbury; and from Bishop's Castle via Stank Lane, Edgton and Long Lane, joining the A49 north of Craven Arms (this formed part of the coaching route from Montgomery to London). A few new roads were also constructed, including that by the Ludlow Second Trust in the late 1750s from Ludlow east over Clee Hill (now the A4117), which was instrumental in opening up new markets for the coal and manufactured goods of the area.

Another new road (now the A488) was constructed in the mid-1830s (with the help of a loan of £4,000 from R.B. More of Linley Hall) north from Lydham through the Hope Valley to Minsterley, replacing the previous Bishop's Castle to Shrewsbury main route which had passed through Pulverbatch and Longden. Each of the new routes constituted a major engineering achievement: the Ludlow Trust road passing through the coal workings, waste heaps and squatter cottages high on Clee Hill, and the Hope Valley road serving the wooded, hilly and remote region of the Stiperstones with its lead and (later in the century) barytes mines.

Turnpikes were not, of course, universally popular and local protests not uncommon. In October 1839, the trustees of the Ludlow First Trust received a petition from the inhabitants of Tenbury against the removal of the Burford gate to a position nearer the town. The petition claimed that the town was 'already nearly surrounded by turnpike gates ... and if this new gate is erected the inhabitants can scarcely move two hundred yards from the Town by any road but one ...' The petitioners argued also that the intended gate was very unfair as it discriminated against the locals when the original intention of the turnpike legislation was to exact tolls from travellers over longer distances. The inhabitants of Ludlow and Bishop's Castle would not have been impressed by these arguments, hemmed in themselves by turnpike gates, and the Ludlow trustees had no difficulty in rejecting Tenbury's petition.

Tollhouses and mileposts represent the best surviving physical evidence of the turnpike system. These, and the roads they served, have been well documented and described by Dr. Barrie Trinder and the late John S. Clarke. Maximum tolls were prescribed by statute and displayed on or near the tollhouse, whilst gates across the road prevented the passage of the traveller until the correct toll had been paid. About 300 tollhouses were built in Shropshire (of which there were approximately 70 in the south-west), and at least 100 survive. Tollhouses varied in design from the semi-octagonal structures of the Ludlow Trusts (for example, Overton south of Ludlow,

Pl. 18 Aston-on-Clun

SO 509725), to the pleasing circular stone building at Aston-on-Clun (SO 394816) and, most commonly, those which look little different from Shropshire vernacular cottages (for example, Crow Gate, Bishop's Castle, SO 331878). There were also one-off designs: the tollhouse in the village of Minsterley (SJ 372051) is a rather crude gothic. A specification for the Sandpits, Ludlow, tollhouse may be found in the minutes of the Ludlow Second Trust. Built in 1756 of stone, brick and tile by John Lumbart, mason, it cost £35 and took only a month to construct. Many mileposts, in stone and cast iron, survive in varying degrees of preservation. Most of the stone mileposts of the Bishop's Castle Trust are painted white with the lettering picked out in black. The late eighteenth-century sandstone obelisk at Craven Arms, which provides a comprehensive record of destinations and distances, is much more unusual.

Shropshire is drained by numerous streams and rivers. Bridges are, therefore, an essential part of the road system, Shropshire possessing over 1,000 county council maintained bridges, many of which have been described by the late Anthony Blackwall. In south-west Shropshire probably the best known of the older bridges are at Clun and Ludlow. Clun

Pl. 19 Milepost,
Upper Mill, Wentnor

Bridge, built about 1450, is in virtually unaltered condition and still able to carry the A488 road over the River Clun. Ludford Bridge, Ludlow, which carried the pre-bypass A49 over the River Teme, is of similar age, but was partly rebuilt at the end of the nineteenth century. Many bridges until the beginning of the nineteenth century were, however, of timber, and most of these rickety structures were rebuilt or replaced under the authority (until the end of the nineteenth century) of the magistrates of the Quarter Sessions, by their county surveyors. Most of the new bridges were of masonry: for example, the Grade II listed Eaton Bridge built in 1842 by Edward Haycock over the River Onny (SO 375897—close to the former Eaton station on the Bishop's Castle line). Others were a combination of masonry and brick: an example is the fine Ashford Bridge built by Thomas Telford in 1797 over the River Teme about two miles south of Ludlow (SO 520711). Iron was also employed: a late example is Onibury Bridge, a wrought-iron lattice girder bridge supported on cast-iron trestles on stone plinths, constructed by Thomas Groves in 1886 over the River Onny (SO 454790). All were a considerable improvement over the structures they replaced. Many of these 'county bridges' survive in south-west Shropshire in original, or near original, condition.

In 1750, Shropshire had few main roads; those wishing to journey from Shrewsbury to London either travelled to Ivetsey Bank for the stagecoach from Chester, or went by Severn wherry to Worcester and from there by road. The first coach service from Shrewsbury to London began in 1753 and took about 3½ days. Most people, not least the drovers driving their flocks and herds to the markets of England, travelled on foot or on horse-back (and a few by private carriage), with goods often carried by pack-horse, along roads which were dusty in summer and deeply rutted and sometimes impassable in winter. These, as already noted, were poorly maintained and the machinery for the repair and maintenance of them inadequate. In many of the more rural and remote areas of the county, including parts of the south-west, postal and carrier services remained infrequent—if any existed at all. None of this was conducive to the development of the internal economy of the region and the introduction of turnpiking represented the first concerted effort to tackle the problem of 'ruinous' roads. Its success can be measured in terms of the number of new coach services appearing after the mid-eighteenth century, and the gradually reducing journey times. In Shropshire, Shrewsbury was the main beneficiary of this process, quickly becoming, from the late 1770s, a hub for routes to and from a number of destinations including London, the Midlands and the Welsh coast. In south-west Shropshire, Ludlow was, historically, a centre of importance, and the turnpike system consolidated this role. By 1822, Ludlow was offering a total of 13 services per week to destinations including London, Bristol and Shrewsbury, and by 1840 the number of weekly services had increased to 25, with reductions in journey times. In 1822, Bishop's Castle could offer services to Ludlow (and from there to London), Shrewsbury and Aberystwyth twice a week from May to September. Church Stretton at the same date had daily coach services to Bristol and Shrewsbury, albeit by virtue of the town being on a through route, rather than as a destination in its own right. Clun remained coachless.

With the coming of the railways, the days of the coach were numbered, although coaches continued until after the 1860s as a means of transport serving those towns without a railway station. Many turnpike trusts had struggled financially, and competition from the railways accelerated their inevitable demise. The process of de-turnpiking started in south-west Shropshire in 1870 and the last turnpike (Hope Valley) removed its gates in 1879.

Water transport was not to assume great importance to the economy of south-west Shropshire. The industry which might have benefited most, lead mining, was located in the Stiperstones where the terrain was unsuitable for the construction of a canal.

The River Severn was navigable in the eighteenth and nineteenth centuries for the whole of its course through Shropshire, but it by-passes the south-west. No other rivers in Shropshire compare. In 1636, William Sandys received permission to improve the River Teme upstream to Ludlow as a means of supplying Herefordshire and Shropshire with wood, iron, coal and seven other commodities, but the scheme appears never to have been carried out. It is possible that the Teme was made navigable for small boats to carry iron from the works at Bringewood to Ludlow, but the evidence is slight.

The Leominster Canal, conceived at the height of 'canal mania', was never finished, and was never profitable. Crossing and re-crossing the border of south Shropshire and north Herefordshire, its intended purpose was to make more accessible the agricultural areas of these counties, and to supply the local towns, including Ludlow and Tenbury, with agricultural produce. In the event, coal from Sir Walter Blount's pits near Mamble, shipped to Woofferton wharf for sale in Ludlow, was probably the most important commodity carried. The canal was intended as part of a larger scheme linking Leominster to Hereford in the south, and extending east-wards to Stourport-on-Severn, a total length of 73km. Further schemes were suggested, including a link to Ludlow and from there to Bishop's Castle and Montgomery to join the Montgomeryshire Canal. The proposed links came to nothing. A section of the canal from above Marlbrook near Mamble (a plateway—L-section rails supporting wheels without flanges—connected the Blount pits) to Woofferton was opened in October 1794, and a further section south to Leominster was commissioned, after severe engineering difficulties, in July 1796. The canal was then about 30km, its maximum length. Despite numerous proposals over the succeeding 40 years for extensions both by means of new sections of canal and tramroad, nothing materialised, and the Leominster Canal was eventually sold to the Shrewsbury and Hereford Railway in 1858. The railway company had considered keeping a section of the canal open between Woofferton and Marlbrook, but in the absence of any prospect of an increase in trade in coal from Sir Edward Blount's pit, it was drained in 1859.

One of the principal surviving monuments to the Leominster Canal is the substantial aqueduct of three arches of brick and stone over the river Teme near Little Hereford (SO 537687). The centre arch was blown up in an army exercise in the last War, but enough survives to make the journey on foot through attractive countryside worthwhile. It is also possible to trace much of the course of the Canal along the southern boundary of the county, and also the site of the wharf at Woofferton (SO 519684).

As the birthplace of the Industrial Revolution, Shropshire possessed some of England's earliest railway lines. The first recorded line (1605), in the Broseley area, was used to transport coal from the pits to the River Severn for onward shipment. In 1802 Richard Trevithick built, at Coalbrookdale, the first steam locomotive to run on rails. But it was not until 1848 that the Shrewsbury and Chester Railway opened the county's first main line railway. In April 1852 the extension from Shrewsbury to Ludlow, via the Stretton Gap, was opened in style by Thomas Brassey, the engineer (and first lessee-operator from Shrewsbury and Hereford Railway Company), who at each stop fired a cannon mounted at the rear of the train. In 1853 the line was extended to Hereford.

On 1st July 1862, following the termination of Thomas Brassey's lease, the Shrewsbury and Hereford Railway Company came under the joint control of GWR and LNWR and these two companies, for many years, ran their trains alternately on the line. By 1862 both the Shrewsbury to Crewe and the Shrewsbury to Hereford lines had been 'doubled up' to cope with the increasing traffic, both of goods and passengers, from the north of England to South Wales, traffic which further increased with the opening of the Severn Tunnel in 1886.

Although there are no major works of engineering on the main line as it passes through south-west Shropshire, a consequence of its construction was the development of a railway junction town, with associated facilities, close to the early nineteenth century inn, The Craven Arms, from which the town took its name. Prior to the coming of the line, and the development of branch lines west to Knighton (1861), north-west to Bishop's Castle (1865) and north-east to Much Wenlock and Buildwas (1867) the nearest local settlements, all of them relatively small, were Newton, Stokesay, Whettleton, and Halford.

Opened in 1865, after much local agitation, the Bishop's Castle line was slow and inefficient, and never achieved profitability in its 70 year life. In consequence its operators were forced to cut corners and bend, or even ignore, the rules in an effort to survive. That is remarkable enough; but the little line is also remarkable for the amount of literature and affection it has generated since closure, out of all proportion to its economic importance when in operation. The line carried passengers and goods, the latter mainly agricultural produce and coal. Branching off the Shrewsbury and Hereford line just north of Craven Arms at Stretford Bridge (SO 431844) it proceeded north-west along the Onny Valley via Horderley, Plowden, Eaton (the three former station buildings survive as houses) and Lydham Heath, to Bishop's Castle. The line from Lydham Heath (SO 346905) to Bishop's Castle had been proposed only as a branch; the original plan was to extend the main line from Lydham Heath to Montgomery to join the Oswestry and Newtown railway; and also proposed was a link via the Rea Valley to Minsterley to connect to the line to Shrewsbury. If the original proposals had been realised, the line might have achieved some degree of profit (although perhaps not prosperity). As it turned out, the necessity for the Bishop's Castle locomotive, on reaching Lydham Heath station, to uncouple from its carriages and wagons and 'run around', re-couple and steam the final few miles to Bishop's Castle in reverse, was a reminder of what might have been. The line (and associated engineering works) is clearly discernible for most of its length, and sections may be walked. The

Pl. 20 Horderley Station, Bishop's Castle railway

Railway and Transport Museum in Bishop's Castle contains much useful information on this independent little line, and many fascinating artifacts.

Another railway line, projected but which failed completely to advance beyond the planning stage, was authorised in 1866 as 'The Presteigne, Clun and Bishop's Castle Railway'. The proposal was to link Clun to Presteigne in the south and to Craven Arms in the north, with a junction to the Central Wales line at Hopton Heath. A plan in 1896 for a light railway from Broome (south-west of Craven Arms on the Central Wales line) to Clun, Bishop's Castle and Minsterley (with a possible extension from the Snailbeach line to Lydham Heath) also came to nothing.

A line from Craven Arms westwards to Bucknell was opened by the Shrewsbury and Hereford Railway (supported by LNWR) in 1860, and extended to Knighton the following year, and thence on to Swansea. The Central Wales line, as it quickly became known, served the developing Welsh inland resorts of Llandrindod Wells and Builth Wells. The Shrewsbury and Hereford also backed the construction by the Tenbury Railway, in 1860/1, of a line from Woofferton to Tenbury. Part of this line ran along the track of the former Leominster Canal. It closed in 1961.

Goods and mineral traffic were of increasing importance after 1860. The Much Wenlock line to Craven Arms was opened in two stages: from Much Wenlock to Presthope in January 1864, and from Presthope to Marsh Farm

Junction, three miles north of Craven Arms, in 1867. Presthope was a busy station for goods, including lime from the Knowle works, and timber, horses and cattle. The line's main function was to serve the limestone quarries on Wenlock Edge, although it also carried passengers. Longville became the terminus of the branch after the line to Marsh Farm closed in 1951; the Buildwas to Longville section ceased to operate in December 1963.

The Snailbeach District Railways, opened in 1877 as part of a scheme of general refurbishment of the lead works by Henry Dennis, was a 2ft 4ins gauge line which linked the standard gauge line at Pontesbury with the lead mines at Crows Nest, Snailbeach above the Hope Valley (SJ 371018). Construction of this line substantially reduced the cost of transporting coal to the mines and smelter, and of conveying the lead and barytes away. Unfortunately, soon after construction, the price of lead fell, and in 1895 the smelter closed. This was not, however, the end: the line continued in service transporting road stone from a quarry north of Eastridge Wood (via a new branch line), and later from the Callow Hill quarry. Shropshire County Council acquired it in 1947 and replaced the steam locomotives with a farm tractor for the final haul up to the Callow Hill quarry. The line finally closed in 1959. The County Council undertook a substantial amount of conservation work at the Snailbeach site in the early 1990s and the narrow gauge rails and restored engine house may still be seen.

The standard gauge Ludlow and Clee Hill Railway line, constructed 1864-7, ran for about 8km from its junction with the Shrewsbury & Hereford line just north of Ludlow east to Bitterley Sidings (SO 574768), and from there a self-acting inclined plane, 2km in length, raised wagons to the dhu-stone quarries at the summit of Clee Hill (SO 595761). The quarrying of dhustone, or dolerite, for the manufacture of setts (stone blocks used for road surfacing) had replaced the mining of coal as the primary industry in the Clee Hills from the 1860s, and it was recognised that the construction of a railway was critical to the success of the quarrying operations. Quarrying duly flourished, and in 1881 an additional self-acting inclined plane with a 3ft gauge line, 2km in length, was constructed from Bitterley Sidings to help open up the Titterstone Clee Hill quarry (SO 595777). Another inclined plane, constructed in 1908, hauled wagons 2.4 km from Ditton Priors station to the dhustone quarries on the top of Brown Clee Hill (SO 610882). The quarries later produced (and still produce) road stone. From the 1930s road transport began to supplement and then supplant rail; the incline to Titterstone Clee Hill closed after 1945 and the Clee Hill incline in 1960; the line between Bitterley and Ludlow followed in 1962.

By the end of the nineteenth century all the towns of south-west Shropshire, with the exception of Clun, were served by rail.

What were the consequences of this revolution in communications and transport? First, the introduction of turnpiking was instrumental in opening up to coach and carriers the remote and hilly areas of south-west Shropshire. Secondly, improved and better maintained roads meant a reduction in journey times, and a reduction in the costs of carriage and of raw materials and goods. Market areas were widened. As mobility increased, new direct links between towns were forged and existing connections developed, and the range of goods and services on offer expanded. The resulting improvement to the economy of each town was, however, relative: Bishop's Castle, Church Stretton and particularly Clun continued to rank low in the hierarchy of Shropshire towns. Ludlow's position as a secondary centre of some importance was strengthened, with Shrewsbury, the county town, maintaining its dominant position as a social and commercial centre at the hub of a communications system.

If the impact of the Leominster Canal was peripheral (in more than one sense), the coming of the railways to south-west Shropshire completed the task started by the turnpike roads and ended the sense of isolation then experienced in many parts of the region. The railway, by competing directly, both nationally and regionally, with the turnpike roads for the carriage of mail, lighter goods and passengers (where speed of delivery was essential), helped bring the turnpike era to a close—albeit the demise of the turnpikes was assisted by their fragile financial state (many had never been profitable). Railways were, however, responsible for a substantial increase in short-haul journeys by road. An Act of 1888 provided that the former turnpike roads were to become main roads, maintainable by the Quarter Sessions, and in 1888 the duty of maintenance was transferred to the newly established county council. In the countryside the parishes were, by Acts of 1862 and 1864, constituted highway districts under the control of highway boards; in 1894 their powers and duties were transferred to the rural district councils, which became the highway authority for these minor roads.

The twentieth century in south-west Shropshire has seen the disappearance of all the branch and mineral railway lines, except the Central Wales line, although this has been balanced by the vast increase in motor transport facilitated by improvements in the lines and surfaces of roads. The region is no longer remote but, lacking as it does a motorway system, it remains off the beaten track. To the inhabitants of this beautiful part of Shropshire that may, or may not, be an advantage.

Bibliography

Blackwall, A. *Historic Bridges of Shropshire* Shropshire County Council, 1985
Clarke, J.S. 'Tollhouses and Turnpikes', *SWSHAS Journal*. No.10, Summer 1999
Morgan, J.S. *Bishop's Castle: Portrait of a Country Railway* 1991
Morriss, R.K. *Canals of Shropshire* Shropshire Books, 1991
   Railways of Shropshire Shropshire Libraries, 1983
Oppitz, L. *Shropshire and Staffordshire Railways Remembered* 1993
Tonks, E.S. *The Snailbeach District Railways* Industrial railway Society, 1974
Trinder, B. *The Industrial Archaeology of Shropshire* Phillimore, 1996

Despite the gathering momentum of industrial society, life in this corner of Shropshire continued to be centred around the rigours of hill-farming. One of the most remote parishes is Mainstone, a group of farms spread around the steep-sided valley of the River Unk. It is still a dynamic and close-knit community, with a church and chapel, and a lively social calendar. Its life has always hinged upon the agricultural uses of large tracts of upland between 500 and 1,200 feet above sea level.

CHAPTER 18

Mainstone:

A Remote Community in the Nineteenth Century
by Patricia Theobald

Mainstone lays no great claim to fame. Situated in beautiful countryside the social history of the parish is largely determined by its geography, a broadening meadow valley running southwards with side valleys running eastwards from the Edenhope, Churchtown and Knuck districts. Between the valleys the hills, often flat-topped pasture with some arable land, extend westwards to the plateau of the Clun Forest. To the east lies similar high pasture in the Reilth area.

Nineteenth-century Mainstone was a thinly-populated parish comprising one Welsh township (Castlewright) and three English townships (Mainstone, Edenhope and Reilth) whose residents were mainly root-crop and sheep farmers and agricultural workers. Possessing a church, chapel, school and smithy it was situated in the overlapping hinterlands of two market towns—Bishop's Castle and Clun. This chapter is concerned with some aspects of the land and population in the English townships of the civil parish of Mainstone in the nineteenth century. In addition to the facts and figures that follow, it must be borne in mind that during the last quarter of the century the consistently poor weather was a major contribution to agricultural depression. Local records tell of prolonged periods of snow and rain, attesting to a wretched working life for the community.

Land has always been the axis on which the rural economy runs. Enclosure of open fields had been practised since the sixteenth century, but by the nineteenth century pressures to increase profitability of the land, due to advancing technology and foreign competition, led to increased enclosure activity. Enclosure then aimed to improve common waste land by division into fields and improving the drainage.

In Shropshire enclosure of land had been achieved 'by agreement' and private Acts of Parliament. By 1820 enclosure in the north of the county exceeded 20,000 acres, almost four times that in the south. A large are, still unenclosed, was Clun forest, which included Mainstone. The main instigators for the parliamentary bill for its enclosure were the major landowners who were negotiating for this between 1825 and 1837. Local freeholders, anxious to see that their rights of common in the forest were recognised (they were extinguished on enclosure, but land was allotted in lieu of them), asked the Earl of Powis (as lord of the manors within the forest), to appoint an agent to act on their behalf at a meeting held in the Six Bells in Clun on 6th February 1830. A collection of letters between landowners, agents and surveyors indicate something of the socio-economic problem attached to the task—from nomination of agents and commissioners, through relative costs of enclosure, to fees payable: commissioners 3 guineas per day; surveyors 7d per acre. In 1830 the value of unenclosed land in the Clun forest was estimated at £6 per acre according to the agent of the Powis Estate. The cost of a private Act of Parliament was set at £1,000 and a commissioner's fee at £945; but three commissioners were required locally and this, combined with other unspecified costs brought the total to £5,030. However, landowners were assured that land values would increase after enclosure.

Unwittingly, this correspondence also shows a social dimension—a tenant whose letter reveals an unexpected articulate diplomacy; one major landowner's plea that he does not understand how to deal with a particular matter; and another, writing on black-edged notepaper, that the whole matter was more than required 'at his time of life'. Most importantly there appears to be a real concern to reach a solution 'beneficial to all parties ... to be of service to the neighbourhood' by mutual agreement between freeholder and the lord of the forest manors.

In hill farming country a dominant concern of landlord and tenant has always been sheep. At the mid-century point, 376 acres in Mainstone township would 'winter' 878 sheep whilst the same numbers could 'summer' on 357 acres of forest. Between 1839-1843, under the direction of the commissioners, wasteland sales were held at the Buffalo's Head, Clun, twice a year

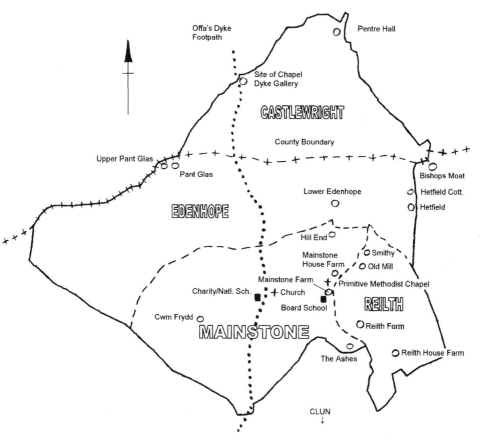

Fig. 10 Plan of Mainstone Parish

in order to defray the expenses of enclosure. Some sales were secured, but bids were frequently too low and land withdrawn. 'The Commissioners were very much annoyed and disappointed at result of sale ... several free-holders did not purchase'.

In some parishes the opportunity was taken in the enclosure of common land to redeem the tithes, and in such cases the creation of a tithe appor-tionment and map under the Tithe Commission Act of 1836 was unneces-sary. This was not the case in Mainstone where these documents exist, dated 1848. The procedure for tithe commutation must therefore have been carried on at the same time as the enclosure was taking place.

The basic unit of civil organisation before the late nineteenth century was the ecclesiastical parish, and communities supported their incumbent by payment of tithes and other dues. The practice of paying tithes originated in the Anglo-Saxon period when the parish acquired a territorial dimension, in most English parishes the glebe terrier, *inter alia*, setting out the custom to be followed, However, no such terrier survives for Mainstone. Tithe disputes are as old as the system itself and in 1710 one Mainstone rector—John Giffard— left 'an account of the Customes and moduses for such Tyths as have not been paid in kind since the memory of man' and a second document containing a veiled threat from the Rector: 'Whereas it is asserted by the inhabitants of the parish of Mainstone that the ancient custom was for the Rector of the said parish to furnish Bread and Wine for the Blessed Sacrament of the Lord's Supper twice at Easter thereupon, while their customs are observed in what they have subscribed to me, I promise to perform the same'. As the country modernised its agricultural practices, the tithe system of payment in kind to clerical and secular tithe owners proved inefficient and was replaced by commutation for cash by tithe apportionment.

The 1836 Tithe Commutation Act was passed in order to rationalise the different practices arising from payment of tithes by commuting them all into money payments, that is rentcharges based on the value of land. Commissioners were appointed and a surveyor drew up a map with a number on each piece of titheable property, and then listed the names of the owners and occupiers, the description of the property, with field names and field use, acreage and the tithe apportioned. The landowners and the parishioners had the opportunity to dispute the boundaries and figures. However, on 19th December 1848 agreement was reached between assistant tithe commissioner George Wingrave Cooke and landowners for Mainstone township to pay £84 10a per annum and Reilth township £63 10s, as rent in lieu of tithes. Thus was created the most complete description of the land since the *Domesday Book*.

The tithe apportionment and map for Mainstone in 1848 gives a complete picture of land use in the parish in the middle of the nineteenth century. Considering land usage first, analysis of the apportionment shows the parish to have comprised some 4,778 acres of which the majority was described as pasture (3,095 acres, 65%). Arable land occupied some 878 acres (18.4%) and meadow 322 acres (6.7%). Woodland was recorded at 266 acres (5.6%) and the remainder was garden (5.5 acres), rough land (2 acres), or undescribed (145 acres). The acreage in the townships was recorded in the preamble to the apportionment (see Table 1): these differ from the modern analysis of the figures.

As for land ownership, it is known that a quarter of Shropshire was owned by county gentlemen and Mainstone was no exception. The Tithe Apportionment reveals that the largest local landowner was the Earl of Powis, Lord of the Manor, owning about 1,370 acres (28.7%), confirmed by

Township	Arable	Meadow	Wood	Forest	Waste	Totals
Mainstone						
& Knuck, Shadwell	177	716	75	899		1,867
Edenhope	483	86		918		1,487
Reilth	150	550			67	767
Totals	810	1,352	75	1,817	67	4,121

Table 1 Land Types and Areas in Mainstone Parish
(Source: Tithe Apportionment Mainstone 1848)

the Powis Estate maps of 1820 and 1825 which show substantial holdings in Mainstone and Edenhope. Next largest was Henry Lyster Esq., related to the Lysters of Rowton Castle, Alberbury, who owned 1,207 acres (25.3%). The Botfield family, prominent figures and one of the richest families in the county, owned about 439 acres (9.2%), whilst Hannah and Elizabeth Beck are recorded as owning 419 acres (8.77%). Together, these landowners controlled nearly three-quarters of the land in Mainstone parish. With powerful landowners Mainstone could be considered a 'closed' village, in which they controlled dwellings and occupations available to the local population. However, the major landowners did not live there and there was no large estate to provide cottages, school or church for the community.

Twenty-nine persons together with the parish itself owned the remaining quarter of the land. Of these, the largest landowners were John and Richard Sankey, (Reilth House Farm) owning 237 acres (5%). One owner, Euphemia Gifford with 167 acres (3.5%), presumably inherited her interest from a former Rector of Mainstone John Giffard (1701-1759) as her parcels of land were centred around the church where one is referred to as 'Giffards Glebe'. The amount of land owned by the parish was very small, comprising 2.7 acres by the Guardians of the Poor and 3 acres by the Surveyors of the Roads and Highways.

Mainstone House

The Tithe Apportionment, together with Census Enumerators Book (CEB) evidence, shows that tenant farmers made up the majority of land users in the parish. The largest tenant farmer was Edward Langford at Lower Edenhope Farm with over 800 acres, later increased to 1,000 acres (22.8%) by the Jones Family who were tenants from 1851-91, followed by Benjamin Beddoes at Mainstone House Farm) with 591 acres (12.4%). Langford's farmland in Edenhope was mainly pasture (772 acres) with some arable (195 acres), woodland (64

Reilth Farm

acres) and a little meadow (32 acres). Beddoes' farmland in Mainstone had about the same proportions of pasture and arable (354 and 139 acres) but more meadow (41 acres) due to its location by a river. Richard and James Owen at Reilth Farm farmed some 300 acres (6.3%) of which 131 acres was pasture, 109 arable, 46 meadow and 5 woodland.

The most important owner-occupier was the Earl of Powis, who farmed some 536 acres (11.2%) of the parish in his own name. Richard Sankey (Reilth House Farm) owned and farmed 237 acres (5%) of similar propor-tions to the Owens, but overall the holdings of the Sankeys amounted to 514 acres. The smallest occupiers with less than 5 acres included the schoolteacher and the blacksmith. Thus tenants, smallholders and agricul-tural labourers populated Mainstone.

During the nineteenth century urbanisation of society brought about rural depopulation and a consequent evolution in village community life. The population of the three English townships of Mainstone in 1801 was 263, peaking in 1821 at 296, before dropping in 1831 to 280, and 276 in 1841. Thereafter, the CEBs for these townships show a steadily decreasing population in line with national trends in England and Wales, from 241 in 1851 to 217 in 1891. (See Table 2)

In Shropshire the number of agricultural workers declined between 1870 and 1914 by 36%, largely due to low wages, poor conditions and compulsory elementary education which removed young people from the labour market. There was also a population exodus of 23% from the Clun area during the 1880s, which is reflected in the figures for Mainstone.

The residential persistence of household heads was studied in the 136 households recorded between 1841 and 1891 within the area, using CEBs and parish registers. Four households retained the same address over 50 years, four over 40 years and twelve over 20 years. Within the parish, two

Year	1841	1851	1861	1871	1881	1891
Male	147	129	127	133	108	111
Female	129	112	93	102	99	106
Total	276	241	220	235	197	217
Houses	50	45	41	44	42	35
Uninhabited	3	3	2	2	3	?
Less than 5 rooms	-	-	-	-	-	15

Table 2 Population of Mainstone
(Source: CEBs 1841 - 1891)

households stayed over a 40 year period and a further two over 20 years, but at different addresses. Four households migrated but had returned by 1881. Thirty-seven households 'disappeared' after one decade, although they may only have migrated to adjacent parishes. Over the period 39 households were terminated by death and 17 more were occupied by the younger generations in these family households. Highest in-migration was recorded in 1841, with highest out-migration in 1851, both comparative 'boom' years in Shropshire agriculture. However, with the exception of Griffith Bason, who is known to have emigrated to America, the remainder probably moved locally. This speculation is supported by census data between 1841 and 1891 which shows 66 of the 88 household heads recorded as born within an 8-mile radius of Mainstone. There does also appear to be a two-way migratory pattern. The decadal data are summarised in Table 3.

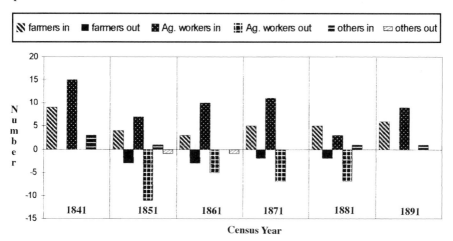

Table 3 In- and Out-Migration of Household Heads
(Source: CEBs 1841 - 1891)

By the mid-point of the nineteenth century conditions in rural cottages were deplorable in most parts of the country. In Shropshire attempts were made by some landowners to rectify the situation and new cottages were built. Mainstone parish consisted mainly of isolated farmsteads with small clusters of dwellings. Mainstone 'village' (which included the blacksmith and wheelwright) and Hetfield, with its collection of cottages adjoining a farm, could both be regarded as loose ribbon developments. However, location and identification of dwellings in nineteenth-century Mainstone is problematic since on the ground the 'village' has almost disappeared. The recorded dwellings for Mainstone 'village' fluctuated between four and 15 properties; differences perhaps explained by a mixture of clerical error, buildings collapsing, households temporarily sharing accommodation and rural depopulation. Enumerated dwellings in the parish fell from 45 (1851) to 35 (1891) with few recorded as uninhabited. Some dwellings were not always identified by name and could 'disappear' at any census point.

In the area identified as 'Hetfield', 'Hatfield' or 'Headfield' (Farm) in the CEBs and maps, the number of cottages varied between two and nine. Only Headfield and nos. 2 and 3 Hatfield Cottages (built in 1874) have survived. Within the parish other dwellings have also survived—recorded in the Tithe Apportionment, in CEBs, or named on estate maps or the Ordnance Survey map of 1884—and are still standing at the end of the twentieth century. These include Cwm Frydd, (Lower) Edenhope Farm, Hill End, Mainstone Farm, Mainstone House Farm, Old Mill, Pant Glas, Reilth Farm, Reilth House Farm, Smithy and The Ashes.

The popular picture of a large Victorian family was not to be found in Mainstone. The majority of the 145 families studied over the period consisted of two to four persons and only ten families contained nine or more members. A significant proportion (ranging from 19% to 43% over the 1851-91 period) of these families did not contain children. Many households contained two family generations with about 10% having three generations at the time of census.

However, family size is not the same as household size, households of the period often containing persons outside the immediate family circle. Many of these were classified as servants although they might be related to the family. Over the period 11 farmers were recorded in the CEBs as having servants. Edenhope Farm had around eight to nine servants covering all the skills expected of an agricultural environment such as that found at Mainstone. The next largest farms (Mainstone House Farm, Reilth House Farm and Reilth Farm) had around five to eight servants. The remaining farms declared one or two servants, but these might well have been members of the family.

In 1851 Shropshire had 18,830 male and 328 female recorded agricultural labourers and 21 male shepherds, the latter number soon to rise. For the Clun area there were 1,019 male and eight female agricultural labourers.By 1891 the number of Shropshire male agricultural workers had decreased to 15,712, with 316 females, but the number of recorded shepherds had increased to 381. The Mainstone data shows a constant proportion of household heads as agricultural labourers but although many women worked in the fields the records give no indication of seasonal employment of women and children.In line with national trends most local servants were aged between 10 and 24 and, as expected, the majority were male.

Although farming was the dominant occupation a number of trades are also recorded for Mainstone: wheelwrights, blacksmiths, schoolteachers, two shoemakers, a lamp maker, a tailor and also 2 shopkeepers (by 1900). Surprisingly, no millers were recorded living in the old mill.However, a working miller and a group of shoemakers were recorded over several decades in the Welsh township of Castlewright.

Data collected from records of births, deaths and marriages in the parish provide a quantitative picture for most of the century (see Table 4). One glimpse behind the figures reveals untimely deaths in 1832: Elizabeth Davies of the old mill, aged 21 years, took a fatal dose of vitriol; Richard Price of Dolvour, aged 10 years, hanged himself in a hedge. There would have been many happy occasions, but the records are silent.

From the available data for Mainstone it has been possible to provide snapshots of three households with varied socio-economic backgrounds.

The first are the residents of Lower Edenhope Farm (1851-91), in Edenhope township, listed in trade directories for the period as farmers working 800-1,000 acres, (one-fifth of the total Mainstone acreage) and significant local employers. In 1851 Edward and Mary Jones were living and working here with eight children aged 6-28 years.This family was

	Marriages	Baptisms	Burials
CEB linked*	52	112	35
Others	103	72	77
Totals	155	184	112
* registry entries linked with household head names in CEBs			

Table 4 Life-cycle Events 1841 - 1891
(Source: CEBs and Parish Registers 1841 - 1891)

Welsh. In a society where late marriage prevailed the local parish register recorded marriages in the Jones family between 1860-63 at the ages of 31, 37 and 39 years, and there were unmarried sons aged 37 and 42 recorded in the 1881 census.

The death of Edward in 1859, aged 65, was followed within five years by those of two adult sons and a daughter. Mary Jones

Lower Edenhope Farm

continued to farm the land with the help of four sons. In 1851 they employed 16 labourers. Between 1861-1881 their employees were described as: a farm bailiff, groom, carters, dairymaid, housekeeper, shepherds, and housemaid. Over the next 20 years it appears that the social status of this family increased for, by the 1881 census, the family of Mary (aged 82) and her unmarried sons George (42) and William (37) are described as 'gentlefolk'. By 1891 Mary Jones had been dead for six years, and the farm was controlled by her elder son John (64) who had returned to Edenhope with his third wife and seven children whose ages ranged from 9 to 26 years. As with the previous generation a familiar pattern of residency, marriage, and death can be traced. Signs of social progress include a daughter who trained to be an elementary school teacher, working for a time in Mainstone. The employment of an 'engine driver' in addition to waggoners highlights advances in farming practice, which provided additional employment for the local blacksmith and wheelwright.

In a rural economy the blacksmith was a significant figure in everyday community life. The Smithy in Mainstone township, consisting of four rooms in the 1891 census, was home and workshop to a branch of the predominantly Mainstone-born Morris family for generations. By 1851 George (from Kerry) and Margaret (from Ratlinghope) with five children, aged between 2 and 18, were well established in the area. Trade directories for the period list them variously as blacksmith, wheelwright and carpenter. Sons, George II and brother Stephen, continued the trade, albeit with separate living accommodation as marriage and family life dictated. By 1871 George had been dead for one year, George II was a widower with three children, and Stephen with his wife and family of four, aged 11 months to

The Smithy

9 years, were living at The Smithy and a cottage nearby. Stephen's second daughter, Alice Beatrice, became the much-respected assistant teacher at Mainstone School for 50 years until 1949. Although there were apparently no servants or employees, an apprentice from Kent was recorded in 1871 and two nephews aged 9 and 14 (the latter apprenticed) in 1881.

However, the majority of inhabitants of the parish were agricultural labourers. The Ashes, Mainstone township, was recorded in the census 1841-71 as home to a branch of the Addis family. Thomas married Sarah Venables (also from Mainstone) in 1813. Their family consisted of eleven children, of whom six were born at The Ashes. Previously listed as a gamekeeper, the 1851 census describes Thomas as a labourer with a wife and only two children resident. At this time a daughter was employed as a general servant by the Sankeys of Reilth House Farm. By 1861 Sarah, then a widow of three years, was farming a smallholding of seven acres (increased to nine acres in 1871) with three of her adult children living at home. One son, James, became gamekeeper on the Garnett-Botfield estate. Another son, Thomas II, married in 1849, was also a gamekeeper living in Mainstone with his wife and eight children (aged between 3 and 19) until the 1870s. Later, in 1881 he is listed as publican in Bishop's Castle. A third son, John, worked as a labourer, married in 1847 and lived just outside the parish in The Goat House, Colebatch until his death in 1892.

Over the 50 year period covered by the census' analysed 25 houses were occupied by the same families and it is these households which provided the hard-core of territorial and social community within the parish.

The 30th March 1851 was Mothering Sunday and the date of a unique census of religious worship in England and Wales. The census provided information on denominational strength at local and national levels at a time when the established church was in disarray. Shropshire returned 64% Anglican and 36% Dissent 'sittings' (seats). In Mainstone there were two recorded places of worship: St. John the Baptist, Churchtown and a Primitive Methodist meeting house (the location of the latter is not recorded). In a total population of 241 the Anglicans returned an attendance of 60 (16 at Sunday School) from a 'capacity' of 201 (including 27 free) sittings at the morning service taken by Rector John Williams with Richard Sankey, Church Warden. The Primitive Methodist afternoon service, taken by Minister Edward Phillips, was attended by 39 faithful from a 'capacity' of approx. 100 spaces. There is no indication whether actual, rounded up or average numbers were recorded, but Mainstone appears close to the county figures.

A watercolour of the church in 1791 by Rev. Williams, showing a building of some length, does not reveal the state of disrepair recorded by the church wardens; the fabric was a constant source of concern for most of the century. The Elizabethan roof timbers and panelling were the only features later retained from this older building which was similar to other churches in the area with deep-set windows, box pews (bought, sold and bartered between households and families) and '6 pews below entrance door [between] font and belfry for the poor'. However, there is some evidence of the music provided at services of the period. According to the records Mainstone church had its 'Mellstock Quire' and, although the music is long forgotten, reference was made to instruments: 'bassoon [purchased] April 1828'; 'clarionet [purchased] April 1829'. More evidence of possible nineteenth music in Mainstone is revealed in the *Shropshire Harmony,* a musical notebook containing anthems and hymns, including a funeral hymn reputedly for Mainstone, written by Thomas Owen, an organist living in an adjacent parish.

Familiar local names appear over the period as church wardens and other community officers: Beddoes, Bowen, Chelmick, Deakin, Griffiths, Hudson, Jones, Langford. Mountford, Price, and Sankey, together with rectors: Samuel D'Elboef Edwards (rector from 1757 to 1805 and the last member of a local eighteenth century gentry family of Pentre Hall [Castlewright]), Oakley, Williams, Herschell (buried in Mainstone 1866), Allen, Griffiths and William Glenn (rector from 1895 to 1935). William Henry Griffiths was rector from 1879 to 1895 during which time unprecedented recorded public building activity took place in the parish. The Board School was erected in 1881 (subsequently enlarged in 1894), the Anglican church rebuilt in 1887 and the Primitive Methodist Chapel was built in 1892.

1887 marked the 50th year of Queen Victoria's reign and celebrations took place throughout the Empire. In Mainstone the 'Rector introduced the question of the Queen's Jubilee Year celebrations. There was much discussion and nothing was done. Parishioners felt that in the present depressed state of agriculture no funds would be forthcoming'. Nevertheless a brass plaque was installed to mark the occasion. This was also an important time

St John the Baptist

in the history of Mainstone, for 1887 was the year when the church of St. John the Baptist was re-built. According to the records the new building replaced one in a poor state, despite the efforts of several generations of parishioners and at least two rectors. From 1882 the need to address the problem was recognised, but funding the project presented a major diffi-culty. By 1886 the Rector 'lay before the [parish] meeting the state of church funds [but] no suggestions made [and] no deci-sions arrived at'. The Earl of Powis (or his agent) suggested another site. Voluntary subscriptions and generous donations, plus £15 from the Incorporated Society, allowed work to proceed on the same site, with the church being re-opened on Sunday 3rd August 1887. This important occasion was recorded in the prayer book of Joseph Sherry, Parish Clerk. That box pews were replaced by free seats and the provision of new flooring and heating, demonstrated policy changes towards making Anglican worship more accessible and pleasant to the local community.

As fixed capital the Anglican Church in Mainstone stood unchallenged for centuries, but even well-established communities are subject to change. Primitive Methodism, strong in industrial Shropshire, spread and market towns adjacent to Mainstone were centres of thriving non-conformist activity. In Flora Thompson's account of religious practice in *Larkrise to Candleford*, Methodists held services in a cottage. Early Primitive Methodist meetings in Mainstone took place in similar surroundings. However, there is a chapel marked on the 1848 Tithe Apportionment Map on the north-west boundary of the Welsh township at Cwm (close to Offa's Dyke), and in 1851 a trade directory lists a Baptist and Independent meeting house close to Offa's Dyke in the same township. Mainstone was mentioned in Primitive Methodist circuit reports and minute books where lectures, revival meetings and services were recorded in 1884 at (Upper) Pantglas—a cottage—'every Sabbath at 6 p.m.' When circuits were being reorganised from Shrewsbury, Mainstone people recorded their wish 'to remain with Bishop's Castle at their request'. There is evidence of an extremely active community in the area having revival, missionary, camp and tea meetings similar to those described in Mary Webb's novel *Gone to Earth*. In 1885 they applied for permission to lease centrally sited land, in Mainstone township, from W. Garnett-Botfield—a prominent Anglican— to build a new chapel. Some years passed and in 1889 the Offa's Dyke chapel (known as the Dyke Gallery by the 1990s) was being rented 'chapel and rooms Offa's Dyke Mainstone [for] 20 sittings; 20 hearers'. Fortunately at this time a bequest of '£32 17s 3d was left to the Primitive Methodists in Mainstone by Mrs [Mary] Jones of Edenhope'. The building of a chapel in Mainstone specifically for Primitive Methodists was duly accomplished and opened in August 1892: 'Freehold. Deeds in Mainstone. Attended services: 40. 11 members in society. Population 187'. The names of some of the local faithful can be gleaned from baptisms between 1887-98: Chester, Hamer, Lloyd and Venables. In 1893 chapel schedules record: '30 sittings (100 free), debt £100, income £7 6s. 11d. outgoings £5 10s. 8d.' The simple unadorned interior satisfied the functional requirement to see and hear the preacher, and simultaneously expressed the religious tenets of the society.

Trade directories for 1851-1891 list five 'gentry' landowners who also appear as benefactors in Anglican records. At the mid-century point eight of the ten employer-farmers listed can be identified as serving officers with the Anglican Church. Only one of the farmers listed had association with Primitive Methodism. Later in the century, 1885-1900, this allegiance increased to six of the twelve listed farmers and craftsmen.

In Mainstone, interest from charities established in the previous century continued to be distributed amongst the needy parishioners on Easter Monday, although after 1824 recipients are not mentioned by name. The Poor Law Act of 1834 affected all parishes in England and Wales with the establishment of union workhouses. As part of the Clun Union, the destitute of Mainstone would have been

Primitive Methodist Chapel

directed to the new 'Bastille' workhouse in Bishop's Castle. The 1851 census recorded only widow Hannah Stokes and her young family as paupers. The saddest entry in the census must be 'Alfred Phillips, 3 weeks old, died 6 January 1867'.

Mainstone Board School

Apart from childbirth and consumption, the problems of the few Mainstone poor, recorded in the Medical Relief Book between 1890-96, are those attributable to the vicious circle of poverty. A most common prescription was '2 lbs. mutton and 1 pint brandy'. However, four entries between November, 1893 and August, 1894 concern 18 year-old Maria Francis of Churchtown who was blind and had a cerebral tumour, for which there was no hope except release in death.

The proceedings of Mainstone Vestry—recorded by the Churchtown schoolteachers for much of the century—spilled over into other public records, which is hardly surprising as the various local offices were filled from amongst the same group of names. Road access in rural areas was a headache for most Highways Boards and comments concerning disrepair appeared in local records from time to time. During 1881 the *Shrewsbury Chronicle* reported a heated discussion where 'John Sankey threatened to take action if Asher [Ashes] Road Mainstone was not repaired. Mr. Beddoes, Mainstone, also applied that another Mainstone road be repaired. Considered of little public use, the Board agreed neglect and responsibility'.

The Education Act 1870 began the drive towards standard elementary education throughout England and Wales. In Mainstone education had been provided earlier in the century at a charity school—later described as a national school—near the church. By 1875, in accordance with the 1870 Act, a local school board was established, but their *laissez-faire* policy earned them a unique place in county educational history—the school board was dismissed and replaced by county-appointed professionals. Eventually a school building was erected, opened in November 1881 and enlarged in 1894. Further along the lane the national school continued to operate until *c*.1900.

Agricultural depression, caused by bad weather and inability to compete with cheap imported grain, seriously affected the rural economy. As a consequence land became a declining asset by the end of the nineteenth century and across the country estates were being sold. In Shropshire the great estates initially continued to provide much needed stability, but within a few years many were being sold off or reduced in size. Lord Powis disposed of some holdings in 1901 and again in 1912 as the First World War loomed. Locally, the Garnett-Botfield estate which encompassed 3,722 acres in Mainstone, Clun and Bettws producing an annual rent of £2,735, was offered for sale in lots at The Three Tuns, Bishop's Castle on Wednesday 22nd September, 1915.

The wedding of Elizabeth Gough of Pant Glas Mainstone in July 1914 may have been one of the last happy occasions before the outbreak of war. Death respected neither rank nor fortune and many great families lost sons. Viscount Clive, heir to the Powis Estate, died on the Somme in 1916, and a member of the local Garnett-Botfield family was also killed. Distant hostilities affected even small rural communities like Mainstone, where at least one man was taken as a prisoner-of-war in Germany. When the Great War ended in 1918 the seven sons of this small community who did not return were recorded in the church for all time.

The nineteenth century saw a great change in land use. In Mainstone three-quarters of the land was owned by four county families. One third of the land was worked by three tenanted farms, with approximately another fifth owned and worked by three families. People migrated in and out over the period largely reflecting national trends. Census data show that many families were small and that most people worked the land. During the last decades of the century the sounds of building never ceased in the Mainstone-Churchtown area of this parish, as the fabric of a modern late-Victorian rural community was constructed. The story of nineteenth century Mainstone is not unique. The documents tell of a parish conforming to a pattern that appears in almost every rural community.

Bibliogrpaphy

Primary Sources
(Deposited in Shropshire Records and Research Centre)

Mainstone
Board School Log Book 1881-1919
Census Enumerator's Books 1841-1891
Church wardens' account book, 1713-1880
Parish Registers
Primitive Methodist papers, 1851-1916
Religious Census Return 1851
Tithe Apportionment and Map
Vestry minutes, 1875-1912

Other
Bishop's Castle Workhouse, Births and Deaths 1866-1914
Census reports for England and Wales, 1851 and 1891
Clun Union District Medical Relief Book 1892-98
Kelly's **Directory of Shropshire**, 1900
Powis estate papers: letters, maps and documents
Thomas Owen, *Shropshire Harmony*

Secondary sources
Best, G. *Mid-Victorian Britain 1851-75* Fontana, 1971
Evans, E.J. *Tithe maps, Apportionment and the 1836 Act* Phillimore, 1993
Harrison, J.F.C, *Early Victorian Britain 1832-1851* Fontana, 1988
                 Late Victorian Britain 1875-1901 Fontana, 1990
Higgs, E. *Making Sense of the Census* Public Records Office, 1989
Lawton, R. *The Census and Social Structure* Cass, 1978
Stamper, P. *The Farmer Feeds us All* Shropshire Books, 1989
Victoria County History of Shropshire, Volumes II, III and IV

The twentieth century brought huge and often traumatic change to the English landscape and its people. The arrival of technology and mobility on the agricultural scene, with their social and economic consequences, the tragedies of two World Wars, and the new thrust towards a united Europe, have all made their mark. At the start of a new millennium, it is important for us to listen to and record the witness of those who lived through the last tumultuous century.

CHAPTER 19

Living History:
Archive & Anecdote
by Janet Preshous

'History is people'
Ken Jones, Oral Historian, Ironbridge Social History Group

The earliest evidence of humankind's activities, apart from archaeology, comes from hearsay—from bards and balladmakers, speaking to us across the centuries about the deeds and events, and sometimes the opinions and emotions, of those who lived in the far distant past. The earliest sagas and ballads may have passed through many stages and been embellished, but at their heart they seem to have a core of fact, and the ring of personal observation. In Britain, there has been a continuous recognition of the value of the folk-tradition, through the collecting of handed-down folk-songs, tunes and stories.

George Ewart Evans, a pioneer of oral history in Suffolk in the 1950s, used the phrase 'Spoken History'. Such evidence alone cannot be relied on entirely for precise facts, but it can serve to flesh out matter-of-fact reporting of events by giving a flavour of 'being there', and 'how it was'. For the local historian, anecdotal material can be corroborated by census returns, probate inventories, tithe maps, parish records, deeds, newspaper and court reports, and so on. The continuity of life in a rural area such as south-west

Shropshire, where significant numbers of people remain firmly rooted in the places in which generations of their forebears have lived, means that handed-down descriptions of events and memories can stretch back over the last hundred years with the immediacy of an eye-witness account. These first hand-memories, together with scraps of ephemera which can still be collected locally (such as postcards, letters, bills, receipts, tickets, and posters), help to bring an era to life. Items preserved at random afford insight into what was thought significant at the time. Diaries, journals, private correspondence, newspapers, and personal accounts have always provided peepholes into the realities of a person's life, or a brief insight into their perception of public events. Portraits and paintings, or drawings of the scene at an event, give a personal point of view.

The advent of photography in the nineteenth century enabled the instant to be pinpointed (although, as with oral recording, there is always the view-point of the person behind the camera or the tape-recorder to be taken into account—why did he or she choose that angle, that moment to take a picture or ask a particular question?). Both techniques have their uses in recording the national, the important, the grand events, but can be of even greater significance in showing what everyday life was like for the ordinary person at different periods.

At a local level, some of the examples given here illustrate how histori-cal information (particularly in otherwise unrecorded areas of study) may, with luck and patience, be pieced together—a picture postcard confirming a tape-recorded recollection; an object providing evidence which can be checked against a document; items in local newspapers, school log-books, town archives, relating to the communal memories which have built up a picture of life in the earlier part of the twentieth century.

Since the formation of the Local History Research Group (now SWSHAS) in 1974, various Oral History Projects have been undertaken arising from several 'Living History' exhibitions organised at The Community College, Bishop's Castle. These brought together documents and archives from the county collections, and items, photographs and memories in the possession of local people. Another important strand in gathering and cross-checking information has been through the RECALL Project, initiated in 1983 for all those at Stone House Residential Home and Hospital (built on the site of Bishop's Castle's former Workhouse).

One of the exhibits at the first exhibition in 1984 was borrowed from Stone House: the heavy iron frame with differently-sized holes in which stone used to be graded. From another source came a pair of wire goggles

Pl. 21 A 'Roadster'

used to protect the eyes when splitting the stones. A picture of a 'roadster' has confirmed first-hand memories of the itinerants who walked from the Workhouse at Forden to the Clun Union at Bishop's Castle, then on to Knighton. For their night's lodging they broke the stone for the roads. Local people remember their mothers keeping pennies and halfpennies to give them, and keeping the kettle on the boil to make them a cup of tea. The late Mr. Grubb (Stone House) remembered seeing them walking towards Knighton Workhouse when he used to be hedging and ditching by the roadside: 'They would ask for a pinch of baccy for their clay pipes—and then ask for a match to light it!'

South-west Shropshire has remained a predominantly agricultural area with a special quality and independence of spirit, which can perhaps be more clearly understood by knowledge of its history and development. It is still recognised officially as an area of low wages: times have never been easy for any but the largest land-owners. Certain places have retained a sense of continuity and community, which even improved transport and road systems and the influence of technology and the pace of modern life have not entirely eroded. In the past, news and information would have to a great extent been spread by word of mouth, when people gathered at the markets and fairs and auctions. The outlying areas would have been kept informed by drovers, itinerant pedlars and travelling'crickers' (who dealt in chinaware), and later by those who delivered goods for the shops in the towns.

Bishop's Castle was, and to a certain extent still is, cut off from larger centres. Because of its status as a town, and its importance as a market centre since medieval times, served from 1865 till 1935 by its own railway, it has retained its autonomy and status, in spite of its small size. Its importance as a Pocket Borough when two Members of Parliament were sent to Westminster is more a matter of national history, but the notoriety of the bribing of the voters is reflected locally in bills (still in the Town Chest) from local hostelries for 'Meat and ale for the Burgesses'. The prevalence

Pl. 22 Courtroom, Bishop's Castle Town Hall, 1907

of contemporary cartoons, jokes, satirical verses and popular songs often highlights the concerns of ordinary people in the face of national and political events and local controversies: for instance, researches in the Town Hall archives have brought to light lampoons of the time, such as 'Starve Beggar The Cause of all the Mischief' — to be sung (intriguingly) to the tune, 'Moses and the Vicar'.

In conversation with older residents one often hears allusions to 'Frenchman's Mile' — a stretch of road on which Napoleonic prisoners (known to have been lodged locally) were reputedly allowed to walk on parole. According to one oral memory, a house in Castle Street has (now beneath the plaster on one wall) an inscription: '*Aujourd'hui je pars pour ma patrie bien-aimee*'; and in the Porch House, one of the most important buildings in Bishop's Castle [see Chapter 14] there is a small oval painting on an eighteenth century wall, possibly of a French castle, thought to have been painted by one of these prisoners. There is firmer evidence of one such French prisoner in a churchyard-inscription (now only partly legible, but quoted in full by Vincent Waite in *Shropshire Hill Country*): '*A la memoire de Louis Paces, Lieut. Colonel de chevaux legers, chevalier des ordres militaires des deux Siciles et de l'Espagne, mort a Bishop's Castle le 1 mai, 1814, age de 40 ans.*'

The diary of a local landowner, Henry Oakeley of Lydham (together with research into the old school log-books, showing absences, both permitted and unlicensed) gives some idea of the high-days and entertainments of the nineteenth century: '7/10/1865: Drove to B.Castle to see a very ordinary circus'; '28/4/1866: Drove to B.Castle to see some menagerie'; '18/9/1866: … thence to a hollow representation of dissolving views at B.Castle'. Commander Oakeley R.N. kept a detailed record of the weather, his estate and his social round, and was particularly interested in the advent of the Bishop's Castle Railway. '24/10/1865: Drove to B.C. to see the opening of the railway. 1 p.m. train arrived. Self, Mrs, and children … got into No.1 1st class carriage just to say we had been there!'; '21/12/1865: The government inspector went over the BC Railway and did not pass it'; '1/2/1866: Walked to Lydham Heath station with Sophy. BC Railway opened for passenger traffic. Took the first two first-class tickets for Craven Arms from this station, numbered respectively 00 and 01. At Craven Arms met Mrs and Katarina who took also the first two from there for Lydham's Heath …' *Eddowes's Journal* (14th March 1877) reports how Henry Oakeley died, rather fittingly, in the Town Clerk's office: '… while engaged listening to a letter which Mr. Griffiths commenced to read, concerning the Bishop's Castle Railway, he fell back and shortly afterwards breathed his last'.

Talking to those who were growing up before the First World War, one feels as if one is witnessing the very end of the purely oral tradition of reciting the deeds of the heroes—words have become ritualised, the story has been honed by frequent repetition, the 'punch-line' polished for the best effect. This is particularly true of stories about the Bishop's Castle Railway, where someone either in authority or 'from away' was outwitted by local people. Mr. Alf Shakespeare (1904-1992, recorded 1987): 'Well, the first Guard, I understand was a fellow of the name of Broome, and he was dressed up there in his uniform, that proud of the train – and up come one of these travellers, a cocky sort of feller: "Is this the Bishop's Castle train?" and he says, "Yes". "Oh this is the train they get out to pick mushrooms from don't they?" And of course, when he got to Bishop's Castle, coming along on the train, like, he was sticking his head out and lost his hat. And he could see Broome, and he kept shouting to Broome to stop; anyhow Broome never stopped. When he got out he said to Broome, "Why didn't you stop to pick my hat up? I shouted at you!" "No," says Broome, "We only stop to pick mushrooms!"'

Mr. Shakespeare and many other members of old local families who had a special connection with the railway and the stations on the line have also provided detailed and vivid accounts of the way in which the railway was vital in its time for the transport of passengers and goods, including timber, milk, stone, coal, cattle and sheep (as well as the mail) to and from Craven Arms. Mrs. Frances Cooper (born 1899), the daughter of one of the engine-drivers, Mr. Sinclair, and the late Mr. Sid Cadwallader (1908-1999), son of the last Guard, 'Tom Cad', have verified details and contributed to the Bishop's Castle Railway Society's remarkable collection of memorabilia and photographs.

Visually, the shape of the centre of Bishop's Castle has changed very little over the centuries: the frontages of the present shops and buildings in the main Church Street/High Street hide the original burgage plots stretching across to the back lanes of Station Street and Union Street. The opportunity to walk in procession from the eighteenth century Town Hall at the top of High Street to the church at the bottom has always been impor-tant to the civic life of the town. A former Mayor, Mr. W.A. Pugh, wrote his impressions of the celebrations at the Fall of Pretoria in June 1900: 'The old Town with its irregular buildings and foreign aspect lends itself well to decoration. The rows of swinging Chinese lanterns, the fairy lights dotted about, the coloured lights, the beautiful floral decorations and waving flags, and the long Procession with its flaring torches winding down the quaint old street formed a spectacle that will long live in the memory of those who witnessed it.'

It is interesting to note that the 'top of the town'—the centre of pro-clamations and gatherings from at least the time of Queen Victoria's Diamond Jubilee in 1897 to the demolition of the Market Hall/Powis Institute in the 1950s—has recently been revitalised with new shops and restaurants, in buildings which originally grew up round the outer walls of the twelfth-century castle. Considerable further research into tenurial reconstruction would be possible; estate and sale maps and plans, and house-deeds are already helping to put together profiles of certain build-ings. For instance, a dwelling and lock-up was built on a space (now No.1 High Street) in 1842 to house the local policeman, following an 1840 decree that every town should have a separate lock-up. The deeds of this house are complete, and oral memories confirm details of successive policemen's families growing up there.

Bishop's Castle still has a Mayor and Town Council, a church and chapel, primary and secondary schools, a small community hospital and residential homes. There is still a market for cattle and sheep, and some industry. The majority of people now have their own transport and can travel further afield to supermarkets (and many of the surrounding villages have lost their school, post office, shop and public house), but the local shops, post office, banks, library, petrol station and pubs are still important (several of the shops and businesses are run by third or fourth generation members of the same family). Any diminution of services is hotly contested, and there is a very strong sense of the town's role in history. This has meant that it is an ideal area for in-depth studies in all aspects of local history. Using the resources and goodwill of local people, all kinds of evidence can be brought together. As one gets to know the present local families, names from the parish registers and census returns spring to life.

In 1979 the memories of Miss Molly Puckle were recorded—her father had been the Doctor and Mayor of Bishop's Castle. The family had moved to Churchstoke in 1919 and Miss Puckle's memories of Bishop's Castle up to that time (together with her aunt's remarkable series of photographs of 'Bishop's Castle Characters 1902'—including the town crier, the postman and even the grave-digger) became the yardstick for all subsequent interviews, which were edited and published as *Bishop's Castle Well-Remembered* in 1990. It became evident that customs and institutions continued longer in this area than elsewhere—for instance that the May Fair had continued as a Hiring Fair as late as the 1930s (confirmed by a comment in the *Shrewsbury Chronicle* in March, 1936). Miss Puckle (1896-1987) remembered that at the Bishop's Castle May Fair before and after the First War 'men and girls stood about, to be engaged for a year by the farmers and their wives, as farm-labourers and domestic servants'. Mr. Alf Shakespeare (1904-1992, recorded 1987) recalled 'They used to grade them! ... They used to feel their muscles in the street!' Mrs. Hemmings (1906-1998, recorded 1985) had a vivid recollection of the scene: 'They had their wages from the last place, you see, and they had ... all the amusements ... and they used to have these stalls all about in the town, selling sweets and fruit and that, and they had these flarey lamps ... paraffin or something—I always remember them.' The May Fair still comes annually to the town, though now only as a fun-fair. Other oral memories frequently refer to the auctions of cattle in the street, and markets for pigs (one end of Union Street was known as Pig Fair, with Horse Fair opposite—now Station Street—near The Boar's Head).

Miss Puckle and others remembered as children being taken to visit the inmates of the Workhouse at Christmas with the Doctor and members of the Board of Guardians: 'I can remember how it upset me, to think that these poor people couldn't have a really good meal, without people going to watch them...' (Miss Marjorie Lamb, 1903-1990, recorded at Stone House, July 1987).

The last link with the workhouse era ended about 90 years later when one of the stalwarts of the RECALL Group died in July 1999. Mary Louise ('Lou') Davies had lived at Stone House for 46 years, and had no other home or family. 'I was born in 1911 in the Union at Knighton ... I was reared on a small-holding—I was adopted at two-and-a-half years old, and I stopped there till they all died. Then I had to come into the old place [Stone House, Bishop's Castle]. It was like a workhouse when I first come, only they'd had it done up. It used to be under the Board of Guardians ... I've been here ever since 1953'. She had always worked very hard for her living, and saw the changes from Workhouse to 'Welfare', to Social Services, to the present Coverage Care Residential Home, and in her last years, with her own comfortable room in the modernised Stone House. She ended her days (in the hospital part of Stone House, under the same roof) as a much valued member of the local community, having contributed many valuable memories to the RECALL Project, and taken part in a video on farm-life made with Acton Scott Farm Museum.

The RECALL Project started by collecting photographs from people in the community, who were asked to identify them and record their memories, which were then used to stimulate reminiscences among those at Stone House. This in turn led to the tape-recording of memories, songs, jokes and anecdotes from the residents themselves—and information on farm life, field names, watercourses, transport, home-management, shopkeeping, apprenticeship, working in-service, methods of dealing with horses, sheep and cattle, and all sorts of other skills, as well as leisure activities and other interests. Old artifacts and tools borrowed from friends and from Acton Scott Farm Museum have proved to be stimulating 'triggers' to unlock memories as well as the expertise of old crafts and skills; and visits to Acton Scott with elderly residents have been most rewarding.

Over the years, a substantial archive has been built up, through those at Stone House, their friends and relatives, and the wider community, of life on the Shropshire/Welsh Border between the 1890s and the end of the Second World War.

One significant photograph discovered by the RECALL Group came from the family of the late Mr. Ned Hotchkiss, who was almost 100 years old. It was a picture of a work-force of miners at the old Wotherton barytes mine near Chirbury, taken in the 1890s, and showing them all wearing bowler hats (which would have been hardened with resin) to which candles had been stuck with lumps of clay. On a RECALL tape-recording Mr. Hotchkiss recalled hearing the whistle of the Mine as he walked to school.

Pl. 23 Lead Miners at Wotherton Mine, Chirbury, c.1900

Mr. H.L. Pugh (1900-1989) remembered that the lead-miners used to come to the Candle Factory in the Market Square for their candles. One of the actual moulds for making a dozen candles at a time has survived, and the 1891 Census Return records 'Hannah Bebb, widow, 52, tallow-chandler'. *The Bishop's Castle Advertiser* carried an account of a disastrous fire which destroyed the building in 1901, describing a chapter of accidents by which the key to the Town Hall (containing the Corporation fire hose) could not be obtained. Several recorded memories mention other occasions when delays in catching the fire-horse prevented the fire-engine from reaching a fire quickly.

Another interesting aspect of a long-term oral history project is the way in which speech-patterns can be seen to reflect continuity with the past in isolated areas. These are the 'upstanding remains' (as the archaeologists say of stone circles or hillforts) of language: the dialect words and local speech rhythms preserved in the way people talk. Many words and phrases used locally today, particularly by the oldest generations, can be traced back to usage defined by Miss Georgina Jackson in her *A Shropshire Word Book* published in 1879. Her examples ring with the rhythm and intonation of Shropshire speech, almost as if she had been using a modern tape-recorder. She entrusted the study of legends, sayings, songs and customs which emerged as a result of her research on Shropshire dialect, to Miss Charlotte Burne, who edited *Shropshire Folk-Lore*, which was published in 1883. These volumes, by two remarkable women, are essential handbooks for the local historian interested in Shropshire traditions.

Amongst local examples of Shropshire dialect words remaining current into this century, Mr. Harry Fletcher (1898-1989, recorded 1986) recalled a visit to Clun May Fair in about 1913, overhearing two old men greeting each other: 'I waited to hear what they'd say, and one got up to the other quietly with his sticks, and he says "Well, George," he says, "And 'ow bist 'ee?" "Oh", he says "A bit in scoots!" ... and then the other one said "Well, Bill, and 'ow bist 'ee goin' on?" And he says "Oh, in 'obs and girds!" ... I've often thought it would take some understanding!' (*Scoots*: an odd piece (often of land); *Hobs and girds*: fits and starts. Jackson.)

Other examples of words still recognised locally for plants, animals, birds, farm-life, include: *Mayflowers* = marsh marigolds; *woller/clogger's woller* = the alder tree, used for clog-making; *oont* = a mole; *oolert* = an owl; *seven-coloured linnet* = a goldfinch; *tallant* = hayloft above a stable; *stiching the shoffs* = stooking sheaves of corn; *tushing* = hauling, especially of timber, and many more. Miss Jackson's own original example '*tining a glat with a brummock*' is still a recognised Shropshire expression for 'mending a hole in the hedge with a billhook'. Less common but very expressive examples of relics of older dialect are the use of 'mushrooms and *frogstools*' (toadstools) and '*slike* [smooth, sleek] holly' ('When the dealers at Christmas was buying holly, they'd rather have the slike holly; there was just a bit of a prick on the end—that other holly's got all pricks all the way round it , but they'd rather buy that slike holly'. Mr. Tom Pryce, of More, b. 1913, recorded 1991).

Miss Jackson also noted many examples of technical words taken from an inventory of Edmund Waring of Owlbury, near Snead. This must have appeared in print when she was compiling her book, because it was published in the *Proceedings of the Society of Antiquaries of London*, 1875. Words such as *Jarsey-hillin* (a bed-covering); *moulding-planke* (for kneading dough); *runlet* (a brewing-tub) were cited, and the reference gave the Local History Research Group clues to the existence of the printed 1625 inventory which gave a great deal of detail on the furnishings of Owlbury Manor at the time of Edmund Waring's death, when the value of his property there was £603 11s 8d.

Charlotte Burne's *Shropshire Folk-Lore* has also been used to confirm many customs and tales referred to by local people, such as 'Halliwell

Wakes', 'The Bull of Bagbury', and the legends of 'Wild Edric' (The 'Edric Sylvaticus' of *Domesday Book*). The late Mr. Bert Challinor, recorded in 1989 at Stone House, remembered a game from his youth in Pontesbury, called 'Buzz and Bandy': 'That was when the pool was frozen over ... you had five that side, five here. Then you had a stick, and the ball—it's almost like ice-hockey'. (*'Buzz-and-bandy*: a local name for hockey, formerly a very popular game among the young men of Shrewsbury and Much Wenlock'. Burne).

Charlotte Burne, in her chapter on Charming and Divination, states that 'a spell is used to work evil, a charm to counteract it'. In 1994, an interesting item came into the possession of The House on Crutches Museum. It was a gravy-salt tin (*c*.1912-1920) containing a 'charm' written in a mixture of English and dog-Latin, with 'abracadabras' and signs, against diseases of cattle. It had been found in the wall of a cowshed at Middle Woodbatch Farm, near Bishop's Castle. Mr. Bill Jones (b.1906), of the RECALL Group, whose father farmed there from 1914-1940, was asked about this, and replied that he remembered that people used to call on a wise man from a 'mountain in mid-Wales' when they needed a charm to protect their animals or home.

Mr. Jones, with an excellent memory at 94, also remembers that when he came to Bishop's Castle Boys' School in 1914, the boys were still playing with the carbines, originally issued for drill at the time of the Boer War: 'Those rifles were there—they were presented to the school from the Boer War, and many a time when there were no schoolteachers about, we would get hold of these rifles and play with them ... they were that heavy you could hardly lift them'. Mr. Jones also remembered the fencing equipment: 'There was like a little basket on the end. [The sticks] are about four foot six long—oh, yes, used them many a time'. These memories are borne out by the *c*.1903 photograph of boys with rifles and fencing equipment, and by entries in the Log-Book of the old Boys' School: 'July 1897 - The following goods received ... Fencing Baskets (Drill)'; 'July 1902 - Board directed me to apply to Ordnance Dept. for 24 carbines at a cost of 1/6 each & carriage'. 'Dec.1902 - Received 24 Martini-Henry Carbines for boys' use in Physical Training'.

The oldest people in this community have in their lifetime seen the very great changes which have taken place during the twentieth century: the replacement of horses by tractors and machinery on the farms, and by lorries, buses and cars on the roads; improvements in communications and enormous innovations in technology. Gas was replaced by electricity, the

Pl. 24 The Boys' School, Bishop's Castle,
with Martini Henry rifles for P.T., c.1903

milliners, dressmakers, and makers of hand-made shoes disappeared. In Bishop's Castle in the 1920s and 1930s there were those who welcomed new inventions—Mr. Leslie Pugh (a fourth-generation tailor in the town) and his friend Mr. Erskine Roberts (landlord of the Three Tuns) welcomed the new 'wireless' and were interested in the exploits of Amy Johnson who flew from the Long Mynd. There were entrepreneurs who saw opportunities to turn their dealing in scrap-metal into businesses as builders and plumbers; the Wood family who had dealt in buying up chickens and rabbits at the Dead Market began to breed chickens and build up the Chukie Chicken enterprise at The Grove, Craven Arms. Others such as Arthur Greenhous & Sons—ironmongers, agricultural merchants and farm machinery dealers—moved into the new motor-vehicle trade, and a grandson of Arthur Greenhous opened up Vincent Greenhous Motors, Shrewsbury. One reason (amongst many others) for the demise of the Bishop's Castle Railway was the improvement and opening-up of the road networks and the advent of lorries and buses, even before private cars were generally affordable. Bishop's Castle became a centre for bus-operators (Rose, Carpenter, Hailstone, Lewis, Roberts, Thomas, Cooke, Robinson, and others) and they came into their own in the Second World War when many servicemen were stationed nearby, and petrol was unobtainable for private use.

As one talks to those who lived in the area during the first half of the twentieth century, one is struck by the similarities of experience and the patterns which emerge, such as the importance of the annual 'wimberry-picking' (verified by absences in the school log-books) to the economy of impoverished households: over and over again one hears of the family outing (on foot, by bus or on the railway) to favourite sites, and how the bilberries would be bought by dealers—'threepence or fourpence a pound', and money saved to buy boots for the winter. The events and eras described come to life, though the details may differ: one person may recall the fascination of seeing the dancing-bear on its regular visits to the area, another may remember with relish the boxing-booths at the May Fair ('the sovereigns was rolling on the ground!'), or the 'cannons' outside the Town Hall and the (now-demolished) Market Hall in the 1920s—recently confirmed by contemporary postcards and photographs as First World War field-guns.

At the turn of the Millennium it is good to know that someone who was born in 1896—Mr. Jack Davies of Edgton—was honoured in February 1999 by the French Government as a surviving veteran of the 1914-18 War. His memories had been tape-recorded in 1987, when he was still in his own home with his wife, having celebrated 60 years of marriage. He was looking back over 90 years, including his time apprenticed to a shoemaker in Bishop's Castle ('in those days, the majority of the boots was all hand-made ... 16s.6d. a pair, and we got half-a crown for making them!') Some of the details he recalled then were of use in confirming his Regiment and war-service when, at the age of 102, he was awarded the Legion d'Honneur at a ceremony in Copthorne Barracks.

Since 1973 when Bishop's Castle celebrated the four hundred years since the granting of its Charter by Queen Elizabeth I, awareness has been growing about the value to the town of the visible history in its buildings and 'streetscape', and in the wealth of experience and knowledge stored in the memories of its older generations. Social history of times past is being documented, fleshing out official reports of national events. Photographs and first-hand memories of the end of the Boer War, and the processions, rejoicings and bonfires that took place; pictures of the Shropshire Yeomanry camped in Walcot Park before and during the First War; memories of the World War Two soldiers billeted there, the placing of ammunition dumps, the queues for the cinema and the crowds of service-people on the buses—all these bring periods of 'history' closer to home for younger generations, and bring into focus the impact of a sudden influx of strangers and times of intense national activity on a normally close-knit and well-regulated community.

Recently former evacuees to the area have been coming forward with memories, and information has been sought from those who settled here after originally being brought as prisoners-of-war to work on the farms. Some recordings have been made of those who served in the Armed Forces in 1939-45, and information collected on those who stayed 'on the Home Front', doing duty in the Home Guard, the Fire Service, the Women's Land Army, or driving buses, producing food or working in the timber industry.

Alongside this body of evidence, further clues continually come to light to reinforce the picture of life in the town between the 1880s and the 1920s, and bring it up to the 1950s and 1960s—details about the railway, the buses, the shops, church and chapel life, schools, work and shared enjoyment, such as the establishment of the 'Castle Players' drama group, and the 'Legionaires' Concert Party in the 1920s, the role of the Town Band, and the huge involvement of the community in carnivals and processions. The establishment of The House on Crutches Museum and the Bishop's Castle Railway and Transport Museum, together with a Brewing Museum at The Three Tuns, ensures that many aspects of the town's history can be preserved and handed on to succeeding generations.

In our own communities here in south-west Shropshire we are learning more and more about how people lived in earlier generations as well as their strength in times of hardship, and we can begin to see why their descendants have inherited such a strong sense of identity. We are fortunate that the evidence is still all around us, and young and old are being encouraged to appreciate and use the memories and artifacts not as nostalgic mementoes, but as strands in an evolving process of understanding the past and preparing for the future.

Bibliography
Burne, C. (ed.) *Shropshire Folk-Lore* EP Publishing Ltd, 1883/Reprinted 1973
Evans, G.E. *Spoken History* Faber & Faber, 1987
Jackson, G. *Shropshire Word-Book* Candle Lane Books, 1879/Reprinted 1982
Lawrence, A. 'A Potent Package', *SWSHAS Journal No. 6*, Spring 1995
Preshous, J. *Bishop's Castle Well-Remembered: Memories and photographs of a small Shropshire market town*, 1990/Reprinted 1995
Waite, V. *Shropshire Hill Country*, Dent, 1970

Bishop's Castle Parish Registers 1559-1663 have been edited by Marion Roberts and the Research Group of SWSHAS, and privately printed for the Shropshire Parish Register Society, 1996.

The year 2000 A.D. will probably not be marked by revolutionary changes in the life of south-west Shropshire. 'The quietest places under the sun' is a sentiment which still rings true, 100 years after A.E. Housman first made it famous. However, our countryside and its new generations will face change, perhaps accelerating change, in the future. Our last picture is of a school, born in the early years of the twentieth century, serving a huge catchment area of around 200 square miles, and developed as a Community College committed to 'education as a life-long process'. The college will bear the responsibility of preparing citizens of the twenty-first century for the new rhythms of life. Two of the present students bring this story to its conclusion.

CHAPTER 20

Hockey Sticks and Bicycles
by Elizabeth Humphreys and Katharine Baker

The summer of 1995 saw Bishop Castle's Community College at the centre of the 'Keep the Heart Beating' campaign. For the second time there was a threat of sixth form closure. All the local institutions likely to be affected—the Hospital and Residential Home (Stone House), the County Branch Library, the Youth Service, the Fire Service and the Highways Department—had come together in unified opposition to government cuts. Elizabeth Humphreys, a new pupil, arrived at the school at the climax of the campaign. She now reflects 'What I experienced on my first day rapidly proved to be not a rare media-oriented protest, but a truly representative example of the ethos of both school and community. The College teaches adults and children the secret of community strength and the value of social acceptance.'

At first sight this icon of equality and freedom may seem a far cry from the disciplinarian days of the school's establishment in 1922. But a deeper examination of the school's development quickly exposes the communal spirit that has been the hallmark of the institution since its foundation.

The friendly but deep-seated rivalry between Bishop's Castle and Clun had surfaced again in 1922. The two towns, along with Craven Arms, fought to be the site of the long-awaited High School. Mr. Jack Bedell, who started as a pupil at the High School in 1922, recalls that Bishop's Castle 'won the day', primarily due to its central location in the catchment area.

The education the High School attempted to offer was in one respect entirely novel. In an area of small village schools the prospect of aiming for higher national qualifications was greeted with excitement, and, no doubt, some apprehension. Higher education, offered in the larger towns of Shrewsbury and Ludlow, was inaccessible to those in the remoter parts of the county when access to public transport was limited or non-existent.

According to Mrs. Florence Beaumond, another early pupil of the school who became headmistress of Lydbury North Primary School, 'many wanted to go on to further education but they had to go to boarding school', and that was only for those families with a large enough income. Miss Pam Norton became a pupil of the High School in 1928. Through the experiences of her elder sisters Miss Norton was aware of the obstructions to higher education before 1922. 'We were at Brunslow then. There wasn't any higher education you see. All my sisters went to ... the GPD school [Girls' Public Day School Trust] in Shrewsbury ... It wasn't a boarding school, but somebody ran a boarding house privately.' Mrs. Jarvis, another of the first pupils, related that 'Mr. Edwards, the saddler, whose daughter later became senior mistress at the High School, was a driving force for secondary education' in Bishop's Castle. But soon the whole community became involved and was anxiously awaiting the new school.

Although the opening of the High School had been long in the pipe-line, people were at first unsure what to expect. It was clear that tight discipline was necessary from the beginning in order to set a positive precedent for the reputation on which the school had to build. As Mrs. Beaumond recalls 'The first morning we stood out on the road because the gates to the school were closed. Mr Dodson [the headmaster] came round and we were all shivering in our shoes. But he was quite nice. I mean he had a fair way about him. He had a VERY gruff voice though!' But 'if the boys did wrong they had the cane from 'Father' Dodson [his nickname]. I never knew a girl to be hit. Miss Thomas' tongue was sufficient.'

During the 1950s and 1960s society's attitude to discipline in education changed. The arrival of Mr. David Preshous as the new headmaster in 1973, heralded a dramatic change within the school community, bringing it into line with national standards. In Mr. Preshous' words 'Even though this was a fairly relaxed and, as schools go, an easy one, there were still difficult pupils. There was an expectation of corporal punishment and severe measures at that time. It took some while, I think, for the staff—and the parents—to mellow to the idea that discipline is a much more complex business. Not just the use of the cane. That [change of attitude] took a few years to materialise.'

Pl. 25 Staff of the County High School, Bishop's Castle in 1922, with Mr. Dodson, Headmaster, seated centre

One could reflect that the intimacy of the community has also minimised the risk of major social problems. 'We come from a rural community where no-one is anonymous' says Mr. Peter Bigglestone who also joined the school in 1973. 'Mr. Hunt [the present headmaster] still teaches. Mr. Preshous taught classics, partly because he loved classics, but also because it meant he got to know every first year student, and if you see them as a first year, you get to know them and they get to know you ... I think in big schools where the heads and deputies don't teach, you get a certain amount of separation.' Mr. Terry Hunt, who arrived as headmaster in 1997, says 'I've worked in schools which are certainly tougher than this, but, because these incidents [acts of serious indiscipline] occur so infrequently here, [when they do] it hurts, it hurts the community. And of course what happens here is that they do stick out, and they magnify themselves. I'm not against that sort of community pressure to make people think about what they're doing. My view about discipline, regardless of the scale of it or frequency, is that it ought, in itself, to be an education.'

The new High School required uniforms to be worn. As Miss Pam Norton recalled 'Uniforms, they were very, very strict on uniform; girls had to wear navy gym tunics, white blouses, thick black stockings, and the winter hats were horrible sort of cap things which had a red binding around and the Bishop's Castle badge. Of course the ties were still the same, red and black. We had panama hats in the summer with those bands on. We used to line up about once a term to have the length of your skirt measured. You had to kneel on the floor and your skirt had to be four inches from the floor, no more. You daren't go up town without your hat. You weren't allowed to wear outside shoes in the school; we had to go straight into the cloakroom and put on our gym shoes. You lived in your gym shoes all day. The boys wore navy suits, or navy jackets and grey shorts.' Apart from a change to 'the cap things' in the 1940s, the uniform was unchanged until the 1980s when it was redesigned to its present form in consultation with students at the school.

The first headmaster was Mr. Charles Dodson, 'a retired army officer who had just been demobbed after the First World War' and Miss Thomas was the senior mistress. Mrs. Jarvis gives a graphic picture of their early days. 'Mr. Dodson lived in the school house [now the Sixth Form Centre]. He was very much the disciplinarian and so was Miss Thomas. 'Father' Dodson and Miss Thomas were the heads and you knew if you put a foot wrong you were sent to them.' Mrs. Beaumond adds 'I was turned out of the lab once, because I was caught sticking a drawing pin in the mayor's son's bum! I later based my own teaching on Miss Thomas' teaching. She was the most wonderful teacher I ever came across. She never had any trouble with discipline in her classes, or any child that wasn't listening. Miss Thomas had eyes everywhere!' In Mr. Bedell's recollection 'She actually lived at the top of Bishop's Castle and she used to cycle to school. She had to push her bike up the hill on the way home, but it was expected, if any pupils were around, they would push the bike up for her.' Mr. Dodson's successor, Mr. Bowman, was headmaster from 1946 to 1949. He was followed by Mr. Hawkin, under whom the County High School became the first Comprehensive non-feepaying school in Shropshire during the 1950s. Mr. Preshous arrived in 1973 and retired in 1997, having seen the school through its transition to a Community College.

As in any school career we all cherish those characters who remain in our memories long after we have forgotten the particulars of routine. Mr. Bigglestone recalls Mr. Roland Harris, once the Head of English. 'He was partly such a character to me because he had taught me in a grammar school in Swindon. In Swindon he struck me very much as a radical new young man. He introduced new poetry that we'd never even read ... stuff that didn't rhyme! And short stories you really had to think about.' The pupils at Bishop's Castle saw this same inspirational quality in Mr. Harris, and, as with all the most stimulating teachers, he had a number of infamous eccentricities. 'He used to type ... single space typing, and some of the letters were either missing or would jump up, so when you came to read his exam papers they were always amazing because they were so hard to read; some of it would be in red and some in black!'

More recent pupils remember one of the school's art teachers: Mrs. Pugh. Stories of her unusual natural dyes haunt the corridors long after her departure. Mr. Bigglestone recollects how 'she used to dye the fabric in natural ways, and she used to treat it with urine. You'd be walking down the old school, as it was then, and she'd suddenly appear with a jam jar and say "go to the toilet and fill this up!" She made no differentiation between staff and pupils when on one of her specimen hunts.'

The access to higher education, which the High School gave, created previously unavailable opportunities for its pupils. The School offered the Oxford School Leaving Certificate to all. Those who did well could then study for the Higher School Certificate in the small sixth form. A favourite teacher of Mrs. Jarvis', Miss Sinclair, had performed highly in the Leaving Certificate and was given the opportunity to stay on as a pupil teacher. 'I thought to myself,' said Mrs. Jarvis, 'If only I could be like Miss Sinclair!' University was also now within reach of some of the most dedicated scholars. Mrs. Jarvis recalls 'the first one that went to university and got his degree. Well, that was really something.' Miss Pam Norton was one of those exalted few, in the 1930s, for whom university became a reality.

The option of further education was, however, not taken up by everyone. Partly because of plentiful agricultural employment many of the first pupils did not take education entirely seriously. 'There were quite a few who were farmers' sons, who went on to the farm.' said Mrs. Jarvis. 'The first building was made of asbestos, and I remember one of the boys put his foot straight through it. He got a terrible telling-off, and he never came back. His parents just kept him at home.' This casual attitude to education has changed dramatically through the raising of the school leaving age to 16, and through wider academic aspirations. But many boys continued to feel their future was mapped out and thus lacked interest in education. This changed rapidly during the Seventies and Eighties when the number of jobs in agriculture and allied industries dwindled. Mr. Bigglestone, who is now Head of History, took over the sixth form in the 1980s, a limb of the school which has perhaps witnessed the most changes during its lifetime. Even then many girls were shying away from higher education. Mr. Bigglestone remembers one incident. 'When I was in charge of the sixth form I had a classic case of a girl who wanted to stay in the sixth form but her parents couldn't see any reason why *a girl* should stay on...' Since then developments in careers advice have successfully encouraged all students to continue their education and the sixth form has continued to grow steadily.

The different treatment of the sexes, which many schools perpetuated during the early twentieth century, was scarcely apparent at the High School. Mrs. Beaumond says 'The only difference was we went to needle-work and they went to woodwork.' She also felt that the girls showed more dedication to their studies, perhaps because opportunities for women were more limited and thus harder to achieve.

During the Fifties and Sixties, after the school became comprehensive, pupils were streamed to a greater degree. Mr. Bigglestone recalls the streams when he arrived in 1973. 'By the end of the first year you went into one of three forms. You either went into the 'C' stream, which meant you would do GCE [note the emphasis] O Levels; or you went into the 'S' stream, which meant, if you stayed on, you would do CSEs; or you went into the 'N' form, which was for non-exam subjects.' Inevitably this created 'quite sharp divisions between the students ... Now all students have aspirations to get some qualifications.'

At the start of the school's life it was fee-paying, although, according to Mr. Bedell and Mrs. Jarvis, 'There was no class distinction ... When the school first started it was £12 a year. But there was a Wright's Charity scholarship and a grant from the council for the people who couldn't afford it. But it was known that if you were C of E you would get it, and if you were non-conformist you wouldn't.' Miss Norton recalls 'In a way it was a Grammar School at that stage, only they did not call it a Grammar School. There were some free places, but it was a fee-paying school. There was a County Major Scholarship, and I had that. I think it was worth about £11 a year or something ridiculous, but I suppose that was the fee in those days.'

However, the attempt to help poorer families and so reduce the risk of class discrimination actually produced the opposite effect. As Mrs. Beaumond recalls, 'The education authority paid for the uniform and paid for bicycles. So of course we all went on worn out bicycles and all the poorer children came cycling by us on posh new bikes. We had to buy all our own games equipment, so we rode to school in the winter with a hockey stick or in the summer with a tennis racquet across our handle bars.' This was partly because, at the start of the school, the majority were given no transport. 'We all cycled from outlying districts. And we didn't ride in lines. We rode in gangs of about 10 or 12, and when one wobbled everybody else wobbled and fell off in a heap.' Mrs. Angela Humphries, a pupil in the 1940s, remembers 'The first bus I went on was a little bus that came from Clun. It belonged to a man named Mr. Wood, and it was a tiny little henhouse; we used to call it "Conky's Henhouse". It was a tiny little yellow and green bus, and it seated 14, and I should think he put 40 children on it.'

The school was quite small at first. 'There were six teachers', Mrs. Beaumond says, 'and I think 22 was the highest number in the classes, and I never remember there being more than four in the sixth form at any one time.' Miss Norton gives a picture of the layout: 'The old buildings were just temporary, asbestos ones, with a quad in the middle. You had a cookery room on one side and the lab. The woodwork room ran along the other side, with the girls' and the boys' cloakrooms at either end. And you had classrooms along the end, and the hall on the last side. The hall sort of jutted out, and there was a verandah all around, sort of servicing the classrooms, not the hall; and my memory of the Head is of him stomping through there in his felt shoes when it was wet, when he didn't go outside.'

The image of the quadrangle as sacred is perhaps a feature of school life that everyone from that time would remember. For a lot of the pupils it symbolised the issues of respect and discipline. As Mrs. Beaumond puts it 'The quadrangle was holy ground and heaven help you if you stepped on it. We used to cut across the corners and you used to get into trouble. You'd hear 'Father' Dodson's voice booming across. My friend wrote a parody of W.H. Davies' 'What is this life' about it:

> What is this life if when at school
> We have no time to play the fool.
> No time before beneath the sod
> To run full tilt across the quad.

The quadrangle was still a part of school life when Mr. Bigglestone arrived. 'The main spine of the building which was built in the Fifties was there. But the old school (now demolished and the site of the bus park) was also there. Between lessons you were not allowed to cross the quad. By the time I came the old building housed the library, art rooms, Maths rooms, and English rooms. It was really cold because they were asbestos clad buildings. Also still standing were three Horsa huts put up in 1947 after the war ... The sixth form lived in a variety of buildings. When I came, it numbered about 20 and had its common room in what is now the small special needs room.' But by the 1970s the number of students was outgrowing the existing buildings.

As the school continued to grow, with added transport, a bigger catchment area, growing population and changing attitudes to education, so did

Pl. 26 The Community College, 1994

the sixth form. It was largely the government-inspired threat to this ever expanding sixth form in the late 1980s that led to the fight for Community College status. Mr. Bigglestone makes the point, 'In all of the discussions about the future of the sixth form it was felt that you couldn't just say "we don't want to lose our sixth form because of this and this". It was felt your argument would carry more weight if you had something positive to put forward and so the Community idea arose out of that.' Mr Preshous' view is 'It raised the status of the school in the eyes of the community. It meant the community now felt, more than ever, that this was their school and they owned it. Before, when there was limited parental involvement and very few evening classes, it was very much a 9 to 4 establishment. Community College status has done an enormous amount of good and the College is still very much a key mover in anything that goes on in Bishop's Castle.' Today it hosts a large number of artistic, cultural and sporting events and a range of day and evening classes. It is a good example of an establishment offering 'cradle to grave' education.

'In the early Eighties,' Mr. Bigglestone again, 'the school's technological resources consisted of an old ink printer which you had to strip down once a week, and a single television, which were both kept in a converted cloakroom.' The Learning Resources Centre quickly expanded with funding that was gained by the Community College's involvement in training adults and this wealth of equipment can now be sustained only because of the community links. As Mr Hunt sees it, 'It is definitely one of the areas that is dramatically changing education. Having access to the Internet and so on takes away some of the problems we have through being so rural.'

Looking to the future, Mr. Preshous remains concerned about the pressures on teachers in the modern world of education. The imaginative aspects of teaching which so attracted many in the past have been over-taken by financial and governmental pressures. 'Teaching has become mechanical in some ways—very exam-orientated. Even in the 1970s obvi-ously there was national interest in education, but that has developed in recent years into something near hysteria. Education is very rarely out of the banner headlines, and usually for the wrong reasons ... The political agenda is strong. Good things have come out of this, but everything, such as curriculum and teaching methods, is now far more under scrutiny than it was.'

Although a more stable period may not yet be visible, the College's future is far from bleak. Advances in technology are shaping a different approach to learning and Mr. Bigglestone senses a corresponding change in the attitudes of students. 'I think a lot of education has been about acquiring information ... In the future, because you can now acquire information so easily, education will be much more about using and managing informa-tion.' Mr. Hunt offers a different but complementary perspective. 'The art of education is learning to be discerning. I am a great believer that maturity has nothing to do with age. It's to do with a state of mind. It's about being able to ask the right questions at the right time to make the right decisions.' Such qualities may prove to be vital in an age such as this, but technology is not the only item on the College's agenda. Mr. Hunt wants to see an extension of the Arts within and without the school. He concludes, 'If we could be known for one thing, we would like to be held up as a beacon for the Arts. I'd like to think when I left here, that would be part of the legacy.' So, as we enter the new millennium, we may see the artistic and techno-logical worlds converging within the bounds of this once isolated commu-nity school.

Envoi

Hollinshed, in his *Chronicles,* a history and description of Britain published in 1577, quoted the Latin proverb 'times change and we change with them'. This collection of essays has illustrated some of the changes which have taken place in the South Shropshire Borderland over the past 2,000 years. Despite its rugged and turbulent history, the area has preserved much of its social and historical character and its physical environment, possibly more than many other parts of Britain. The remoteness, sparse population, and the tenacious and independent nature of the people have combined to maintain, through centuries of change, a wealth of tradition, an unspoilt landscape, and a gentle and harmonious quality of life. Those who live and work in the area and those who visit it on holiday appreciate and cherish these facets.

However, the pace of life and with it the pace of change accelerated greatly during the twentieth century. Education, transport, housing, health care, employment, agriculture, religion, distribution of wealth, local and national identity—all have changed radically since 1900, and science and technology are continuing to change dramatically our perception of the world round us.

With the undeniable benefits of progress have come serious consequences for our historical heritage. Society is awakening to the importance of preserving this and caring for our environment, while recognising the needs of a living and working landscape. The editors hope that the insights into our past, which the authors of these essays offer, will contribute to the understanding and recognition of our rare local inheritance. This must now be commended to the vigilant care of the new generations of the Third Millennium.

Biographical Notes

ROBERT ANTHONY earns his living as a solicitor and is co-author of the standard book on the Law of Markets and Fairs. In the early 1990s he gained a Master's Degree in Industrial Archaeology from the Ironbridge Institute (University of Birmingham) studying under Dr. Barrie Trinder. He is currently struggling to complete a PhD from the Centre for Urban History, University of Leicester. He is a joint-owner of the Three Tuns Inn and Brewery, Bishop's Castle.

KATHARINE BAKER was born, a twin, in 1981 in Chertsey. She lived for three years in the Yemen before moving to Lydbury North. She attended Lydbury Primary School and is currently a sixth former at the Community College, Bishop's Castle. She is studying A Levels in Electronics, French, Mathematics, and Physics, and intends to read Civil Engineering at university. Her interests include music, sport, and animals, and she is an active member of a number of local community groups.

PETER BIGGLESTONE was born in London in 1948, but in 1955 his family moved to Swindon in Wiltshire where he attended the local grammar school. He trained as a teacher and gained a B.Ed in Bristol. He began his teaching career in Chipping Norton, Oxfordshire. In 1973 he became Head of History at the County High School (Community College) Bishop's Castle, where he has remained to the present. With his A Level classes he has specialised in the period of the English Revolution, but has also a personal interest in family and local history.

SALLY CHAPPELL and ANNE LAWRENCE are the present curators of the House on Crutches Museum Collection in Bishop's Castle. Their backgrounds contain no hint of historical scholarship. Sally is a professional photographer who spent several years in the photographic studios of the Victoria and Albert Museum, London. Anne spent her professional life as a primary school teacher on Merseyside. They are both, however, intrigued by the development of Bishop's Castle and hope that their contribution will provide for others a basis for an equal fascination with the long history of this small town.

MARGARET GELLING. Dr Gelling has been engaged in place-name research since 1946, when she was appointed research assistant to the English Place-Name Society, a post she relinquished in 1953, when her late husband became lecturer in Ancient History and Archaeology at the University of Birmingham. She is honorary reader in English Place-Name studies at that university, lectures widely, and has written many books on the subject. She is President of the English Place-Name Society and for that society, in collaboration with the late H.D.G. Foxall, has produced two publications on *The Place-Names of Shropshire*—Part One on the names of Shropshire parishes, and Part Two on the township, hamlet, farm, and field names within the parishes of Ford and Condover Hundred. Further volumes are planned as the topographical volumes of the *Victoria County History* appear.

DAVID HILL. Dr Hill is Senior Research Fellow in the Centre for Anglo-Saxon Studies in the University of Manchester. He first came to the Dyke when the late Frank Noble spoke to a course he was helping to run at Preston Montford Field Centre. His explorations of the Dyke, based on the Blue Bell at Brompton, began in the winter of 1971-2, when he was Staff Tutor in Archaeology in the Manchester University Department of Extra-Mural Studies. He has carried out extensive fieldwork and excavation on the Dyke over the past 27 years, and is continuing these and other studies in the Bishop's Castle area with his co-director, Margaret Worthington.

NEIL HIRD. Neil's interest in history began at Merchant Taylors' School, Crosby, and continued during National Service in the Royal Navy in the Mediterranean. Working in Africa and South-East Asia gave further opportunities to continue an interest which retirement in historically-rich Shropshire has allowed him to maintain.

ROBIN HOWARD was ordained in 1953. After parish ministry in the dioceses of Durham, Ely, Hong Kong, Chester, Birmingham, and Salisbury, he and Mary retired to Aston-on-Clun in 1993. Retirement activity includes the management committee of Coverage Care (Shropshire) which runs Stone House and eight other residential homes in the county. Robin is a member of Hopesay Parish Council and serves as Treasurer of the Friends of the Church in China, of the Marches Rural Theology Association, and of Hopesay Parish Church.

ELIZABETH HUMPHREYS was born in St. Thomas' Hospital, London, and lived in the capital for 12 years. She moved to Shropshire with her parents and elder sister in 1995. She is currently studying A Levels in English, History, and Politics, at the Community College, Bishop's Castle, and hopes to pursue a career in some kind of investigative journalism.

ALAN HURLEY was educated at Nottingham High School and University College, Oxford where he read Law, and obtained his MA Degree. He practised as a solicitor in Nottingham, and, on retirement, has come to live in Clun.

JOHN LEONARD is a retired consultant physician, who has written several books on county parish churches.

MADGE MORAN was educated at Newport High School and Calder College, Liverpool, and was a lecturer at Radbrook College, Shrewsbury for 25 years. She has made her name by her expertise in vernacular architecture, for which she was elected a Fellow of the Society of Antiquaries. She currently lectures in the subject for the Birmingham University School of Continuing Studies and Keele University Extra-Mural Department. She is a member of the Vernacular Architecture Group and runs the dendrochronological project for Shropshire. The author of a number of articles, she has recently published a book on the vernacular architecture of the Whitchurch area of Shropshire.

DAVID PRESHOUS, O.B.E., was born in Shrewsbury and educated there at Prestfelde School and Priory Boys' Grammar School, before reading Classics at Bristol University (MA, 1961). He taught Classics at Letchworth Grammar School, Hertfordshire, and at The Bulmershe School, Woodley, Reading. In 1973 he was appointed headmaster of the County

High School (later The Community College) Bishop's Castle, from which post he retired in 1997. He was a founder-member of SWSHAS and is its current Chairman.

JANET PRESHOUS was educated in Devon and London (BA Hons, English, Birkbeck College 1957). She worked in administration at London and Exeter Universities. Since coming to Bishop's Castle in 1973 she has been involved with the community and worked as a volunteer at Stone House Residential Home and Hospital. She co-founded the RECALL Project there, and is now on the executive Committee of Shropshire Reminiscence. In 1990 she published *Bishop's Castle Well-Remembered*: *memories and photographs of a small market town.*

MARION ROBERTS was educated at Berkhamsted Girls' School, St. Andrew's University (Hons. Degree in Modern & Medieval History) and University College, London (Diploma in Archive Admin.). Her working life was spent in Shropshire Records Office (1957-1989); she became County Archivist in 1975. As well as being Secretary of Shrops. Archaeol. & Hist. Soc., Vice-President of SWSHAS, and Bishop's Castle's Honorary Archivist, she continues to conduct local history / palaeography courses for Birmingham School of Continuing Studies.

JOHN SAXBEE is Bishop and Archdeacon of Ludlow, and lives in Craven Arms. He was born and brought up in Bristol, reading for a Theology Degree at the university there. He gained a Ph.D at Durham University, where he also trained for Ordination. After ten years as a parish priest in Plymouth, he became Director of Training for the Exeter Diocese and in 1992 was appointed Archdeacon of Ludlow. He became Bishop two years later, and combines both roles.

NOEL SHEPHERDSON, after training as a painter and printmaker, taught in Art Schools for 13 years. In 1973 he moved with his wife and two sons to Clunton. His ambition was to paint full-time, particularly the landscape of south-west Shropshire. Twenty-six years and over 60 one-man exhibitions later, his enthusiasm for his subject is as strong as ever.

JOHN SMYTH read History at Trinity College, Dublin in the 1950s, and, some years later, embarked on a career as a history teacher. In 1984 he and his wife took a smallholding near Bishop's Castle which, 15 years later, still occupies most of their time. He was a founder-member of SWSHAS and edits the Society's Journal. He is a part-time local bus driver.

PATRICIA THEOBALD came to Shropshire in 1990 from Normandy in Surrey, after careers in libraries and music. Having the former Mainstone village school at the bottom of her garden stimulated her interest in local history. She first studied the development of education in Mainstone after completing a number of local history courses. She hopes to broaden her studies of this fascinating rural community. She lives in the Old School House, Mainstone, with her husband, an academic working in London, and two cats.

CHRISTOPHER TRAIN, C.B., M.A.(Oxon), was educated at Nottingham High School and Christ Church, Oxford where he read Classics. He taught Classics at St. Paul's School, London, for ten years before joining the Home Civil Service to work in the Home Office. He now lives in Clunbury.

ROGER WHITE, after attending North Hampstead Comprehensive School, went up to Liverpool University where he read Ancient and Medieval History and Archaeology for his first degree. He then took his Doctorate in History at the same university, where he was appointed temporary lecturer in archaeology for two years. From 1976 onwards he was the supervisor of excavations at Wroxeter, and was the senior investigator on the Wroxeter Hinterland Project 1994-97. He is currently a Research Fellow at Birmingham University.

ALAN WILSON has lived at Anchor, beside the Kerry Ridgeway for ten years. Before that he was an outside broadcast engineer for the BBC, based in London. He is secretary of the Bettws-y-Crwyn PCC.

MAURICE YOUNG was born in 1932 and brought up on Viscount Ridley's Northumbrian estates, attending King Edward VI Grammar School in Morpeth. He joined the army for National Service before accepting a regular commission, serving for almost 30 years and reaching the rank of Lieutenant-Colonel, before deciding upon a new career. He studied Theology at St. John's College, Nottingham, and, after ordination into the Church of England Ministry, served as a curate in Shrewsbury and, for ten years, as Vicar of Hadley, Telford. He bought a house in Clun in 1982 and retired there in 1994.

INDEX

INDEX

INDEX

259

SOUTH-WEST SHROPSHIRE HISTORICAL & ARCHAEOLOGICAL SOCIETY

Bishop's Castle Historical Research Group was formed in 1974 by the late Keith Ritherden, and, under the guidance of James Lawson and Barrie Trinder, worked on local projects such as tithe maps, census returns, probate inventories, family and church records and parish histories.

In 1988, with the inception of the Community College, Bishop's Castle, the group became the nucleus of The South-West Shropshire Historical & Archaeological Society (SWSHAS). It has continued to flourish, supporting local research and offering members a programme of lectures and outings. It frequently organises or participates in exhibitions on local history and archaeology, and publishes an annual Journal with articles by members and other material of local interest.

Research work has included the publication of the first volume of Bishop's Castle Parish Registers—with another to follow. Members' individual interests and researches have resulted in the production of publications on many subjects including oral history, photographic records, dialect, education, church buildings, village histories, guide-books and town-trails.

The Society, which usually meets at The Community College, Bishop's Castle, has over 100 members and warmly welcomes new members and visitors at its functions. Its broad aim is to promote active involvement in the study of history and archaeology, with particular emphasis on south-west Shropshire and the Welsh Border.